VC £3·75

CASEBOOK SERIES

PUBLISHED

Jane Austen: *Emma* DAVID LODGE
Jane Austen: *'Northanger Abbey' and 'Persuasion'* B. C. SOUTHAM
Jane Austen: *'Sense and Sensibility', 'Pride and Prejudice' and 'Mansfield Park'*
B. C. SOUTHAM
William Blake: *Songs of Innocence and Experience* MARGARET BOTTRALL
Charlotte Brontë: *'Jane Eyre' and 'Villette'* MIRIAM ALLOTT
Emily Brontë: *Wuthering Heights* MIRIAM ALLOTT
Browning: *'Men and Women' and Other Poems* J. R. WATSON
Bunyan: *The Pilgrim's Progress* ROGER SHARROCK
Byron: *'Childe Harold's Pilgrimage' and 'Don Juan'* JOHN JUMP
Chaucer: *Canterbury Tales* J. J. ANDERSON
Coleridge: *'The Ancient Mariner' and Other Poems* ALUN R. JONES AND
WILLIAM TYDEMAN
Conrad: *The Secret Agent* IAN WATT
Dickens: *Bleak House* A. E. DYSON
Donne: *Songs and Sonets* JULIAN LOVELOCK
George Eliot: Middlemarch PATRICK SWINDEN
George Eliot: *'The Mill on the Floss' and 'Silas Marner'* R. P. DRAPER
T. S. Eliot: *Four Quartets* BERNARD BERGONZI
T. S. Eliot: *'Prufrock', 'Gerontion', 'Ash Wednesday' and Other Shorter Poems* B. C.
SOUTHAM
T. S. Eliot: *The Waste Land* C. B. COX AND ARNOLD P. HINCHLIFFE
Farquhar: *'The Recruiting Officer' and 'The Beaux' Stratagem'* RAYMOND A.
ANSELMENT
Henry Fielding: *Tom Jones* NEIL COMPTON
E. M. Forster: *A Passage to India* MALCOLM BRADBURY
Hardy: *The Tragic Novels* R. P. DRAPER
Gerard Manley Hopkins: *Poems* MARGARET BOTTRALL
Jonson: *Volpone* JONAS A. BARISH
Jonson: *'Every Man in His Humour' and 'The Alchemist'* R. V. HOLDSWORTH
James Joyce: *'Dubliners' and 'A Portrait of the Artist as a Young Man'* MORRIS
BEJA
John Keats: *Odes* G. S. FRASER
D. H. Lawrence: *Sons and Lovers* GĀMINI SALGĀDO
D. H. Lawrence: *'The Rainbow' and 'Women in Love'* COLIN CLARKE
Marlowe: *Doctor Faustus* JOHN JUMP
Milton: *'Comus' and 'Samson Agonistes'* JULIAN LOVELOCK
Milton: *Paradise Lost* A. E. DYSON AND J JULIAN LOVELOCK
John Osborne: *Look Back in Anger* JOHN RUSSELL TAYLOR
Peacock: *The Satirical Novels* LORNA SAGE
Pope: *The Rape of the Lock* JOHN DIXON HUNT
Shakespeare: *Antony and Cleopatra* JOHN RUSSELL BROWN
Shakespeare: *Coriolanus* B. A. BROCKMAN
Shakespeare: *Hamlet* JOHN JUMP
Shakespeare: *Henry IV Parts I and II* G. K. HUNTER
Shakespeare: *Henry V* MICHAEL QUINN
Shakespeare: *Julius Caesar* PETER URE
Shakespeare: *King Lear* FRANK KERMODE
Shakespeare: *Macbeth* JOHN WAIN
Shakespeare: *Measure for Measure* G. K. STE

Shakespeare: *The Merchant of Venice* JOHN WILDERS
Shakespeare: *Othello* JOHN WAIN
Shakespeare: *Richard II* NICHOLAS BROOKE
Shakespeare: *The Sonnets* PETER JONES
Shakespeare: *The Tempest* D. J. PALMER
Shakespeare: *Troilus and Cressida* PRISCILLA MARTIN
Shakespeare: *Twelfth Night* D. J. PALMER
Shakespeare: *The Winter's Tale* KENNETH MUIR
Shelley: *Shorter Poems and Lyrics* PATRICK SWINDEN
Spenser: *The Faerie Queene* PETER BAYLEY
Swift: *Gulliver's Travels* RICHARD GRAVIL
Tennyson: *In Memoriam* JOHN DIXON HUNT
Thackeray: *Vanity Fair* ARTHUR POLLARD
Webster: *'The White Devil' and 'The Duchess of Malfi'* R. V. HOLDSWORTH
Virginia Woolf: *To the Lighthouse* MORRIS BEJA
Wordsworth: *Lyrical Ballads* ALUN R. JONES AND WILLIAM TYDEMAN
Wordsworth: *The Prelude* W. J. HARVEY AND RICHARD GRAVIL
Yeats: *Last Poems* JON STALLWORTHY
Drama Criticism: Developments since Ibsen ARNOLD P. HINCHLIFFE
The English Novel: Developments in Criticism since Henry James STEPHEN HAZELL
The Metaphysical Poets GERALD HAMMOND
The Romantic Imagination JOHN SPENCER HILL

TITLES IN PREPARATION INCLUDE
Congreve: *'Love for Love' and 'The Way of the World'* PATRICK LYONS
Conrad: *'Heart of Darkness', 'Lord Jim', 'Nostromo' and 'Under Western Eyes'* C. B. COX
Hardy: *Poems* JAMES GIBSON AND TREVOR JOHNSON
Marvell: *Poems* ARTHUR POLLARD
Shakespeare: *'Much Ado about Nothing' and 'As You Like It'* JOHN RUSSELL BROWN
Shakespeare: *A Midsummer Night's Dream* ANTONY W. PRICE
Wilde: *Comedies* WILLIAM TYDEMAN

Poetry Criticism: Developments since the Symbolists A. E. DYSON
Comedy: Developments in Criticism D. J. PALMER
Tragedy: Developments in Criticism R. P. DRAPER
Poetry of the First World War DOMINIC HIBBERD

Hardy

The Tragic Novels

The Return of the Native
The Mayor of Casterbridge
Tess of the d'Urbervilles
Jude the Obscure

A CASEBOOK

EDITED BY

R. P. DRAPER

First edition 1975
Reprinted 1978, 1979

Published by
THE MACMILLAN PRESS LTD
London and Basingstoke
Associated companies in Delhi Dublin
Hong Kong Johannesburg Lagos Melbourne
New York Singapore and Tokyo

ISBN O 333 15502 5

Printed in Hong Kong

FOR ANNE, ISABEL AND SOPHIA

CONTENTS

ACKNOWLEDGEMENTS

The author and publishers wish to thank the following, who have kindly given permission for the use of copyright material: Jean Brooks for extract from *Thomas Hardy: the Poetic Structure* by permission of Paul Elek Ltd, and Cornell University Press; Douglas Brown for extract from 'Novels of Character and Environment' from *Thomas Hardy*, by permission of Longman Group Ltd; Leonard Deen for 'Heroism and Pathos', in *Return of the Native*, © 1960 by The Regents of the University of California, reprinted from *Nineteenth-Century Fiction*, vol. 15, no. 3 (December 1960) pp. 207–19, by permission of the Regents; Ian Gregor for extract from 'An End and a Beginning' from *The Great Web*, reprinted by permission of Faber & Faber Ltd; Robert Heilman for *Hardy's Sue Bridehead*, © 1966 by the Regents of the University of California, reprinted from *Nineteenth-Century Fiction*, vol. 20, no. 4 (March 1966) pp. 307–23, by permission of the Regents; D. H. Lawrence for extract from 'Study of Thomas Hardy' from *Phoenix*, by permission of Laurence Pollinger Ltd, and the Estate of the late Mrs Frieda Lawrence; David Lodge for 'Tess, Nature and the Voices of Hardy' from *Language of Fiction*, by permission of Routledge & Kegan Paul Ltd, and Columbia University Press; F. Manning for *Novels of Character and Environment*, by permission of *Spectator*; J. C. Maxwell for 'The "Sociological" Approach to *The Mayor of Casterbridge*' from *Imagined Worlds*; Robert Schweik for 'Character and Fate in *The Mayor of Casterbridge*,' © 1966 by the Regents of the University of California, reprinted from *Nineteenth-Century Fiction*, vol. 21, no. 3 (December 1966) pp. 249–62, by permission of the Regents; Tony Tanner for 'Colour and Movement in Hardy's *Tess of the d'Urbervilles*'; Raymond Williams for extract from *The English Novel from Dickens to Lawrence*, by permission of Chatto & Windus Ltd, and Oxford

University Press Inc., New York; Virginia Woolf for 'The Novels of Thomas Hardy' from *The Second Common Reader* by permission of the Author's Literary Estate, The Hogarth Press Ltd, and Harcourt Brace Jovanovich, Inc. The publishers have made every effort to trace the copyright-holders, but if they have inadvertently overlooked any they will be pleased to make the necessary arrangement at the first opportunity.

GENERAL EDITOR'S PREFACE

Each of this series of Casebooks concerns either one well-known and influential work of literature or two or three closely linked works. The main section consists of critical readings, mostly modern, brought together from journals and books. A selection of reviews and comments by the author's contemporaries is also included, and sometimes comments from the author himself. The Editor's Introduction charts the reputation of the work from its first appearance until the present time.

The critical forum is a place of vigorous conflict and disagreement, but there is nothing in this to cause dismay. What is attested is the complexity of human experience and the richness of literature, not any chaos or relativity of taste. A critic is better seen, no doubt, as an explorer than as an 'authority', but explorers ought to be, and usually are, well equipped. The effect of good criticism is to convince us of what C. S. Lewis called 'the enormous extension of our being which we owe to authors'. A Casebook will be justified if it helps to promote the same end.

A single volume can represent no more than a small selection of critical opinions. Some critics have been excluded for reasons of space, and it is hoped that readers will follow up the further suggestions in the Select Bibliography. Other contributions have been severed from their original context, to which some readers may wish to return. Indeed, if they take a hint from the critics represented here, they certainly will.

A. E. DYSON

INTRODUCTION

'Wanted: Good Hardy Critic' is the title of a review article by Philip Larkin in the *Critical Quarterly* (Summer 1966). The obvious retort (cf. J. C. Maxwell, p. 155) is that there are many good Hardy critics; but it is true that there is no single critic who seems to have taken the full measure of his subject and whose book one could recommend to the newcomer to Hardy as *the* critical account. But in this respect Hardy is no worse served than certain major writers, D. H. Lawrence, for example, and it is perhaps even a relief that there is no established, 'authoritative' view of him, no stone that has to be rolled away before one can start looking for oneself at the embalmed corpse. The body still breathes, and at any moment will walk, run, spring upon us, or hide, with all the elusiveness and unpredictability of life.

There is, however, perhaps a special problem connected with Hardy in that he so often strikes his readers as being greater than there is any apparent cause for him to be. E. M. Forster, the most engagingly frank of literary critics, illustrates this reaction in *Aspects of the Novel* (1927), where he comments that Meredith knows better how to combine plot and character, but 'the work of Hardy is my home and that of Meredith cannot be'. This would seem to be the cue for a generous appraisal of Hardy's achievement as a novelist, but most of what Forster has to say proves to be on the negative side: Hardy's characters are dominated by a plot. They 'are ordered to acquiesce in its requirements'. The sense of a tragic fate is strong, but 'fate above us, not the fate working through us'. He is more successful in *The Dynasts* where the great engine of Fate is really seen working out the destinies of his characters. In the novels, however, with the one exception of the character of Tess, who 'conveys the feeling that she is greater than destiny', the machine works, but 'never catches humanity in its teeth'. And of *Jude the Obscure* Forster says, 'there is some vital problem that has not been answered, or even

posed in the misfortunes of Jude the Obscure'. His misgivings
are summed up in the remark that Hardy 'has emphasized caus-
ality more strongly than his medium permits'. This adds up to
something like a statement of failure. Yet one senses that all these
comments are made against the grain, as if Forster feels himself
bound by some external commitment (possibly the fact that he is
giving a lecture on 'Plot') to expose the inadequacies of Hardy's
novelistic technique, while feeling that all this is fundamentally
irrelevant to the deeply moving poetic effect which Hardy's novels
have upon him. The most telling comment is: 'Hardy seems to
me essentially a poet . . .', a tacit admission that the greatness of
Hardy is not explicable in the usual terms of novel criticism.

Though never an angry young man, or leader of a literary
revolt, Hardy was from the first in uneasy relationship with the
publishing practices and reading public of his day. His first
attempt at novel-writing, *The Poor Man and the Lady*[1] written
supposedly 'By the Poor Man', is described in *The Life of Thomas
Hardy* (nominally by Florence Emily Hardy, Hardy's second
wife, but now recognised to be effectively the work of Hardy himself) as 'a striking socialistic novel'. In 1869 it was read, among
others, by George Meredith, then publisher's reader for Chapman
and Hall, who thought it was too outspoken for a young man's
first novel. The meeting between the new and the already established author is described in the *Life* :

Meredith had the manuscript in his hand, and began lecturing
Hardy upon it in a sonorous voice. No record was kept by the latter
of their conversation, but the gist of it he remembered very well. It
was that the firm were willing to publish the novel as agreed, but
that he, the speaker, strongly advised its author not to 'nail his colours
to the mast' so definitely in a first book, if he wished to do anything
practical in literature; for if he printed so pronounced a thing he
would be attacked on all sides by the conventional reviewers, and his
future injured.[2]

This reference to 'conventional reviewers' is ominous, though
the tastes of conventional readers were to constitute a more real
problem for Hardy.

Meredith further suggested that Hardy should 'attempt a novel
with a purely artistic purpose, giving it a more complicated "plot"

than was attempted with *The Poor Man and the Lady*. As can be seen in his next, and first published, novel, *Desperate Remedies* (1871), the young writer, whose wish to do something 'practical in literature' included a legitimate hope for a modicum of reputation and financial success, bent his will to this advice; but his *prédilection d'artiste* (to use the term employed by D. H. Lawrence in his 'Study of Thomas Hardy') for romantically uncompromising characters and his instinctive sense of the falsity of conventional values asserted itself in forms that increasingly disturbed his attempts to write for the market, and particularly alarmed the editors of magazines to which Hardy sold the serial rights of his novels.

Problems of this kind arose more especially with the later work, i.e. with *The Return of the Native* (1878) and subsequent novels.[3] As a result of editorial pressures various details, and some whole episodes, were bowdlerised to satisfy the moral prejudices of the late Victorian reading public. Thus, from the manuscript version of *The Return of the Native* it would appear that Hardy originally intended Thomasin to go through an illegal marriage ceremony with Wildeve and be away from home for a whole week – a more compromising experience than her merely returning the same day because the licence is found to be invalid. At the same time Hardy's revisions suggest that his own imagination was increasingly fired by the unconventional character of Eustacia, who became a more 'Promethean' figure, and that the world of the novel grew less 'pastoral' in the manner of such earlier successes with the public as *Under the Greenwood Tree* (1872) and *Far From the Madding Crowd* (1874), and through increased mythological reference acquired the aura of 'the more comprehensive world of classical Greece'.[4] In the serial versions of *The Mayor of Casterbridge* (1886) and *Tess of the d'Urbervilles* (1891) further steps were taken to appease the Mrs Grundys of the magazines : Lucetta's Jersey affair with Henchard was glossed over as a marriage undertaken in the belief that Henchard was now a free man; and in the case of *Tess* two episodes, described by Hardy as 'more especially addressed to adult readers', were excised from the text and printed separately (though they were restored to the book version) in presumably more 'adult' periodicals. These episodes were Tess's seduction by Alec (chapters 10 and 11 of the book), published in a Special Literary Supplement of the *National Observer* (14 November 1891) under the ironic title of 'Saturday Night in Arcady', and the unorthodox baptising by Tess of her baby (chapter 14), published in the *Fortnightly Review* (May 1891). In the serial version of *Tess* the hoary device of a seemingly legal marriage was used yet again, and towards the end of the novel, in the crucial episode of Alec d'Urberville and Tess at the Sandbourne boarding-house, a feeble attempt was made to suggest that they were simply staying there as friends. Most ludicrous of all was the change in detail in chapter 23 so that Angel could wheel the dairymaids in a barrow instead of actually carrying them in his arms over the flooded lane.

More serious problems were encountered with *Jude the Obscure* (1895). Serialisation, in *Harper's New Monthly Magazine*, was agreed in principle in 1893 on condition that the story should be 'in every respect suitable for a family magazine', and Hardy said that 'it would be a tale that could not offend the most fastidious maiden'. But it did not work out that way, and several adjustments had to be made for the serial version. For example, Arabella's device for tricking Jude into marriage became simply the pretence that a former sweetheart is offering to marry her, and a letter is produced to 'prove' the point. Jude's night with Arabella in Aldbrickham was made quite innocuous by their going to separate lodgings, and Sue and Jude likewise were placed in separate, though contiguous, houses. In the serial Sue never gives in to Jude sexually, as she does in the book when she fears the rivalry of Arabella; she merely promises marriage. Above all, Sue's confiding in Little Time about the coming baby is also omitted from the serial, thus destroying a vital element in the tragedy.

All this is perhaps mainly an illustration of the queasy literary stomachs of late Victorian magazine readers; but that Hardy should have written scenes so offensive to contemporary taste, while still wishing to benefit from serialisation, is an indication not, as Mary Ellen Chase would suggest, of his lack of integrity as an artist,[5] but of the strength of the imaginative compulsion within him towards the expression of unpalatable truths.

The reviews of his work, and his reactions to them, suggest once again the uneasiness of his relationship with his contemporaries, though by no means a uniformly unfavourable response. The two novels which, as might be expected, most aroused the moral indignation of propriety-conscious reviewers were *Tess* and *Jude*. In *The Life of Thomas Hardy* the intemperate comments of a 'maiden lady' critic on *Jude* are quoted, including such phrases as 'I thought that *Tess of the d'Urbervilles* was bad enough, but that is milk for babes compared to this. . . . Aside from its immorality there is coarseness which is beyond belief. . . . When I finished the story I opened the windows and let in the fresh air.'[6] At the beginning of chapter 24 of the *Life* occurs the remark that misrepresentations 'wellnigh compelled [Hardy], in his own judgment at any rate, if he wished to retain any shadow of self-respect, to abandon at once a form of literary art he had long intended to abandon at some indefinite time', and turn to poetry. How seriously the adverse reviews of *Tess* and *Jude* (and they were not all adverse) influenced Hardy's decision to abandon novel-writing is open to debate. But the implication of this passage is that he was already prepared to make the change from prose to verse before he read the reviews. The likelihood is that such factitious moral outbursts were no more influential than they were true criticism; but it is worth paying attention to them since they further exemplify the uncongenial publishing conditions in which Hardy had to work. He was a man who wished to be on good terms with his readers yet felt he could not trust the moral judgement of many of them. This is evident in the tone of the later novels, and not least in the title page of *Tess*. The sub-title, 'A Pure Woman', was added as an afterthought when Hardy had read the final proofs, 'as being the estimate left in a candid mind of the heroine's character – an estimate that nobody would be likely to dispute. It was disputed more than anything else in the book.'[7] But this is slightly disingenuous. The sub-title defies conventional opinion, and is reinforced by the words 'Faithfully Presented' and the quotation from the *Two Gentlemen of Verona*: '. . . Poor wounded name! My bosom as a bed/Shall lodge thee.' If this is written to indicate the true interpretation, it also seems to anticipate misinterpretation.

Saner and more penetrating criticism came from men like
Havelock Ellis, R. H. Hutton, William Watson and Edmund
Gosse.[8] These praised him while adding strictures, which, though
in the end one may have to reject them, started a critical debate
of an altogether more serious kind, to be continued by the authors
of books and articles produced at greater leisure and after time
had been given for the sifting processes of reflection and discussion. Thus Hutton begins to question Hardy's pessimism and
Watson and Gosse his touches of pedantry in style.[9] Havelock
Ellis, on the other hand, takes up the issue of what is fit reading
for the 'Young Person' and argues for a more enlightened attitude
in a way that must have given Hardy great satisfaction.

Even before the publication of *Jude the Obscure* Lionel Johnson
wrote his book, *The Art of Thomas Hardy* (1894), which, as shown
in the extract printed here, combined disagreement with Hardy's
'general sentiments, about the meaning of the unconscious universe, or of conscious mankind' with considerable admiration for
his art; and his list of the characteristics of Hardy's work – the
concentration on Wessex, the choice of powerful characters set
off by others less powerful and their clash with men of 'more
modern experiences', the focus on erotic love, the preference for
a certain tragic curve in the development of his plots – provides
a useful summation of the Hardy world. F. Manning, in his
article on 'Novels of Character and Environment' (1912), goes
further. He identifies tragedy as the central preoccupation of
Hardy's later novels, and, while deploring the passivity of a
character like Tess because this diminishes the sense of free will
on which the ennobling effect of tragedy depends, he recognises
quite clearly that the special tragic power of Hardy's work derives
from 'the depth and richness of his emotional nature' which finds
its fullest expression in *Tess* and *Jude*.

The feeling that Hardy is great in spite of a curious wrong-
headedness is a widespread critical reaction. D. H. Lawrence,
however, is more confident than most in defining what is right
and what is wrong. For him the tragedy of Hardy is the tragedy
of those who answer the call of individual fulfilment instead of
submitting to 'the comparative imprisonment' of conventional
standards of behaviour, but in so doing are destroyed. He senses

the anti-conventionality of Hardy, but is impatient because Hardy does not go far enough in asserting it. It is commonly said that the 'Study of Thomas Hardy' tells us more about Lawrence than about Hardy, and it is true that the interpretation of tragedy which Lawrence attributes to Hardy reflects Lawrence's own impatience with the inhibitive power of convention. Hardy, like Tolstoy, is condemned for making his characters submit to society, or a morality which is socially induced, instead of allowing them to assert, and live by, their own innate vitality. Nevertheless in his comments on *The Return of the Native* Lawrence shows his awareness of the importance in Hardy of the relationship between the human and the natural, and he gives an analysis of Egdon Heath which initiates a long series of attempts to account for the peculiarly evocative power of Hardy's descriptions of it.

For Virginia Woolf, too, man in the tragic context of Nature is the special subject of Hardy and, like Forster, she finds the poet at work in the novels, though in her view poet and novelist are not at odds with each other, but join their forces together : 'In short, nobody can deny Hardy's power – the true novelist's power – to make us believe that his characters are fellow-beings driven by their own passions and idiosyncrasies, while they have – and this is the poet's gift – something symbolical about them which is common to us all.'

A rather different kind of emphasis is given to the poetic element by one of Hardy's most recent critics, Jean Brooks. Acknowledging the truth of the sentence just quoted from Virginia Woolf, she none the less goes on to argue that 'the poetic structure' informing Hardy's work, not simply the presence of the 'poet's gift' in parts of his work, demands central critical attention, for this explains and justifies, as other critical approaches do not, the tensions and seeming contradictions of his art. The 'poetic' principle as thus understood is the more or less explicit assumption on which many recent studies of particular novels are based. Examples in this collection are the studies of *Tess of the d'Urbervilles* (the Hardy novel which most seems to invite this approach) by Tony Tanner and David Lodge. Tanner uses a favourite method of modern critics, the selection and analysis of significant images, to show that Hardy's poetic impressionism depicts in Tess a type of human life drawn out from Nature, but doomed to be destroyed by Nature, and 'a universe of radical opposition, working to destroy what it works to create . . .'. Lodge, on the other hand, studies the details of Hardy's style, taking up the well-tried theme of its unevenness and attempting to establish with greater precision where it is successful and where it fails.

The poetic approach is on the whole the most satisfactory approach to Hardy. It largely invalidates the preoccupation of earlier critics with such matters as the supposedly deterministic philosophy of Hardy and his excessive use of chance and coincidence. If Hardy is not seeking to present a fictional imitation of character and circumstance as they actually interact in observable day-to-day existence, if he is not, that is to say, a realist (and he certainly denied that he was), such offences against plausibility are no more to be held against him, as Virginia Woolf suggests, than the similar offences of the Elizabethan dramatists. The appropriate question to ask, then, with regard to Hardy's fiction is whether characters, setting, plot and language combine in an imaginatively effective whole. The novels must be judged by their inner coherence as works of art rather than by their faithfulness in reflecting the real conditions of the external world.

But as soon as this is said it appears to be an overstatement. In the 'General Preface to the Novels and Poems', written for the 1912 Wessex Edition of his works, Hardy speaks of the trouble he has taken to authenticate the detail of his presentation of 'Wessex' (at once the actual, and a fictional version of south-western England) 'in order to preserve for my own satisfaction a fairly true record of a vanishing life'. Much of the background, he says, 'has been done from the real – that is to say, has something real for its basis, however illusively treated'.[10] Such a juxtaposition of 'real' and 'illusively' may seem confusing, but it probably springs from Hardy's quite legitimate desire to retain the freedom of the artist creating a work of fiction, and yet to keep close to the 'feel' of the experiences which he himself had had as boy and young man in the region of which he writes. Moreover, the attitudes and habits of 'Wessex' touched him all the more keenly as he appreciated the quality of the social and intellectual forces which were detaching him from that life. As a result there is also an entirely justifiable biographical and sociological strain to be found in some Hardy criticism. This, in its turn, has generated a reaction. The historical accuracy, for example, of Douglas Brown's suggestion that the tragic novels, and *The Mayor of Casterbridge* in particular, are about the agricultural tragedy of 1870–1902 is questioned by J. C. Maxwell in his essay 'The "Sociological" Approach to *The Mayor of Casterbridge*'. Maxwell reminds us that Hardy's 1912 Preface to that novel alludes to an earlier period, involving 'the uncertain harvest which immediately preceded the repeal of the Corn Laws',[11] and, while conceding that the struggle between Henchard and Farfrae does reflect in a general manner the conflict between old and new styles of life, he shows that Farfrae cannot seriously be identified with the new financial methods and cold ruthlessness of modern enterprise encroaching on the warm, passionate ways of old Wessex. The essence of Brown's argument remains, however : all the later novels are permeated by Hardy's 'sensuous understanding' of the organically integrated agricultural life, and a tragic sense of its decay; though in some ways it is *Tess of the d'Urbervilles* rather than *The Mayor of Casterbridge* which best illustrates this thesis. His deep feeling for 'Wessex' makes Tess at once a very real woman and a representative, almost at times a mythic, figure, 'a visionary essence of woman'.

If we are in danger, by following this train of thought, of losing once more the elements of immediate knowledge which Hardy draws upon to create his Wessex world (and one should remember that it is Angel to whom Tess appears 'visionary'; she herself prefers to be taken as simply 'Tess' the milkmaid), Raymond Williams' chapter on Hardy in *The English Novel from Dickens to Lawrence* is another salutary reminder of Hardy's grasp of the complex reality. The particular vantage point given him by his background – neither of the agricultural labouring class nor of the farmers and landowners, but son of a builder, and himself trained to a professional career as an architect – enabled Hardy to write about 'Wessex' as 'both the educated observer and the passionate participant', and an important consequence of this combination of detachment and sympathy was that he could represent the pressures to which his characters were subjected as 'pressures from within the system of living, not outside it'.

To some extent all criticism proceeds by disagreement and qualification compelling a return to whatever text is being considered for renewed impressions and reappraisal. The question of the realism or ultra-realism of Hardy's fiction can in this light be seen as a fruitful contradiction resulting from shifting critical points of view. The essays in this volume on *The Return of the Native* by John Paterson and Leonard W. Deen are further examples of such contradiction. Paterson's researches into the making of *The Return* brought out for him the double theme of the romantic enlargement of the novel in the process of revision and the pretentiousness of its too explicit claims to tragic grandeur.[12] Deen's argument, however, is that *The Return*, though it 'invites comparison with grand tragedy', is not essentially a tragic achievement of that kind. Rather, it constitutes a stage in Hardy's development towards the special mode of his later tragedies which are not heroic in the traditional manner, but ironic and pathetic. (Another critical disagreement is also involved here, for the very qualities that had led Manning in 1912 to rate *Tess* below *The Return* lead Deen to reverse that judgement and see *The Return* as the imperfect forerunner of *Tess*.) So much is the heroism played down that the appropriateness of the word 'tragedy' becomes matter for doubt. Deen is inclined to reject the term and would prefer to see *The Return* as a forerunner of the twentieth-century novel of 'disillusioned scepticism', introspection and the 'sense of isolation in an alien society'.

The consideration of conflicting interpretations of *The Mayor of Casterbridge* by previous critics leads Robert C. Schweik to the discovery of a change of posture on Hardy's part as the novel advanced – a change from presenting Henchard's career as an illustration of the dictum, 'character is fate', which implies that the universe is morally ordered, to seeing him as victim in a morally neutral world. The transition from one to the other is effectively disguised by the overall structure of the novel, consisting of successive wave-like movements of hope, anxiety and catastrophe. The reason that Schweik suggests for this modulation of the tragic concept underlying *The Mayor* – that in Hardy traditional beliefs were at variance with intellectually acquired doubt – is speculative; but the analysis is excellent in its tracing of the shifting values of the novel.

Among Hardy's novels the most problematical is *Jude the Obscure*. There is considerable disagreement among critics as to whether it is the greatest of his novels, or his most perverse; a true 'Wessex' novel, or a curious outsider; a tragedy, or a case-history; late, but still essentially Victorian, or the novel in which Hardy finally breaks with the conventional prejudices of the Victorian reading public and allows himself to step forward as a distinctively 'modern' author. It is even a matter of dispute whether Jude or Sue is the central character. Structurally the two are in balance; or, rather, together with Phillotson and Arabella they create a quartet whose sexual relations form something like a geometrical pattern of alternating partnerships,[13] and, as Hardy himself writes in his letter to Gosse, 'the book is all contrasts' (see p. 34).

For Robert Heilman, however, Sue Bridehead is a character who 'has taken off on her own, and developed as a being whose brilliant and puzzling surface provides only partial clues to the depths in which we can sense the presence of profound and representative problems'. She is a psychological study of coquettishness, i.e. the desire to dominate men through attractiveness coupled with denial, which she indulges in for unconscious, and often self-protective, motives. Sue professes unconventional opinions, but is dangerously unaware of the extent to which she remains, at the level of emotional response, fundamentally conventional. Therefore, after her crisis, irrationally, but with a curiously relevant emotional logic, she punishes herself by returning to the most rigid extreme of conventionality. This is a profoundly typical Hardy theme, interpreted by Heilman as an instance of modern man's 'habitual rational analysis that tends to destroy the forms of feeling developed by the historical community'. As an example of close reading for a particular purpose Heilman's analysis is a model of its kind, but his conclusion that Sue's fate is more an 'illness' than a tragedy does suggest that concentration on the psychology of a single character can distort the imaginative effect of the novel as an artistic whole.

Heilman is none the less right in focusing attention on the diseased consciousness as a distinguishing mark of *Jude the Obscure*. As Ian Gregor remarks, 'With her [Sue] we find displayed the consciousness of self, the innate uncertainties, the psychic disturbance with which the fiction of our own day is to make us familiar'. This points also to the modernity of *Jude* as compared with the rest of the Wessex novels. Not that the break is absolute. Gregor finds it still a very nineteenth-century novel in that it bears very markedly the stamp of the authorial presence (it is recognisably the work of 'the novelist as sage'); but it is twentieth-century in its emphasis on rhythm, its orchestration of themes, and its sometimes extravagant defiance of realism. Thus the Father Time episode and the death of the children, which Gregor describes as 'the most terrible scene in Hardy's fiction', indeed it might reasonably be argued in English fiction, transcends realism and aims at 'an impersonal tragic dimension'. The novel becomes what Hardy himself in the Preface to *Jude* called 'a series of seemings'. At the same time what Gregor shows to be the growing insulation of Sue from the feelings of others, counterpointed by Jude's increasing awareness of his involvement 'with time, place and person', suggests that this tokens not a retreat from, but a more intense engagement with, actual experience.

The old and the new meet in *Jude* in other ways as well. This new intensity of response to the actual is accompanied by a magnification of those grotesque misalliances of incident and impression so characteristic of Hardy from his earliest work. Jude's death scene is a potent example : By ten o'clock that night Jude was lying on the bedstead at his lodging covered with a sheet, and straight as an arrow. Through the partly opened window the joyous throb of a waltz entered from the ball-room at Cardinal.' On one level this is savage irony; on another it is representative of the nature of tragedy especially as it affects the modern sensibility – something poignant and wringing but which, with a shift of attitude, easily becomes farce. 'If you look beneath the surface of any farce', wrote Hardy in 1888, 'you see a tragedy; and, on the contrary, if you blind yourself to the deeper issues of a tragedy you see a farce.' This perception, implicit in each of the tragic novels, reaches its culmination, and its most conscious expression, in *Jude*. There tragedy and farce are the closest of neighbours, and it is Hardy's purpose to intensify this impression; but it is also his purpose to act upon the compassion and indignation of the reader so that the reader is never blind to the deeper issues, seeing only the farce and not the tragedy.

NOTES

1. This novel was never published in its original form, but parts of it may have been used in *Under the Greenwood Tree* and *An Indiscretion in The Life of an Heiress*. (See Carl J. Weber's edition of the latter, 1935; reissued, New York, 1965.)

2. Florence Emily Hardy, *The Life of Thomas Hardy, 1840–1928* (Macmillan, 1962, reprinted 1972) p. 61. (Originally printed in two vols, *The Early Life of Thomas Hardy, 1840–1891*, 1928 and *The Later Years of Thomas Hardy, 1892–1928*, 1930.)

3 For details see John Paterson, *The Making of 'The Return of the Native'* (University of California Press, 1960); Mary Ellen Chase, *Thomas Hardy from Serial to Novel* (University of Minnesota Press, 1922; rev. ed., New York, 1964); and R. L. Purdy, *Thomas Hardy: A Bibliographical Study* (Oxford University Press, 1954). The following discussion of Hardy's publication difficulties is indebted to the above sources and the *Life*.

4. Paterson, *The Making of 'The Return of the Native'*, p. 30.

5. See *Thomas Hardy from Serial to Novel*, pp. 198–201.

6. *Life*, p. 279. The review appeared in the New York *World* (8 December 1895). The critic responsible for this outburst was Jeannette Gilder, who later sought a journalistic interview with Hardy 'to get your side of the argument'. Hardy replied, 'Those readers who, like yourself, could not see that *Jude* (though a book quite without a "purpose" as it is called) makes for morality more than any other book I have written, are not likely to be made to do so by a newspaper article, even from your attractive pen.' (*Life*, p. 280.)

7. 1912 Preface to *Tess*. In Purdy's Bibliography there is a photograph (opposite p. 71) of the MS. draft of the title-page bearing the words, 'To supersede copy previously sent'.

8. Havelock Ellis, 'Thomas Hardy's Novels', *Westminster Review* (April 1883), and 'Concerning *Jude the Obscure*', *Savoy Magazine* (October 1896); R. H. Hutton, review of *The Mayor of Casterbridge*, *Spectator* (5 June 1886); William Watson, review of *Tess, Academy*

(6 February 1892); Edmund Gosse, review of *Jude, Cosmopolis* (January 1896). (See R. G. Cox, ed., *Thomas Hardy, the Critical Heritage*, Routledge & Kegan Paul, London, 1970).

9. For further discussion of Hardy's style see David Lodge's 'Tess, Nature, and the Voices of Hardy' included in this selection. Most critics comment on Hardy's so-called pessimism, but see, in particular, Roy Morrell, *Thomas Hardy, the Will and the Way* (University of Malaya Press, 1965). Morrell argues that Hardy is not a pessimist, but simply anxious that people shall not deceive themselves with easy hopes : '. . . no Being, or Force, is going to change the course of things for us . . . we must do something ourselves.' (pp. 37–8).

10. *Thomas Hardy's Personal Writings*, ed. Harold Orel (Macmillan, 1967) p. 46.

11. *Personal Writings*, p. 18.

12. See above, p. 13 and footnote 3. Paterson's conclusions are summarised in his Preface to Harper & Row's 1966 edition of *The Return of the Native*, which also contains his considered critical judgments on the novel and is, therefore, the piece chosen for reprinting here.

13. A detailed analysis of this structure is given by the French critic, Fernand Lagarde in 'A propos de la construction de *Jude the Obscure*', *Caliban* (January 1966). Though brilliant this analysis is carried out with such thoroughgoing efficiency as to make the novel seem more of an artificial *tour de force* than a moving human document.

PART ONE

Comments by Hardy

1. EXTRACTS FROM *THE LIFE OF THOMAS HARDY*

April 1878. Note. A Plot, or Tragedy, should arise from the gradual closing in of a situation that comes of ordinary human passions, prejudices, and ambitions, by reason of the characters taking no trouble to ward off the disastrous events produced by the said passions, prejudices, and ambitions. (p. 120)

19 April 1885. [Hardy had just finished *The Mayor of Caster-bridge* two days before.] The business of the poet and novelist is to show the sorriness underlying the grandest things, and the grandeur underlying the sorriest things. (p. 171)

21–2 November 1885. . . . Tragedy. It may be put thus in brief: a tragedy exhibits a state of things in the life of an individual which unavoidably causes some natural aim or desire of his to end in a catastrophe when carried out. (p. 176)

21 December 1885. The Hypocrisy of things. Nature is an arch-dissembler. A child is deceived completely; the older members of society more or less according to their penetration; though even they seldom get to realize that *nothing* is as it appears. (p. 176)

15–21 October 1888. . . . If you look beneath the surface of any farce you see a tragedy; and, on the contrary, if you blind yourself to the deeper issues of a tragedy you see a farce. (p. 215)

5 May 1889. . . . That which, socially, is a great tragedy, may be in Nature no alarming circumstance. (p. 218)

5 August 1890. Reflections on Art. Art is a changing of the actual proportions and order out of things, so as to bring out more

forcibly than might otherwise be done that feature in them which appeals most strongly to the idiosyncrasy of the artist. The changing, or distortion, may be of two kinds : (1) The kind which increases the sense of vraisemblance : (2) That which diminishes it. (1) is high art : (2) is low art.

High art may choose to depict evil as well as good, without losing its quality. Its choice of evil, however, must be limited by the sense of worthiness.

Art is a disproportioning – (i.e. distorting, throwing out of proportion) – of realities, to show more clearly the features that matter in those realities, which, if merely copied or reported inventorially, might possibly be observed, but would more probably be overlooked. Hence 'realism' is not Art. [Last paragraph added a little later than the rest.] (pp. 228–9)

24 October 1892. The best tragedy – highest tragedy in short – is that of the WORTHY encompassed by the INEVITABLE. The tragedies of immoral and worthless people are not of the best. (p. 251)

1895? [The outcome of some reviews of *Jude the Obscure*.] Tragedy may be created by an opposing environment either of things inherent in the universe, or of human institutions. If the former be the means exhibited and deplored, the writer is regarded as impious; if the latter, as subversive and dangerous; when all the while he may never have questioned the necessity or urged the non-necessity of either. . . . (p. 274)

ON 'THE RETURN OF THE NATIVE'

22 April 1878. The method of Boldini, the painter of 'The Morning Walk' in the French Gallery two or three years ago (a young lady beside an ugly blank wall on an ugly highway) – of Hobbema, in his view of a road with formal lopped trees and flat tame scenery – is that of infusing emotion into the baldest external objects either by the presence of a human figure among them, or by mark of some human connection with them.

This accords with my feeling about, say, Heidelberg and Baden *versus* Scheveningen – as I wrote at the beginning of *The Return of the Native* – that the beauty of association is entirely superior to the beauty of aspect, and a beloved relative's old battered tankard to the finest Greek vase. Paradoxically put, it is to see the beauty in ugliness. (pp. 120–1)

September 1878. [Hardy writes to his publishers.] I enclose a sketch-map of the supposed scene in which *The Return of the Native* is laid, copied from the one I used in writing the story; and my suggestion is that we place an engraving of it as frontispiece to the first volume. Unity of place is so seldom preserved in novels that a map of the scene of action is as a rule quite impracticable. But since the present story affords an opportunity of doing so I am of opinion that it would be a desirable novelty. (p. 122)

[In a letter of 1923? Hardy wrote about his play, *The Queen of Cornwall*, that it 'strictly preserved' the unities, and added : 'I, myself, am old-fashioned enough to think there *is* a virtue in it, if it can be done without artificiality. The only other case I remember attempting it in was *The Return of the Native*' (p. 422).]

ON 'THE MAYOR OF CASTERBRIDGE'

1886 – 2 January, *The Mayor of Casterbridge* begins to-day in the *Graphic* newspaper and *Harper's Weekly*. – I fear it will not be so good as I meant, but after all, it is not improbabilities of incident but improbabilities of character that matter. (p. 176)

The Mayor of Casterbridge was issued complete about the end of May [1886]. It was a story which Hardy fancied he had damaged more recklessly as an artistic whole, in the interest of the newspaper in which it appeared serially, than perhaps any other of his novels, his aiming to get an incident into almost every week's part causing him in his own judgment to add events to the narrative somewhat too freely. However, as at this time he called his novel-writing 'mere journeywork' he cared little about it as art, though it must be said in favour of the plot, as he admitted later,

that it was quite coherent and organic, in spite of its complication.
(p. 179)

ON 'TESS OF THE D'URBERVILLES'

And it was about this date [1853–4] that he [Hardy] formed
one of a trio of youths (the vicar's sons being the other two) who
taught in the Sunday School of the parish, where as a pupil in
his class he had a dairymaid four years older than himself, who
afterwards appeared in *Tess of the d'Urbervilles* as Marian –
one of the few portraits from life in his works. This pink and
plump damsel had a marvellous power of memorizing whole
chapters in the Bible, and would repeat to him by heart in class,
to his boredom, the long gospels before Easter without missing a
word, and with evident delight in her facility; though she was
by no means a model of virtue in her love-affairs. (p. 25)

. . . the business immediately in hand [ca October 1889] was the
new story *Tess of the d'Urbervilles*, for the serial use of which
Hardy had three requests, if not more, on his list; and in October
as much of it as was written was offered to the first who had asked
for it, the editor of *Murray's Magazine*. It was declined and
returned to him in the middle of November virtually on the score
of its improper explicitness. It was at once sent on to the second,
the editor of *Macmillan's Magazine*, and on the 25th was declined
by him for practically the same reason. Hardy would now have
much preferred to finish the story and bring it out in volume form
only, but there were reasons why he could not afford to do this;
and he adopted a plan till then, it is believed, unprecedented in
the annals of fiction. This was not to offer the novel intact to the
third editor on his list (his experience with the first two editors
having taught him that it would be useless to send it to the third
as it stood), but to send it up with some chapters or parts of chapters cut out, and instead of destroying these to publish them, or
much of them, elsewhere, if practicable, as episodic adventures
of anonymous personages (which in fact was done, with the omission of a few paragraphs); till they could be put back in their

places at the printing of the whole in volume form. In addition several passages were modified. Hardy carried out this unceremonious concession to conventionality with cynical amusement, knowing the novel was moral enough and to spare. But the work was sheer drudgery, the modified passages having to be written in coloured ink, that the originals might be easily restored, and he frequently asserted that it would have been almost easier for him to write a new story altogether. Hence the labour brought no profit. He resolved to get away from the supply of family fiction to magazines as soon as he conveniently could do so. (pp. 221–2)

As the year [1891] drew to a close an incident that took place during the publication of *Tess of the d'Urbervilles* as a serial in the *Graphic* might have prepared him for certain events that were to follow. The editor objected to the description of Angel Clare carrying in his arms, across a flooded lane, Tess and her three dairymaid companions. He suggested that it would be more decorous and suitable for the pages of a periodical intended for family reading if the damsels were wheeled across the lane in a wheel-barrow. This was accordingly done. (p. 240)

1892. [Hardy on 'The President of the Immortals had finished his sport with Tess', in reply to a critic who wrote that 'Hardy postulates an all-powerful being endowed with the baser human passions . . .'] As I need hardly inform any thinking reader, I do not hold, and never have held, the ludicrous opinions here assumed to be mine – which are really, or approximately, those of the primitive believer in his man-shaped tribal god. And in seeking to ascertain how any exponent of English literature could have supposed that I held them I find that the writer of the estimate has harked back to a passage in a novel of mine, printed many years ago, in which the forces opposed to the heroine were allegorized as a personality (a method not unusual in imaginative prose or poetry) by the use of a well-known trope, explained in that venerable work, Campbell's *Philosophy of Rhetoric*, as 'one in which life, perception, activity, design, passion, or any property of sentient beings, is attributed to things inanimate'.

Under this species of criticism if an author were to say 'Aeolus maliciously tugged at her garments, and tore her hair in his wrath', the sapient critic would no doubt announce that author's evil creed to be that the wind is 'a powerful being endowed with the baser human passions', etc., etc.

However, I must put up with it, and say as Parrhasius of Ephesus said about his pictures : There is nothing that men will not find fault with. (p. 244)

15 April 1892. *Good Friday.* Read review of *Tess* in *The Quarterly.* A smart and amusing article; but it is easy to be smart and amusing if a man will forgo veracity and sincerity. . . . How strange that one may write a book without knowing what one puts into it – or rather, the reader reads into it. Well, if this sort of thing continues no more novel-writing for me. A man must be a fool to deliberately stand up to be shot at. (p. 246)

ON 'JUDE THE OBSCURE'

28 April 1888. A short story of a young man – 'who could not go to Oxford' – His struggles and ultimate failure. Suicide. [Probably the germ of *Jude the Obscure.*] There is something [in this] the world ought to be shown, and I am the one to show it to them – though I was not altogether hindered going, at least to Cambridge, and could have gone up easily at five-and-twenty. (pp. 207–8; the square brackets here are in *The Life*)

20 September 1926. [Concerning 'a proposed dramatisation of *Jude the Obscure*':] Would not Arabella be the villain of the piece? – or Jude's personal constitution? – so far as there is any villain more than blind Chance. Christminster is of course the tragic influence of Jude's drama in one sense, but innocently so, and merely as crass obstruction. By the way it is not meant to be exclusively Oxford, but any old-fashioned University about the date of the story, 1860–1870, before there were such chances for poor men as there are now. I have somewhere printed that I had no feeling against Oxford in particular. (p. 433)

THREE LETTERS TO EDMUND GOSSE (1895-6)

I. 10 November 1895

. . . . Your review (of *Jude the Obscure*) is the most discriminating that has yet appeared. It required an artist to see that the plot is almost geometrically constructed – I ought not to say *constructed*, for, beyond a certain point, the characters necessitated it, and I simply let it come. As for the story itself, it is really sent out to those into whose souls the iron has entered, and has entered deeply at some time of their lives. But one cannot choose one's readers.

It is curious that some of the papers should look upon the novel as a manifesto on 'the marriage question' (although, of course, it involves it), seeing that it is concerned first with the labours of a poor student to get a University degree, and secondly with the tragic issues of two bad marriages, owing in the main to a doom or curse of hereditary temperament peculiar to the family of the parties. The only remarks which can be said to bear on the *general* marriage question occur in dialogue, and comprise no more than half a dozen pages in a book of five hundred. And of these remarks I state that my own views are not expressed therein. I suppose the attitude of these critics is to be accounted for by the accident that, during the serial publication of my story, a sheaf of 'purpose' novels on the matter appeared.

You have hardly an idea how poor and feeble the book seems to me, as executed, beside the idea of it that I had formed in prospect.

I have received some interesting letters about it already – yours not the least so. Swinburne writes, too enthusiastically for me to quote with modesty. . . .

P.S. One thing I did not answer. The 'grimy' features of the story go to show the contrast between the ideal life a man wished to lead, and the squalid real life he was fated to lead. The throwing of the pizzle, at the supreme moment of his young dream, is to sharply initiate this contrast. But I must have lamentably failed, as I feel I have, if this requires explanation and is not self-evident. The idea was meant to run all through the novel. It is, in fact, to be discovered in *everybody's* life, though it lies

H.T.T.N.—B

less on the surface perhaps than it does in my poor puppet's.
(pp. 271-2)

II. 20 November 1895

I am keen about the new magazine. How interesting that you
should be writing this review for it! I wish the book were more
worthy of such notice and place.

You are quite right; there is nothing perverted or depraved in
Sue's nature. The abnormalism consists in disproportion, not in
inversion, her sexual instinct being healthy as far as it goes, but
unusually weak and fastidious. Her sensibilities remain painfully
alert notwithstanding, as they do in nature with such women. One
point illustrating this I could not dwell upon : that, though she
has children, her intimacies with Jude have never been more than
occasional, even when they were living together (I mention that
they occupy separate rooms, except towards the end), and one of
her reasons for fearing the marriage ceremony is that she fears it
would be breaking faith with Jude to withhold herself at pleasure,
or altogether, after it; though while uncontracted she feels at
liberty to yield herself as seldom as she chooses. This has tended
to keep his passion as hot at the end as at the beginning, and helps
to break his heart. He has never really possessed her as freely
as he desired.

Sue is a type of woman which has always had an attraction
for me, but the difficulty of drawing the type has kept me from
attempting it till now.

Of course the book is all contrasts – or was meant to be in its
original conception. Alas, what a miserable accomplishment it is,
when I compare it with what I meant to make it! – e.g. Sue and
her heathen gods set against Jude's reading the Greek testament;
Christminster academical, Christminster in the slums; Jude the
saint, Jude the sinner; Sue the Pagan, Sue the saint; marriage,
no marriage; &c., &c.

As to the 'coarse' scenes with Arabella, the battle in the schoolroom, etc., the newspaper critics might, I thought, have sneered
at them for their Fieldingism rather than for their Zolaism. But
your everyday critic knows nothing of Fielding. I am read in

Zola very little, but have felt akin locally to Fielding, so many of his scenes having been laid down this way, and his home near.

Did I tell you I feared I should seem too High-Churchy at the end of the book where Sue recants? You can imagine my surprise at some of the reviews. . . . (pp. 272–3)

III. 4 January 1896

For the last three days I have been tantalized by a difficulty in getting *Cosmopolis*, and had only just read your review when I received your note. My sincere thanks for the generous view you take of the book, which to me is a mass of imperfections. We have both been amused – or rather delighted – by the sub-humour (is there such a word?) of your writing. I think it a rare quality in living essayists, and that you ought to make more of it – I mean write more in that vein than you do.

But this is apart from the review itself, of which I will talk to you when we meet. The rectangular lines of the story were not premeditated, but came by chance : except, of course, that the involutions of four lives must necessarily be a sort of quadrille. The only point in the novel on which I feel sure is that it makes for morality; and that delicacy or indelicacy in a writer is according to his object. If I say to a lady 'I met a naked woman', it is indelicate. But if I go on to say 'I found she was mad with sorrow', it ceases to be indelicate. And in writing Jude my mind was fixed on the ending. . . . (p. 273)

December 1895. When they [Hardy and his wife] got back to Dorchester during December Hardy had plenty of time to read the reviews of *Jude* that continued to pour out. Some paragraphists knowingly assured the public that the book was an honest autobiography, and Hardy did not take the trouble to deny it till more than twenty years later, when he wrote to an inquirer with whom the superstition still lingered that no book he had ever written contained less of his own life, which of course had been known to his friends from the beginning. Some of the incidents were real in so far as that he had heard of them, or come in contact with them when they were occurring to people he knew;

but no more. It is interesting to mention that on his way to
school he did once meet with a youth like Jude who drove the
bread-cart of a widow, a baker, like Mrs. Fawley, and carried
on his studies at the same time, to the serious risk of other drivers
in the lanes; which youth asked him to lend him his Latin grammar. But Hardy lost sight of this fearful student, and never knew
if he profited by his plan. (p. 274)

S o u r c e : Florence Emily Hardy, *The Life of Thomas Hardy*
(1962).

2. FROM 'THE DORSETSHIRE LABOURER' (1883)

It seldom happens that a nickname which affects to portray a class is honestly indicative of the individuals composing that class. The few features distinguishing them from other bodies of men have been seized on and exaggerated, while the incomparably more numerous features common to all humanity have been ignored. In the great world this wild colouring of so-called typical portraits is clearly enough recognised. Nationalities, the aristocracy, the plutocracy, the citizen class, and many others have their allegorical representatives, which are received with due allowance for flights of imagination in the direction of burlesque.

But when the class lies somewhat out of the ken of ordinary society the caricature begins to be taken as truth. Moreover, the original is held to be an actual unit of the multitude signified. He ceases to be an abstract figure and becomes a sample. Thus when we arrive at the farm-labouring community we find it to be seriously personified by the pitiable picture known as Hodge; not only so, but the community is assumed to be a uniform collection of concrete Hodges.

This supposed real but highly conventional Hodge is a degraded being of uncouth manner and aspect, stolid understanding, and snail-like movement. His speech is such a chaotic corruption of regular language that few persons of progressive aims consider it worth while to enquire what views, if any, of life, of nature, or of society are conveyed in these utterances. Hodge hangs his head or looks sheepish when spoken to, and thinks Lunnon a place paved with gold. Misery and fever lurk in his cottage, while, to paraphrase the words of a recent writer on the labouring classes, in his future there are only the workhouse and the grave. He hardly dares to think at all. He has few thoughts of joy, and little hope of rest. His life slopes into a darkness not 'quieted by hope'.

If one of the many thoughtful persons who hold this view were
to go by rail to Dorset, where Hodge in his most unmitigated form
is supposed to reside, and seek out a retired district, he might by
and by certainly meet a man who, at first contact with an intelligence fresh from the contrasting world of London, would seem to
exhibit some of the above-mentioned qualities. The latter items
in the list, the mental miseries, the visitor might hardly look for
in their fulness, since it would have become perceptible to him
as an explorer, and to any but the chamber theorist, that no un-
educated community, rich or poor, bond or free, possessing average
health and personal liberty, could exist in an unchangeable slough
of despond, or that it would for many months if it could. Its
members, like the accursed swine, would rush down a steep place
and be choked in the waters. He would have learnt that wherever
a mode of supporting life is neither noxious nor absolutely inade-
quate, there springs up happiness, and will spring up happiness,
of some sort or other. Indeed, it is among such communities as
these that happiness will find her last refuge on earth, since it is
among them that a perfect insight into the conditions of existence
will be longest postponed.

That in their future there are only the workhouse and the grave
is no more and no less true than that in the future of the average
well-to-do householder there are only the invalid chair and the
brick vault.

Waiving these points, however, the investigator would insist
that the man he had encountered exhibited a suspicious blankness
of gaze, a great uncouthness and inactivity; and he might truly
approach the unintelligible if addressed by a stranger on any but
the commonest subject. But suppose that, by some accident, the
visitor were obliged to go home with this man, take pot-luck with
him and his, as one of the family. For the nonce the very sitting
down would seem an undignified performance, and at first, the
ideas, the modes, and the surroundings generally, would be puzzling – even impenetrable; or if in a measure penetrable, would
seem to have but little meaning. But living on there for a few days
the sojourner would become conscious of a new aspect in the life
around him. He would find that, without any objective change
whatever, variety had taken the place of monotony; that the man

who had brought him home – the typical Hodge, as he conjectured – was somehow not typical of anyone but himself. His host's brothers, uncles, and neighbours, as they became personally known, would appear as different from his host himself as one member of a club, or inhabitant of a city street, from another. As, to the eye of a diver, contrasting colours shine out by degrees from what has originally painted itself of an unrelieved earthy hue, so would shine out the characters, capacities, and interests of these people to him. He would, for one thing, find that the language, instead of being a vile corruption of cultivated speech, was a tongue with grammatical inflection rarely disregarded by his entertainer, though his entertainer's children would occasionally make a sad hash of their talk.. Having attended the National School they would mix the printed tongue as taught therein with the unwritten, dying, Wessex English that they had learnt of their parents, the result of this transitional state of theirs being a composite language without rule or harmony.

Six months pass, and our gentleman leaves the cottage, bidding his friends good-bye with genuine regret. The great change in his perception is that Hodge, the dull, unvarying, joyless one, has ceased to exist for him. He has become disintegrated into a number of dissimilar fellow-creatures, men of many minds, infinite in difference; some happy, many serene, a few depressed; some clever, even to genius, some stupid, some wanton, some austere; some mutely Miltonic, some Cromwellian; into men who have private views of each other, as he has of his friends; who applaud or condemn each other; amuse or sadden themselves by the contemplation of each other's foibles or vices; and each of whom walks in his own way the road to dusty death. . . .

To see the Dorset labourer at his worst and saddest time, he should be viewed when attending a wet hiring-fair at Candlemas, in search of a new master. His natural cheerfulness bravely struggles against the weather and the incertitude; but as the day passes on, and his clothes get wet through, and he is still unhired, there does appear a factitiousness in the smile which, with a self-repressing mannerliness hardly to be found among any other class, he yet has ready when he encounters and talks with friends who have been more fortunate. In youth and manhood, this disappoint-

ment occurs but seldom; but at threescore and over, it is frequently
the lot of those who have no sons and daughters to fall back upon,
or whose children are ingrates, or far away.

Here, at the corner of the street, in this aforesaid wet hiring-
fair, stands an old shepherd. He is evidently a lonely man. The
battle of life has always been a sharp one with him, for, to begin
with, he is a man of small frame. He is now so bowed by hard
work and years that, approaching from behind, you can scarcely
see his head. He has planted the stem of his crook in the gutter,
and rests upon the bow, which is polished to silver brightness by
the long friction of his hands. He has quite forgotten where he is
and what he has come for, his eyes being bent on the ground.
'There's work in en,' says one farmer to another, as they look
dubiously across; 'there's work left in en still; but not so much as
I want for my acreage.' 'You'd get en cheap,' says the other. The
shepherd does not hear them, and there seems to be passing
through his mind pleasant visions of the hiring successes of his
prime – when his skill in ovine surgery laid open any farm to him
for the asking, and his employer would say uneasily in the early
days of February, 'You don't mean to leave us this year?'

But the hale and strong have not to wait thus, and having
secured places in the morning, the day passes merrily enough
with them. . . .

Of all the days in the year, people who love the rural poor of
the south-west should pray for a fine day then [i.e. Lady Day, the
day when workers move to new employment]. Dwellers near the
highways of the country are reminded of the anniversary surely
enough. They are conscious of a disturbance of their night's rest
by noises beginning in the small hours of darkness, and intermit-
tently continuing till daylight – noises as certain to recur on that
particular night of the month as the voice of the cuckoo on the
third or fourth week of the same. The day of fulfilment has come,
and the labourers are on the point of being fetched from the old
farm by the carters of the new. For it is always by the waggon and
horses of the farmer who requires his services that the hired man
is conveyed to his destination; and that this may be accomplished
within the day is the reason that the noises begin so soon after midnight. Suppose the distance to be an ordinary one of a dozen or

fifteen miles. The carter at the prospective place rises 'when Charles's Wain is over the new chimney', harnesses his team of three horses by lantern light, and proceeds to the present home of his coming comrade. It is the passing of these empty waggons in all directions that is heard breaking the stillness of the hours before dawn. The aim is usually to be at the door of the removing household by six o'clock, when the loading of goods at once begins; and at nine or ten the start to the new home is made. From this hour till one or two in the day, when the other family arrives at the old house, the cottage is empty, and it is only in that short interval that the interior can be in any way cleaned and lime-whitened for the new comers, however dirty it may have become, or whatever sickness may have prevailed among members of the departed family.

Should the migrant himself be a carter there is a slight modification in the arrangement, for carters do not fetch carters, as they fetch shepherds and general hands. In this case the man has to transfer himself. He relinquishes charge of the horses of the old farm in the afternoon of 5 April, and starts on foot the same afternoon for the new place. There he makes the acquaintance of the horses which are to be under his care for the ensuing year, and passes the night sometimes on a bundle of clean straw in the stable, for he is as yet a stranger here, and too indifferent to the comforts of a bed on this particular evening to take much trouble to secure one. From this couch he uncurls himself about two o'clock, a.m. (for the distance we have assumed), and, harnessing his new charges, moves off with them to his old home, where, on his arrival, the packing is already advanced by the wife, and loading goes on as before mentioned.

The goods are built up on the waggon to a well-nigh unvarying pattern, which is probably as peculiar to the country labourer as the hexagon to the bee. The dresser, with its finger-marks and domestic evidence thick upon it, stands importantly in front, over the backs of the shaft horses, in its erect and natural position, like some Ark of the Covenant, which must not be handled slightingly or overturned. The hive of bees is slung up to the axle of the waggon, and alongside it the cooking pot or crock, within which are stowed the roots of garden flowers. Barrels are largely used for crockery, and budding gooseberry bushes are suspended by the roots; while on the top of the furniture a circular nest is made of the bed and bedding for the matron and children, who sit there through the journey. If there is no infant in arms, the woman holds the head of the clock, which at any exceptional lurch of the waggon strikes one, in thin tones. The other object of solicitude is the looking-glass, usually held in the lap of the eldest girl. It is emphatically spoken of as *the* looking-glass, there being but one in the house, except possibly a small shaving-glass for the husband. But labouring men are not much dependent upon mirrors for a clean chin. I have seen many men shaving in the chimney corner, looking into the fire; or, in summer, in the garden, with their eyes fixed upon a gooseberry-bush, gazing as steadfastly as if there were a perfect reflection of their image – from which it would seem that the concentrated look of shavers in general was originally demanded rather by the mind than by the eye. On the other hand, I knew a man who used to walk about the room all the time he was engaged in the operation, and how he escaped cutting himself was a marvel. Certain luxurious dandies of the furrow, who could not do without a reflected image of themselves when using the razor, obtained it till quite recently by placing the crown of an old hat outside the window-pane, then confronting it inside the room and falling to – a contrivance which formed a very clear reflection of a face in high light.

The day of removal, if fine, wears an aspect of jollity, and the whole proceeding is a blithe one. A bundle of provisions for the journey is usually hung up at the side of the vehicle, together with a three-pint stone jar of extra strong ale; for it is as impossible to move house without beer as without horses. Roadside inns, too, are patronized, where, during the halt, a mug is seen ascending and descending through the air to and from the feminine portion of the household at the top of the waggon. The drinking at these times is, however, moderate, the beer supplied to travelling labourers being of a preternaturally small brew; as was illustrated by a dialogue which took place on such an occasion quite recently. The liquor was not quite to the taste of the male travellers, and they complained. But the landlady upheld its merits. ' 'Tis our own brewing, and there is nothing in it but malt and hops', she said, with rectitude. 'Yes, there is', said the traveller. 'There's water.' 'Oh, I forgot the water', the landlady replied. 'I'm d——d if you did, mis'ess', replied the man; 'for there's hardly anything else in the cup.'

Ten or a dozen of these families, with their goods, may be seen halting simultaneously at an out-of-the-way inn, and it is not possible to walk a mile on any of the high roads this day without meeting several. This annual migration from farm to farm is much in excess of what it was formerly. For example,. on a particular farm where, a generation ago, not more than one cottage on an average changed occupants yearly, and where the majority remained all their lifetime, the whole number of tenants were changed at Lady Day just past, and this though nearly all of them had been new arrivals on the previous Lady Day. Dorset labourers now look upon an annual removal as the most natural thing in the world, and it becomes with the younger families a pleasant excitement. Change is also a certain sort of education. Many advantages accrue to the labourers from the varied experience it brings, apart from the discovery of the best market for their abilities. They have become shrewder and sharper men of the world, and have learnt how to hold their own with firmness and judgment. Whenever the habitually-removing man comes into contact with one of the old-fashioned stationary sort, who are still to be found, it is impossible not to perceive that the former is much more wide awake than his fellow-worker, astonishing him with stories of the wide world comprised in a twenty-mile radius from their homes.

They are also losing their peculiarities as a class; hence the humorous simplicity which formerly characterised the men and the unsophisticated modesty of the women are rapidly disappearing or lessening, under the constant attrition of lives mildly approximating to those of workers in a manufacturing town. It is the common remark of villagers above the labouring class, who know the latter well as personal acquaintances, that 'there are no nice homely workfolk now as there used to be'. There may be, and is, some exaggeration in this, but it is only natural that, now different districts of them are shaken together once a year and redistributed, like a shuffled pack of cards, they have ceased to be so local in feeling or manner as formerly, and have entered on the condition of inter-social citizens, 'whose city stretches the whole county over'. Their brains are less frequently than they once were 'as dry as the remainder biscuit after a voyage', and they vent less often the result of their own observations than what they have heard to be the current ideas of smart chaps in towns. The women have, in many districts, acquired the rollicking air of factory hands. That seclusion and immutability, which was so bad for their pockets, was an unrivalled fosterer of their personal charm in the eyes of those whose experiences had been less limited. But the artistic merit of their old condition is scarcely a reason why they should have continued in it when other communities were marching on so vigorously towards uniformity and mental equality. It is only the old story that progress and picturesqueness do not harmonise. They are losing their individuality, but they are widening the range of their ideas, and gaining in freedom. It is too much to expect them to remain stagnant and old-fashioned for the pleasure of romantic spectators. . . .

Women's labour, too, is highly in request, for a woman who, like a boy, fills the place of a man at half the wages, can be better depended on for steadiness. Thus where a boy is useful in driving a cart or a plough, a woman is invaluable in work which, though somewhat lighter, demands thought. In winter and spring a farmwoman's occupation is often 'turnip-hacking' – that is, picking out from the land the stumps of turnips which have been eaten off by the sheep – or feeding the threshing-machine, clearing away straw from the same, and standing on the rick to hand forward the sheaves. In mid-spring and early summer her services are required for weeding wheat and barley (cutting up thistles and other noxious plants with a spud), and clearing weeds from pasture-land in like manner. In late summer her time is entirely engrossed by haymaking – quite a science, though it appears the easiest thing in the world to toss hay about in the sun. The length to which a skilful raker will work and retain command over her rake without moving her feet is dependent largely upon practice, and quite astonishing to the unitiated.

Haymaking is no sooner over than the women are hurried off

to the harvest-field. This is a lively time. The bonus in wages
during these few weeks, the cleanliness of the occupation, the
heat, the cider and ale, influence to facetiousness and vocal strains.
Quite the reverse do these lively women feel in the occupation
which may be said to stand, emotionally, at the opposite pole to
gathering in corn: that is, threshing it. Not a woman in the
county but hates the threshing machine. The dust, the din, the
sustained exertion demanded to keep up with the steam tyrant,
are distasteful to all women but the coarsest. I am not sure
whether, at the present time, women are employed to feed the
machine, but some years ago a woman had frequently to stand
just above the whizzing wire drum, and feed from morning to
night – a performance for which she was quite unfitted, and
many were the manœuvres to escape that responsible position. A
thin saucer-eyed woman of fifty-five, who had been feeding the
machine all day, declared on one occasion that in crossing a field
on her way home in the fog after dusk, she was so dizzy from the
work as to be unable to find the opposite gate, and there she
walked round and round the field, bewildered and terrified, till
three o'clock in the morning, before she could get out. The farmer
said that the ale had got into her head, but she maintained that it
was the spinning of the machine. The point was never clearly settled between them; and the poor woman is now dead and buried.

To be just, however, to the farmers, they do not enforce the
letter of the Candlemas agreement in relation to the woman, if
she makes any reasonable excuse for breaking it; and indeed,
many a nervous farmer is put to flight by a matron who has a
tongue with a tang, and who chooses to assert, without giving
any reason whatever, that, though she had made fifty agreements,
'be cust if she will come out unless she is minded' – possibly terrifying him with accusations of brutality at asking her, when he
knows 'how she is just now'. A farmer of the present essayist's
acquaintance, who has a tendency to blush in the presence of
beauty, and is in other respects a bashful man for his years, says
that when the ladies of his farm are all together in the field, and
he is the single one of the male sex present, he would as soon put
his head into a hornet's nest as utter a word of complaint, or even
a request beyond the commonest.

The changes which are so increasingly discernible in village life by no means originate entirely with the agricultural unrest. A depopulation is going on which in some quarters is truly alarming. Villages used to contain, in addition to the agricultural inhabitants, an interesting and better-informed class, ranking distinctly above those – the blacksmith, the carpenter, the shoemaker, the small higgler, the shopkeeper (whose stock-in-trade consisted of a couple of loaves, a pound of candles, a bottle of brandy-balls and lumps of delight, three or four scrubbing-brushes, and a frying-pan), together with nondescript-workers other than farm-labourers, who had remained in the houses where they were born for no especial reason beyond an instinct of association with the spot. Many of these families had been life-holders, who built at their own expense the cottages they occupied, and as the lives dropped, and the property fell in they would have been glad to remain as weekly or monthly tenants of the owner. But the policy of all but some few philanthropic landowners is to disapprove of these petty tenants who are not in the estate's employ, and to pull down each cottage as it falls in, leaving standing a sufficient number for the use of the farmer's men and no more. The occupants who formed the backbone of the village life have to seek refuge in the boroughs. This process, which is designated by statisticians as 'the tendency of the rural population towards the large towns', is really the tendency of water to flow uphill when forced. The poignant regret of those who are thus obliged to forsake the old nest can only be realised by people who have witnessed it – concealed as it often is under a mask of indifference. It is anomalous that landowners who are showing unprecedented activity in the erection of comfortable cottages for their farm labourers, should see no reason for benefiting in the same way these unattached natives of the village who are nobody's care. They might often expostulate in the words addressed to King Henry the Fourth by his fallen subject : –

> Our house, my sovereign liege, little deserves
> The scourge of greatness to be used on it;
> And that same greatness, too, which our own hands
> Have holp to make so portly.

The system is much to be deplored, for every one of these banished people imbibes a sworn enmity to the existing order of things, and not a few of them, far from becoming merely honest Radicals, degenerate into Anarchists, waiters on chance, to whom danger to the State, the town – nay, the street they live in, is a welcomed opportunity.

A reason frequently advanced for dismissing these families from the villages where they have lived for centuries is that it is done in the interests of morality; and it is quite true that some of the 'liviers' (as these half-independent villagers used to be called) were not always shining examples of churchgoing, temperance, and quiet walking. But a natural tendency to evil, which develops to unlawful action when excited by contact with others likeminded, would often have remained latent amid the simple isolated experiences of a village life. The cause of morality cannot be served by compelling a population hitherto evenly distributed over the country to concentrate in a few towns, with the inevitable results of overcrowding and want of regular employment. But the question of the Dorset cottager here merges in that of all the houseless and landless poor, and the vast topic of the Rights of Man, to consider which is beyond the scope of a merely descriptive article.

S o u r c e : *Longman's Magazine* (July 1883); reprinted in *Thomas Hardy's Personal Writings*, ed. Harold Orel (1967) pp. 168–89.

3. FROM 'CANDOUR IN ENGLISH FICTION' (1890)

. . . By a sincere school of Fiction we may understand a Fiction that expresses truly the views of life prevalent in its time, by means of a selected chain of action best suited for their exhibition. What are the prevalent views of life just now is a question upon which it is not necessary to enter further than to suggest that the most natural method of presenting them, the method most in accordance with the views themselves, seems to be by a procedure mainly impassive in its tone and tragic in its developments.

Things move in cycles; dormant principles renew themselves, and exhausted principles are thrust by. There is a revival of the artistic instincts towards great dramatic motives – setting forth that 'collision between the individual and the general' – formerly worked out with such force by the Periclean and Elizabethan dramatists, to name no other. More than this, the periodicity which marks the course of taste in civilised countries does not take the form of a true cycle of repetition, but what Comte, in speaking of general progress, happily characterises as 'a looped orbit' : not a movement of revolution but – to use the current word – evolution. Hence, in perceiving that taste is arriving anew at the point of high tragedy, writers are conscious that its revived presentation demands enrichment by further truths – in other words, original treatment : treatment which seeks to show Nature's unconsciousness not of essential laws, but of those laws framed merely as social expedients by humanity, without a basis in the heart of things; treatment which expresses the triumph of the crowd over the hero, of the commonplace majority over the exceptional few.

But originality makes scores of failures for one final success, precisely because its essence is to acknowledge no immediate precursor or guide. It is probably to these inevitable conditions of further acquisition that may be attributed some developments of naturalism in French novelists of the present day, and certain crude results from meritorious attempts in the same direction by intellectual adventurers here and there among our own authors.

Anyhow, conscientious fiction alone it is which can excite a reflective and abiding interest in the minds of thoughtful readers of mature age, who are weary of puerile inventions and famishing for accuracy; who consider that, in representations of the world, the passions ought to be proportioned as in the world itself. This is the interest which was excited in the minds of the Athenians by their immortal tragedies, and in the minds of Londoners at the first performance of the finer plays of three hundred years ago. They reflected life, revealed life, criticised life. Life being a physiological fact, its honest portrayal must be largely concerned with, for one thing, the relations of the sexes, and the substitution for such catastrophes as favour the false colouring best expressed by the regulation finish that 'they married and were happy ever after', of catastrophes based upon sexual relations as it is. To this expansion English society opposes a well-nigh insuperable bar.

The popular vehicles for the introduction of a novel to the public have grown to be, from one cause and another, the magazine and the circulating library; and the object of the magazine and circulating library is not upward advance but lateral advance; to suit themselves to what is called household reading, which means, or is made to mean, the reading either of the majority in a household or of the household collectively. The number of adults, even in a large household, being normally two, and these being the members which, as a rule, have least time on their hands to bestow on current literature, the taste of the majority can hardly be, and seldom is, tempered by the ripe judgment which desires fidelity. However, the immature members of a household often keep an open mind, and they might, and no doubt would, take sincere fiction with the rest but for another condition, almost generally co-existent: which is that adults who would desire true views for their own reading insist, for a plausible but questionable reason, upon false views for the reading of their young people.

As a consequence, the magazine in particular and the circulating library in general do not foster the growth of the novel which reflects and reveals life. They directly tend to exterminate it by monopolising all literary space. Cause and effect were never more clearly conjoined, though commentators upon the result, both French and English, seem seldom if ever to trace their connection. A sincere and comprehensive sequence of the ruling passions, however moral in its ultimate bearings, must not be put on paper as the foundation of imaginative works, which have to claim notice through the above-named channels, though it is extensively welcomed in the form of newspaper reports. That the magazine and library have arrogated to themselves the dispensation of fiction is not the fault of the authors, but of circumstances over which they, as representatives of Grub Street, have no control.

What this practically amounts to is that the patrons of literature – no longer Peers with a taste – acting under the censorship of prudery, rigorously exclude from the pages they regulate subjects that have been made, by general approval of the best judges, the bases of the finest imaginative compositions since literature rose to the dignity of an art. The crash of broken commandments is as necessary an accompaniment to the catastrophe of a tragedy as the noise of drum and cymbals to a triumphal march. But the crash of broken commandments shall not be heard; or, if at all, but gently, like the roaring of Bottom – gently as any sucking dove, or as 'twere any nightingale, lest we should fright the ladies out of their wits. More precisely, an arbitrary proclamation has gone forth that certain picked commandments of the ten shall be preserved intact – to wit, the first, third, and seventh; that the ninth shall be infringed but gingerly; the sixth only as much as necessary; and the remainder alone as much as you please, in a genteel manner.

S O U R C E : *New Review* (January 1890); reprinted in *Thomas Hardy's Personal Writings*, ed. Orel (1967) pp. 126–9.

4. FROM THE GENERAL PREFACE TO THE NOVELS AND POEMS

. . . It has sometimes been conceived of novels that evolve their action on a circumscribed scene – as do many (though not all) of these – that they cannot be so inclusive in their exhibition of human nature as novels wherein the scenes cover large extents of country, in which events figure amid towns and cities, even wander over the four quarters of the globe. I am not concerned to argue this point further than to suggest that the conception is an untrue one in respect of the elementary passions. But I would state that the geographical limits of the stage here trodden were not absolutely forced upon the writer by circumstances; he forced them upon himself from judgment. I considered that our magnificent heritage from the Greeks in dramatic literature found sufficient room for a large proportion of its action in an extent of their country not much larger than the half-dozen counties here reunited under the old name of Wessex, that the domestic emotions have throbbed in Wessex nooks with as much intensity as in the palaces of Europe, and that, anyhow, there was quite enough human nature in Wessex for one man's literary purpose. So far was I possessed by this idea that I kept within the frontiers when it would have been easier to overleap them and give more cosmopolitan features to the narrative.

Thus, though the people in most of the novels (and in much of the shorter verse) are dwellers in a province bounded on the north by the Thames, on the south by the English Channel, on the east by a line running from Hayling Island to Windsor Forest, and on the west by the Cornish coast, they were meant to be typically and essentially those of any and every place where

Thought's the slave of life, and life time's fool,

– beings in whose hearts and minds that which is apparently local should be really universal.

But whatever the success of this intention, and the value of these novels as delineations of humanity, they have at least a humble supplementary quality of which I may be justified in reminding the reader, though it is one that was quite unintentional and unforeseen. At the dates represented in the various narrations things were like that in Wessex: the inhabitants lived in certain ways, engaged in certain occupations, kept alive certain customs, just as they are shown doing in these pages. And in particularizing such I have often been reminded of Boswell's remarks on the trouble to which he was put and the pilgrimages he was obliged to make to authenticate some detail, though the labour was one which would bring him no praise. Unlike his achievement, however, on which an error would as he says have brought discredit, if these country customs and vocations, obsolete and obsolescent, had been detailed wrongly, nobody would have discovered such errors to the end of Time. Yet I have instituted inquiries to correct tricks of memory, and striven against temptations to exaggerate, in order to preserve for my own satisfaction a fairly true record of a vanishing life.

SOURCE: Volume I of the 'Wessex Edition' of Hardy's Works (1912); reprinted in *Thomas Hardy's Personal Writings*, ed. Orel (1967).

PART TWO

Early and More Recent Comments

Lionel Johnson

THE CHARACTERISTICS OF HARDY'S ART (1894)

Throughout the preceding essays, I have laid stress upon the strength and the stability of character, which Mr. Hardy loves to present; upon his souls of a somewhat pagan severity, grand in the endurance of dooms; upon their simplicity, resoluteness, and power: yet I have also spoken of Mr. Hardy, as a novelist typical of modern literature in this, that he loves the complexity of things, the clash of principles and of motives, the encounter of subtle emotions. Both criticisms, as I dare think, are true: and in these two characteristics, brought together, contrasted, made to illustrate each other, lies the power of Mr. Hardy's art. For he chooses to present the play of life, tragic and comic, first of all, in a definite tract or province of England; in the Kingdom of Wessex: whither new influences penetrate but slowly. Secondly, he takes for his chief characters, men of powerful natures, men of the country, men of little acquired virtue in mind and soul: but men disciplined by the facts and by the necessities of life, as a primitive experience manifests them. Thirdly, he surrounds them with men of the same origin and class, but men of less strongly marked a power, of less finely touched a spirit: the rank and file of country labour. Fourthly, he brings his few men of that stronger and finer nature, his rustic heroes, into contact and into contrast with a few men, commonly their superiors in education, and sometimes in position, but their inferiors in strength and fineness of nature: men, whom more modern experiences have redeemed from being clowns, at the risk of becoming curs. Fifthly, he makes this contact and this contrast most effective, through the passion of love: to which end, he brings upon the scene women of various natures; less plainly marked in character than the men; for the most part, nearer to the flashy prigs and pretty fellows in outward sentiment, fashion, and culture; but nearer to the stronger and finer men, in the depths of their souls. Sixthly, the narratives are conducted slowly at the first, and great pains are given to make clear the spirit of the country, with its works and ways : when that has been made clear, the play quickens into passion, the actors come into conflict, there is strong attraction and strong repulsion, 'spirits are finely touched' : then, there is a period of waiting, a breathing space, an ominous stillness and a pause; till, at the last, with increased force and motion, the play goes forward to its 'fine issues'; all the inherent necessities of things cause their effects, tragic or comic, triumphs of the right or of the wrong; and the end of all is told with a soft solemnity, a sense of pity striving against a sense of fate.

I do not say that any one novel presents those features, in precisely that way : it is but an attempt to construct a mechanical type, to which all Mr. Hardy's novels tend to conform. At the least, it is true of them all, that they present, either the resolution of a discord into a harmony, or the breaking of a harmony by a discord : always the contrast, and the various issue, according to the worth of the performers with that strange organ, the human mind. Tess was changing from peasant ignorance and convention, when she met Clare, changing from the conventional culture and belief of a higher station; the woman struggling up from superstition, the man struggling free from prejudice : the two natures, breaking with the past, came together, she straining towards his level of thought, he stooping to her level of life : the result was a tragic discord. It might be interpreted in many ways. Perhaps the superstitious faith of the Durbeyfield household, and the Calvinist faith of the Clare household, were more nearly in accord with the essential verities of life, than the new aims and impulses of their offspring : perhaps Tess and Clare carried right theories into wrong practice : perhaps one alone did so : certainly, we have in this story a singular presentation of the struggle between old and new, in various ranks of life and ranges of thought; of the contact of the new in one rank and range with the new in another; of the curious reversion, in each case, of the new to the old. Tess acts, on several occasions, from impulses and in ways, which derive, so her maker hints, from her knightly ancestors : Clare, at the crisis of her life and of his own, falls back in cruel cowardice to the conventional standards of that society, which he so greatly scorns. Tess, again, having learned by ear and heart Clare's arguments against Christian theology, repeats them to her old betrayer, Alec d'Urberville, then a fanatical convert to the Calvinism of Clare's father : and she enables him thereby to become a second time her betrayer. Finally, this tangled play of new things upon old comes to its wretched end at Stonehenge, the most ancient of religious monuments in England, and at Winchester, the ancient capital of England : religion, however stern, society, however cruel, are vindicated in the presence of their august memorials. The old, we are meant to feel, was wrong, and the new was right : but the inhuman irony of fate turned all to misunderstanding and to despair : the new devil quoted the new scriptures in the ears of the new believers; and they went to the old destruction.

But the human comedy of Tess must be elsewhere discussed in detail : now it merely serves to illustrate a characteristic common to almost all Mr. Hardy's books. Norris of Bemerton, 'the English Malebranche', has this saying in his third *Contemplation* : ' 'Twas a Celebrated Problem among the Ancient Mythologists, What was the *strongest* thing, what the *wisest*, and what the *greatest*? Concerning which 'twas this determin'd, that the *strongest* Thing was *Necessity*, the *wisest* was *Time*; and the *greatest* was the *Heart* of Man.' That would seem to be the determination of Mr. Hardy also, at his best and deepest : almost over conscious of the fatal strength, ever delighted with the growing wisdom, strongly moved by the unsatisfied greatness, he sends out his characters to that forlorn hope, life : forlorn, but not lost, and promising at least the noblest of defeats. I remember but few of Mr. Hardy's general sentiments, about the meaning of the unconscious universe, or of conscious mankind, with which I do not disagree : his tone of thought about human progress, about the province and the testimony of physical science, about the sanctions of natural and social ethics, neither charms, nor compels, me to acquiescence : but it is because I am thus averse from the attitude of a disciple, that I admire Mr. Hardy's art so confidently.

S O U R C E : *The Art of Thomas Hardy* (1894) pp. 406–10.

F. Manning

'NOVELS OF CHARACTER AND ENVIRONMENT' (1912)

In the preface to the new edition of his works Mr. Hardy has the following passage :

Positive views on the whence and wherefore of things have never been advanced by this pen as a consistent philosophy. Nor is it likely, indeed, that imaginative writings extending over more than forty years would exhibit a coherent scientific theory of the universe, even if it had been attempted – of that universe concerning which Spencer owns to the 'paralysing thought' that possibly there exists no comprehension of it anywhere. But such objectless consistency never has been attempted, and the sentiments in the following pages have been stated truly to be mere impressions of the moment, and not convictions or arguments. That these impressions have been condemned as 'pessimistic' – as if that were a very wicked adjective – shows a curious muddle-mindedness. It must be obvious that there is a higher characteristic of philosophy than pessimism, or than meliorism, or even than the optimism of these critics – which is truth.

There is in this last sentence, and perhaps we may be forgiven if we draw attention to it, a touch of *naïveté*. Mr. Hardy probably was not blind to it himself, since he continues :

Differing natures find their tongue in the presence of differing spectacles. Some natures become vocal at tragedy, some are made vocal by comedy, and it seems to me that to whichever of these aspects of life a writer's instinct for expression the more readily responds, to that he should allow it to respond. That before a contrasting side of things he remains undemonstrative need not be assumed to mean that he remains unperceiving.

We have every sympathy with these remarks in so far as they represent a protest gainst the habit of classifying all writers under convenient heads, even though we recognize that such a scheme of classification upon proper occasions may be extremely useful. Great art is representative of life, not critical of it. The great artist has a delicacy and mobility of mind by which he is able to capture and reflect the most various and fluid moods, to seize upon the contrasting aspects of life and present each with a perfect impartiality. Such a mind is delicate in the way it realizes with an exquisite tact the essential character of every object; and mobile in its range, in the comprehensive nature of its sympathy. In our own conscious life the sensations of pain or of pleasure, emotions of hatred or of love, moods of joy or of sorrow, have no definite and objective existence for us, though we may connect them in our minds with the realities about us which have this definite existence. They flow through us; but, though they may leave some traces of their passage, they do not remain with us. To the normal mind, life, not being a solid block, but a continuous flux, is neither to be viewed from an entirely pessimistic nor from an entirely optimistic standpoint; it is an affair of compensations. Some natures, as Mr. Hardy observes, may be more responsive to the tragedy of life, and yet perceive another side, for our consciousness is always dissolving, and the aspects of life continually changing under it. On the other hand, a nature which only becomes vocal at tragedy, and which perceives another aspect of life without responding to it, is a nature in which the will has inclined the balance upon one side; and to view life almost entirely in its tragic significance is to view it incompletely. Great art, the art of Sophocles or of Shakespeare, does not leave our minds impressed by a pessimistic conception of existence. It represents the flux of all things, the cessation of pain and grief as well as of joy and pleasure. It has its compensating values. The effect of tragedy upon the mind is ultimately one of relief at the cessation of pain. We consider the quality or characteristic from which the tragic development proceeds less as an essential than as an accidental feature, a flaw in the material; and the solution of a tragic situation brings with it a sense of relief at the eradication of this flaw, the restoration to some extent of ideal conditions, and thus the recovery of balance. The significance of tragedy is not merely tragic. It leaves upon our mind the idea of compensation and readjustment; and when literature ceases to have this effect upon us it ceases to be great literature; it is no longer representative, but didactic. This, we think, is an objection which may be urged in all fairness against the art of Mr. Hardy. His nature is one which responds instinctively to tragedy, and this responsiveness to one particular aspect of life has been cultivated to the neglect of another kind of responsiveness. Truth, that higher characteristic of philosophy, to some extent, however slightly still appreciably, suffers and diminishes in proportion as a habit of thought is formed. Not only his critics, but his admirers and disciples, are apt to find in Mr. Hardy's work a didactic tendency. Well, in so far as that tendency is present in his work it is present as a flaw.

Moreover, that kind of tragedy which is based upon the idea of an ultimate compensation, and which presents life to us as a perpetual collision and readjustment of opposed forces, the effects of which are being dissolved, and from which new forces are being generated continually and in infinite variety, implies naturally a certain activity and freedom of will. Whether the notion of ourselves which we have gained from experience in practical affairs be true or false, it is at least sufficiently true to say that we regard ourselves as active agents to whom is allowed a certain freedom of choice, and upon whom ultimately falls the sole responsibility for the choice. Possibly this notion of ourselves may be an illusion, but it is an illusion which life compels us to accept. We are not concerned here with a philosophic but with an artistic conception of truth. We do not wish to be involved in the damnation of those who have attributed a consistent philosophy to Mr. Hardy. To us Mr. Hardy's nature is not a rational but an emotional nature. It is in the depth and richness of his emotional nature that he is great, and it is in *Tess of the d'Urbervilles* and *Jude the Obscure* that his nature has found its most complete expression. At the same time we do not think that, considered purely as works of art, these are Mr. Hardy's best novels. In *Tess of the d'Urbervilles* the whole of the reader's attention is focused upon a single aspect of life, and that aspect is reflected in a single person. Considered apart from Tess, Alec d'Urberville and Angel Clare are purely superficial characters. It is only in their relation to her, only whɛn we see them bathed in the light of her own consciousness, only in so far as she turns from one to the other of them, that they interest us. On the other hand, Tess herself is an almost entirely passive character. She interests us, not by what she does or says, but entirely by what she feels, entirely by her capacity for suffering. To understand such a nature *il faut s'abêtir*, as Pascal said; it is spontaneous, instinctive, moody; it lacks both the control of will and the control of reason. It is one of the simplest organisms, in which the nerve-centres are not localized, but spread over the whole surface of the body, and in which thought is practically identical with sensation. It is essentially feminine. The passivity of her character is so firmly insisted upon by her author, in his eagerness to retain our sympathy, as in some measure to defeat his end, for in order that our sympathy with her should be complete we must realize her own responsibility. 'Why was it that upon this beautiful feminine tissue, sensitive as gossamer, and practically blank as snow as yet, there should have been traced such a coarse pattern as it was doomed to receive; why so often the coarse appropriates the finer thus, the wrong man the woman, the wrong woman the man, many thousand years of analytical philo- sophy have failed to explain to our sense of order. One may, indeed, admit the possibility of a retribution lurking in the present catastrophe. . . . As Tess's own people down in those retreats are never tired of saying among each other in their fatalistic way: "It was to be." There lay the pity of it.' This is partly ironical, no doubt; practically all Mr. Hardy's references to justice and retribution are ironical; the conflict for him resolves itself mainly into a conflict between natural instincts and social regulations. But thus to shift the responsibility for the catastrophe to God, or Nature, or Fate, or Chance, is a fault in art. The passage may be admirable as a criticism of life, or as an expression of feeling; but it destroys the illusions of an individual will and of individual activity. Sympathy is not regulated by any considera- tions of justice, of which it is quite independent; but we do require that the person or character with whom we are asked to sympathize should be a responsible agent. Shakespeare's Cleopatra, Euripides Phædra, Thackeray's Becky Sharp, are all severally and in their different ways loaded with will. With the first two the question we put to ourselves is not whether their will is directed towards a proper object, but whether it is sufficiently intense. When a character is willing to sacrifice everything else in order to attain the object desired we no longer measure it by ordinary standards. The sacrifice purges the offence; and even if the object be not attained the catastrophe is the consummation of desire, the final effort of the will. Any return would be fatal to our sympathy; the will, finally immolating itself for the sake of its object, achieves some measure of triumph. It is a fault in art to substitute for this individual will the blind, impersonal forces of nature.

If, however, the tendency of Mr. Hardy's mind has been towards the expression of one particular aspect of life, the tendency is only discernible when we view the novels in their chronological order, and that is not a proper way to criticize his work. *Tess* is a great work of subjectivity, a masterpiece of its kind, but of a very special kind. No other writer, we think, of the Victorian age has shown such emotional power or so intuitive a vision. Considered, however, from another point of view, we prefer *The Return of the Native. Tess*, perhaps, is more complete as an expression of the peculiar qualities of Mr. Hardy's genius, but *The Return of the Native* is more complete as a representation of life. Life in it is more fluid and more various, the contrasting aspects are more impartially presented, the blind forces of nature and the tragic grandeur of humanity pitted against them are there, but implied rather by the wild expanse of Egdon Heath than expressed in any particular action. Every incident is perfectly realized : the bonfires on the heath, the stones thrown into the pond as a signal to Eustacia, the mummers, the sympathetic magic, the game of dice played by Wildeve and the reddleman by the light of glow-worms, the drowning. An unreal glamour plays over the whole, and yet it is full of a human warmth; full, too, of that almost Shakespearean humour with which Mr. Hardy has endowed his clowns, a humour occasionally suffused with tears, as in that scene from *The Mayor of Casterbridge* when the village gossips talk over Mrs. Henchard's death. It is by this intuitive sympathy with humanity in all its moods that Mr. Hardy is great. His pessimism, after all, is only a habit of thought, a weariness with life that comes upon all of us sometimes, if it does not remain with us always; and that, too, springs from his sympathy with mankind, from the depth and richness of his emotional nature.

S o u r c e : *Spectator* (7 September 1912).

D. H. Lawrence

THE REAL TRAGEDY (1914)

It is urged against Thomas Hardy's characters that they do unreasonable things – quite, quite unreasonable things. They are always going off unexpectedly and doing something that nobody would do. That is quite true, and the charge is amusing. These people of Wessex are always bursting suddenly out of bud and taking a wild flight into flower, always shooting suddenly out of a tight convention, a tight, hide-bound cabbage state into something quite madly personal. It would be amusing to count the number of special marriage licenses taken out in Hardy's books. Nowhere, except perhaps in Jude, is there the slightest development of personal action in the characters : it is all explosive. Jude, however, does see more or less what he is doing, and acts from choice. He is more consecutive. The rest explode out of the convention. They are people each with a real, vital, potential self, even the apparently wishy-washy heroines of the earlier books, and this self suddenly bursts the shell of manner and convention and commonplace opinion, and acts independently, absurdly, without mental knowledge or acquiescence.

And from such an outburst the tragedy usually develops. For there does exist, after all, the great self-preservation scheme, and in it we must all live. Now to live in it after bursting out of it was the problem these Wessex people found themselves faced with. And they never solved the problem, none of them except the comically, insufficiently treated Ethelberta.

This because they must subscribe to the system in themselves. From the more immediate claims of self-preservation they could free themselves : from money, from ambition for social success. None of the heroes or heroines of Hardy cared much for these things. But there is the greater idea of self-preservation, which is formulated in the State, in the whole modelling of the community. And from this idea, the heroes and heroines of Wessex, like the heroes and heroines of almost anywhere else, could not free themselves. In the long run, the State, the Community, the established form of life remained, remained intact and impregnable, the individual, trying to break forth from it, died of fear, of exhaustion, or of exposure to attacks from all sides, like men who have left the walled city to live outside in the precarious open.

This is the tragedy of Hardy, always the same : the tragedy of those who, more or less pioneers, have died in the wilderness, whither they had escaped for free action, after having left the walled security, and the comparative imprisonment, of the established convention. This is the theme of novel after novel : remain quite within the convention, and you are good, safe, and happy in the long run, though you never have the vivid pang of sympathy on your side : or, on the other hand, be passionate, individual, wilful, you will find the security of the convention a walled prison, you will escape, and you will die, either of your own lack of strength to bear the isolation and the exposure, or by direct revenge from the community, or from both. This is the tragedy, and only this : it is nothing more metaphysical than the division of a man against himself in such a way : first, that he is a member of the community, and must, upon his honour, in no way move to disintegrate the community, either in its moral or its practical form; second, that the convention of the community is a prison to his natural, individual desire, a desire that compels him, whether he feels justified or not, to break the bounds of the community, lands him outside the pale, there to stand alone, and say : 'I was right, my desire was real and inevitable; if I was to be myself I must fulfil it, convention or no convention', or else, there to stand alone, doubting, and saying : 'Was I right, was I wrong? If I was wrong, oh, let me die !' – in which case he courts death.

The growth and the development of this tragedy, the deeper and deeper realization of this division and this problem, the coming towards some conclusion, is the one theme of the Wessex novels. ...

The real sense of tragedy [in *The Return of the Native*] is got from the setting. What is the great, tragic power in the book? It is Egdon Heath. And who are the real spirits of the Heath? First,

Eustacia, then Clym's mother, then Wildeve. The natives have little or nothing in common with the place.

What is the real stuff of tragedy in the book? It is the Heath. It is the primitive, primal earth, where the instinctive life heaves up. There, in the deep, rude stirring of the instincts, there was the reality that worked the tragedy. Close to the body of things, there can be heard the stir that makes us and destroys us. The heath heaved with raw instinct. Egdon, whose dark soil was strong and crude and organic as the body of a beast. Out of the body of this crude earth are born Eustacia, Wildeve, Mistress Yeobright, Clym, and all the others. They are one year's accidental crop. What matters if some are drowned or dead, and others preaching or married: what matter, any more than the withering heath, the reddening berries, the seedy furze, and the dead fern of one autumn of Egdon? The Heath persists. Its body is strong and fecund, it will bear many more crops beside this. Here is the sombre, latent power that will go on producing, no matter what happens to the product. Here is the deep, black source from whence all these little contents of lives are drawn. And the contents of the small lives are spilled and wasted. There is savage satisfaction in it: for so much more remains to come, such a black, powerful fecundity is working there that what does it matter?

Three people die and are taken back into the Heath: they mingle their strong earth again with its powerful soil, having been broken off at their stem. It is very good. Not Egdon is futile, sending forth life on the powerful heave of passion. It cannot be futile, for it is eternal. What is futile is the purpose of man.

Man has a purpose which he has divorced from the passionate purpose that issued him out of the earth into being. The Heath threw forth its shaggy heather and furze and fern, clean into being. It threw forth Eustacia and Wildeve and Mistress Yeobright and Clym, but to what purpose? Eustacia thought she wanted the hats and bonnets of Paris. Perhaps she was right. The heavy, strong soil of Egdon, breeding original native beings, is under Paris as well as under Wessex, and Eustacia sought herself in the gay city. She thought life there, in Paris, would be tropical, and all her energy and passion out of Egdon would there come into handsome flower. And if Paris real had been Paris as she imagined it, no doubt she was right, and her instinct was soundly expressed. But Paris real was not Eustacia's imagined Paris. Where was her imagined Paris, the place where her powerful nature could come to blossom? Beside some strong-passioned, unconfined man, her mate.

Which mate Clym might have been. He was born out of passionate Egdon to live as a passionate being whose strong feelings moved him ever further into being. But quite early his life became narrowed down to a small purpose: he must of necessity go into business, and submit his whole being, body and soul as well as mind, to the business and to the greater system it represented. His feelings, that should have produced the man, were suppressed and contained, he worked according to a system imposed from without. The dark struggle of Egdon, a struggle into being as the furze struggles into flower, went on in him, but could not burst the enclosure of the idea, the system which contained him. Impotent to *be*, he must transform himself, and live in an abstraction, in a generalization, he must identify himself with the system. He must live as Man or Humanity, or as the Community, or as Society, or as Civilization. 'An inner strenuousness was preying on his outer symmetry, and they rated his look as singular. . . . His countenance was overlaid with legible meanings. Without being thought-worn, he yet had certain marks derived from a perception of his surroundings, such as are not infrequently found on man at the end of four or five years of endeavour which follow the close of placid pupilage. He already showed that thought is a disease of the flesh, and indirectly bore evidence that ideal physical beauty is incompatible with emotional development and a full recognition of the coil of things. Mental luminousness must be fed with the oil of life, even if there is already a physical seed for it; and the pitiful sight of two demands on one supply was just showing itself here.'

But did the face of Clym show that thought is a disease of flesh, or merely that in his case a dis-ease, an un-ease, of flesh produced thought? One does not catch thought like a fever: one produces it. If it be in any way a disease of flesh, it is rather the rash that indicates the disease than the disease itself. The 'inner strenuousness' of Clym's nature was not fighting against his physical symmetry, but against the limits imposed on his physical movement. By nature, as a passionate, violent product of Egdon, he should have loved and suffered in flesh and in soul from love, long before this age. He should have lived and moved and had his being, whereas he had only his business, and afterwards his inactivity. His years of pupilage were past, 'he was one of whom something original was expected', yet he continued in pupilage. For he produced nothing original in being or in act, and certainly no original thought. None of his ideas were original. Even he himself was not original. He was over-taught, had become an echo. His life had been arrested, and this activity turned into repetition. Far from being emotionally developed, he was emotionally undeveloped, almost entirely. Only his mental faculties were developed. And, hid, his emotions were obliged to work according to the label he put upon them : a ready-made label.

Yet he remained for all that an original, the force of life was in him, however much he frustrated and suppressed its natural movement. 'As is usual with bright natures, the deity that lies ignominiously chained within an ephemeral human carcass shone out of him like a ray.' But was the deity chained within his ephemeral human carcass, or within his limited human consciousness? Was it his blood, which rose dark and potent out of Egdon, which hampered and confined the deity, or was it his mind, that house built of extraneous knowledge and guarded by his will, which formed the prison?

He came back to Egdon – what for? To re-unite himself with the strong, free flow of life that rose out of Egdon as from a source? No – 'to preach to the Egdon eremites that they might rise to a serene comprehensiveness without going through the process of enriching themselves'. As if the Egdon eremites had not already far more serene comprehensiveness than ever he had himself, rooted as they were in the soil of all things, and living from the root! What did it matter how they enriched themselves, so long as they kept this strong, deep root in the primal soil, so long as their instincts moved out to action and to expression? The system was big enough for them, and had no power over their instincts. They should have taught him rather than he them.

And Egdon made him marry Eustacia. Here was action and life, here was a move into being on his part. But as soon as he got her, she became an idea to him, she had to fit in his system of ideas. According to his way of living, he knew her already, she was labelled and classed and fixed down. He had got into this way of living, and he could not get out of it. He had identified himself with the system, and he could not extricate himself. He did not know that Eustacia had her being beyond his. He did not know that she existed untouched by his system and his mind, where no system had sway and where no consciousness had risen to the surface. He did not know that she was Egdon, the powerful, eternal origin seething with production. He thought he knew. Egdon to him was the tract of common land, producing familiar rough herbage, and having some few unenlightened inhabitants. So he skated over heaven and hell, and having made a map of the surface, thought he knew all. But underneath and among his mapped world, the eternal powerful fecundity worked on heedless of him and his arrogance. His preaching, his superficiality made no difference. What did it matter if he had calculated a moral chart from the surface of life? Could that affect life, any more than a chart of the heavens affects the stars, affects the whole stellar universe which exists beyond our knowledge? Could the sound of his words affect the working of the body of Egdon, where in the unfathomable womb was begot and conceived all that would ever come forth? Did not his own heart beat far removed and immune from his thinking and talking? Had he been able to put even his own heart's mysterious resonance upon his map, from which he charted the course of lives in his moral system? And how much more completely, then, had he left out, in utter ignorance, the dark, powerful source whence all things rise into being, whence they will always continue to rise, to struggle forward to further being? A little of the static surface he could see, and map out. Then he thought his map was the thing itself. How blind he was, how utterly blind to the tremendous movement carrying and producing the surface. He did not know that the greater part of every life is underground, like roots in the dark in contact with the beyond. He preached, thinking lives could be moved like hen-houses from here to there. His blindness indeed brought on the calamity. But what matter if Eustacia

or Wildeve or Mrs. Yeobright died : what matter if he himself
became a mere rattle of repetitive words – what did it matter ?
It was regrettable; no more. Egdon, the primal impulsive body,
would go on producing all that was to be produced, eternally,
though the will of man should destroy the blossom yet in bud,
over and over again. At last he must learn what it is to be at one,
in his mind and will, with the primal impulses that rise in him.
Till then, let him perish or preach. The great reality on which the
little tragedies enact themselves cannot be detracted from. The
will and words which militate against it are the only vanity.

This is a constant revelation in Hardy's novels : that there exists
a great background, vital and vivid, which matters more than
the people who move upon it. Against the background of dark,
passionate Egdon, of the leafy, sappy passion and sentiment of
the woodlands, of the unfathomed stars, is drawn the lesser
scheme of lives : *The Return of the Native*, *The Woodlanders*, or
Two on a Tower. Upon the vast, incomprehensible pattern of
some primal morality greater than ever the human mind can
grasp, is drawn the little, pathetic pattern of man's moral life and
struggle, pathetic, almost ridiculous. The little fold of law and
order, the little walled city within which man has to defend
himself from the waste enormity of nature, becomes always too
small, and the pioneers venturing out with the code of the walled
city upon them, die in the bonds of that code, free and yet unfree,
preaching the walled city and looking to the waste.

This is the wonder of Hardy's novels, and gives them their
beauty. The vast, unexplored morality of life itself, what we call
the immorality of nature, surrounds us in its eternal incomprehensibility, and in its midst goes on the little human morality
play, with its queer frame of morality and its mechanized movement; seriously, portentously, till some one of the protagonists
chances to look out of the charmed circle, weary of the stage,
to look into the wilderness raging round. Then he is lost, his
little drama falls to pieces, or becomes mere repetition, but the
stupendous theatre outside goes on enacting its own incomprehensible drama, untouched. There is this quality in almost all
Hardy's work, and this is the magnificent irony it all contains,
the challenge, the contempt. Not the deliberate ironies, little

tales of widows or widowers, contain the irony of human life as we live it in our self-aggrandized gravity, but the big novels, *The Return of the Native*, and the others.

And this is the quality Hardy shares with the great writers, Shakespeare or Sophocles or Tolstoi, this setting behind the small action of his protagonists the terrific action of unfathomed nature; setting a smaller system of morality, the one grasped and formulated by the human consciousness within the vast, uncomprehended and incomprehensible morality of nature or of life itself, surpassing human consciousness. The difference is, that whereas in Shakespeare or Sophocles the greater, uncomprehended morality, or fate, is actively transgressed and gives active punishment, in Hardy and Tolstoi the lesser, human morality, the mechanical system is actively transgressed, and holds, and punishes the protagonist, whilst the greater morality is only passively, negatively transgressed, it is represented merely as being present in background, in scenery, not taking any active part, having no direct connexion with the protagonist. Œdipus, Hamlet, Macbeth set themselves up against, or find themselves set up against, the unfathomed moral forces of nature, and out of this unfathomed force comes their death. Whereas Anna Karenina, Eustacia, Tess, Sue, and Jude find themselves up against the established system of human government and morality, they cannot detach themselves, and are brought down. Their real tragedy is that they are unfaithful to the greater unwritten morality, which would have bidden Anna Karenina be patient and wait until she, by virtue of greater right, could take what she needed from society; would have bidden Vronsky detach himself from the system, become an individual, creating a new colony of morality with Anna; would have bidden Eustacia fight Clym for his own soul, and Tess take and claim her Angel, since she had the greater light; would have bidden Jude and Sue endure for very honour's sake, since one must bide by the best that one has known, and not succumb to the lesser good.

Had Œdipus, Hamlet, Macbeth been weaker, less full of real, potent life, they would have made no tragedy; they would have comprehended and contrived some arrangement of their affairs, sheltering in the human morality from the great stress and attack of the unknown morality. But being, as they are, men to the fullest capacity, when they find themselves, daggers drawn, with the very forces of life itself, they can only fight till they themselves are killed, since the morality of life, the greater morality, is eternally unalterable and invincible. It can be dodged for some time, but not opposed. On the other hand, Anna, Eustacia, Tess or Sue – what was there in their position that was necessarily tragic? Necessarily painful it was, but they were not at war with God, only with Society. Yet they were all cowed by the mere judgment of man upon them, and all the while by their own souls they were right. And the judgment of men killed them, not the judgment of their own souls or the judgment of Eternal God.

Which is the weakness of modern tragedy, where transgression against the social code is made to bring destruction, as though the social code worked our irrevocable fate. Like Clym, the map appears to us more real than the land. Shortsighted almost to blindness, we pore over the chart, map out journeys, and confirm them: and we cannot see life itself giving us the lie the whole time.

S O U R C E : *Study of Thomas Hardy* (1914), reprinted in *Phoenix* (1936).

Virginia Woolf

THE NOVELS OF THOMAS HARDY (1928)

In every book three or four figures predominate, and stand up like lightning conductors to attract the force of the elements. Oak and Troy and Bathsheba; Eustacia, Wildeve, and Venn; Henchard, Lucetta, and Farfrae; Jude, Sue Bridehead, and Phillotson. There is even a certain likeness between the different groups. They live as individuals and they differ as individuals; but they also live as types and have a likeness as types. Bathsheba is Bathsheba, but she is woman and sister to Eustacia and Lucetta and Sue; Gabriel Oak is Gabriel Oak, but he is man and brother to Henchard, Venn, and Jude. However lovable and charming Bathsheba may be, still she is weak; however stubborn and ill-guided Henchard may be, still he is strong. This is a fundamental part of Hardy's vision; the staple of many of his books. The woman is the weaker and the fleshlier, and she clings to the stronger and obscures his vision. How freely, nevertheless, in his greater books life is poured over the unalterable framework! When Bathsheba sits in the wagon among her plants, smiling at her own loveliness in the little looking-glass, we may know, and it is proof of Hardy's power that we do know, how severely she will suffer and cause others to suffer before the end. But the moment has all the bloom and beauty of life. And so it is, time and time again. His characters, both men and women, were creatures to him of an infinite attraction. For the women he shows a more tender solicitude than for the men, and in them, perhaps, he takes a keener interest. Vain might their beauty be and terrible their fate, but while the glow of life is in them their step is free, their laughter sweet, and theirs is the power to sink into the breast of Nature and become part of her silence and solemnity, or to rise and put on them the movement of the clouds and the wildness of the flowering woodlands. The men who suffer, not like the women through dependence upon other human beings, but through conflict with fate, enlist our sterner sympathies. For such a man as Gabriel Oak we need have no passing fears. Honour him we must, though it is not granted us to love him quite so freely. He is firmly set upon his feet and can give as shrewd a blow, to men at least, as any he is likely to receive. He has a prevision of what is to be expected that springs from character rather than from education. He is stable in his temperament, steadfast in his affections, and capable of open-eyed endurance without flinching. But he, too, is no puppet. He is a homely, humdrum fellow on ordinary occasions. He can walk the street without making people turn to stare at him. In short, nobody can deny Hardy's power – the true novelist's power – to make us believe that his characters are fellow-beings driven by their own passions and idiosyncrasies, while they have – and this is the poet's gift – something symbolical about them which is common to us all.

And it is when we are considering Hardy's power of creating men and women that we become most conscious of the profound differences that distinguish him from his peers. We look back at a number of these characters and ask ourselves what it is that we remember them for. We recall their passions. We remember how deeply they have loved each other and often with what tragic results. We remember the faithful love of Oak for Bathsheba; the tumultuous but fleeting passions of men like Wildeve, Troy, and Fitzpiers; we remember the filial love of Clym for his mother, the jealous paternal passion of Henchard for Elizabeth Jane. But we do not remember how they have loved. We do not remember how they talked and changed and got to know each other, finely, gradually, from step to step and from stage to stage. Their relationship is not composed of those intellectual apprehensions and subtleties of perception which seem so slight yet are so profound. In all the books love is one of the great facts that mould human life. But it is a catastrophe; it happens suddenly and overwhelmingly, and there is little to be said about it. The talk between the lovers when it is not passionate is practical or philosophic, as though the discharge of their daily duties left them with more desire to question life and its purpose than to investigate each other's sensibilities. Even if it were in their power to analyse their emotions, life is too stirring to give them time. They need all their strength to deal with the downright blows, the freakish ingenuity, the gradually increasing malignity of fate. They have none to spend upon the subtleties and delicacies of the human comedy.

Thus there comes a time when we can say with certainty that we shall not find in Hardy some of the qualities that have given us most delight in the works of other novelists. He has not the perfection of Jane Austen, or the wit of Meredith; or the range of Thackeray, or Tolstoy's amazing intellectual power. There is in the work of the great classical writers a finality of effect which places certain of their scenes, apart from the story, beyond the reach of change. We do not ask what bearing they have upon the narrative, nor do we make use of them to interpret problems which lie on the outskirts of the scene. A laugh, a blush, half a dozen words of dialogue, and it is enough; the source of our delight is perennial. But Hardy has none of this concentration and completeness. His light does not fall directly upon the human heart. It passes over it and out on to the darkness of the heath and upon the trees swaying in the storm. When we look back into the room the group by the fireside is dispersed. Each man or woman is battling with the storm, alone, revealing himself most when he is least under the observation of other human beings. We do not know them as we know Pierre or Natasha or Becky Sharp. We do not know them in and out and all round as they are revealed to the casual caller, to the Government official, to the great lady, to the general on the battlefield. We do not know the complication and involvement and turmoil of their thoughts. Geographically, too, they remain fixed to the same stretch of the English country-side. It is seldom, and always with unhappy results, that Hardy leaves the yeoman or farmer to describe the class above theirs in the social scale. In the drawing-room and club-room and ballroom, where people of leisure and education come together, where comedy is bred and shades of character revealed, he is awkward and ill at ease. But the opposite is equally true. If we do not know his men and women in their relations to each other, we know them in their relations to time, death, and fate. If we do not see them in quick agitation against the lights and crowds of cities, we see them against the earth, the storm, and the seasons. We know their attitude towards some of the most tremendous problems that can confront mankind. They take on a more than mortal size in memory. We see them, not in detail but enlarged and dignified. We see Tess reading the baptismal service in her nightgown 'with an impress of dignity that was almost regal'. We see Marty South, 'like a being who had rejected with indifference the attribute of sex for the loftier quality of abstract humanism', laying the flowers on Winterborne's grave. Their speech has a Biblical dignity and poetry. They have a force in them which cannot be defined, a force of love or of hate, a force which in the men is the cause of rebellion against life, and in the women implies an illimitable capacity for suffering, and it is this which dominates the character and makes it unnecessary that we should see the finer features that lie hid. This is the tragic power; and, if we are to place Hardy among his fellows, we must call him the greatest tragic writer among English novelists.

But let us, as we approach the danger-zone of Hardy's philosophy, be on our guard. Nothing is more necessary, in reading an imaginative writer, than to keep at the right distance above his page. Nothing is easier, especially with a writer of marked idiosyncrasy, than to fasten on opinions, convict him of a creed, tether him to a consistent point of view. Nor was Hardy any exception to the rule that the mind which is most capable of receiving impressions is very often the least capable of drawing conclusions. It is for the reader, steeped in the impression, to supply the comment. It is his part to know when to put aside the writer's conscious intention in favour of some deeper intention of which perhaps he may be unconscious. Hardy himself was aware of this. A novel 'is an impression, not an argument', he has warned us, and, again : 'Unadjusted impressions have their value, and the road to a true philosophy of life seems to lie in humbly recording diverse readings of its phenomena as they are forced upon us by chance and change'.

Certainly it is true to say of him that, at his greatest, he gives us impressions; at his weakest, arguments. In *The Woodlanders*,

The Return of the Native, Far from the Madding Crowd, and, above all, in *The Mayor of Casterbridge*, we have Hardy's impression of life as it came to him without conscious ordering. Let him once begin to tamper with his direct intuitions and his power is gone. 'Did you say the stars were worlds, Tess?' asks little Abraham as they drive to market with their beehives. Tess replies that they are like 'the apples on our stubbard-tree, most of them splendid and sound – a few blighted'. 'Which do we live on – a splendid or a blighted one?' 'A blighted one', she replies, or rather the mournful thinker who has assumed her mask speaks for her. The words protrude, cold and raw, like the springs of a machine where we had seen only flesh and blood. We are crudely jolted out of that mood of sympathy which is renewed a moment later when the little cart is run down and we have a concrete instance of the ironical methods which rule our planet.

That is the reason why *Jude the Obscure* is the most painful of all Hardy's books, and the only one against which we can fairly bring the charge of pessimism. In *Jude the Obscure* argument is allowed to dominate impression, with the result that though the misery of the book is overwhelming it is not tragic. As calamity succeeds calamity we feel that the case against society is not being argued fairly or with profound understanding of the facts. Here is nothing of that width and force and knowledge of mankind which, when Tolstoy criticises society, makes his indictment formidable. Here we have revealed to us the petty cruelty of men, not the large injustice of the gods. It is only necessary to compare *Jude the Obscure* with *The Mayor of Casterbridge* to see where Hardy's true power lay. Jude carries on his miserable contest against the deans of colleges and the conventions of sophisticated society. Henchard is pitted, not against another man, but against something outside himself which is opposed to men of his ambition and power. No human being wishes him ill. Even Farfrae and Newson and Elizabeth Jane whom he has wronged all come to pity him, and even to admire his strength of character. He is standing up to fate, and in backing the old Mayor whose ruin has been largely his own fault, Hardy makes us feel that we are backing human nature in an unequal contest. There is no pessimism here. Throughout the book we are aware of the sublimity of the issue, and yet it is presented to us in the most concrete form. From the opening scene in which Henchard sells his wife to the sailor at the fair to his death on Egdon Heath the vigour of the story is superb, its humour rich and racy, its movement large-limbed and free. The skimmity ride, the fight between Farfrae and Henchard in the loft, Mrs. Cuxsom's speech upon the death of Mrs Henchard, the talk of the ruffians at Peter's Finger with Nature present in the background or mysteriously dominating the foreground, are among the glories of English fiction. Brief and scanty, it may be, is the measure of happiness allowed to each, but so long as the struggle is, as Henchard's was, with the decrees of fate and not with the laws of man, so long as it is in the open air and calls for activity of the body rather than of the brain, there is greatness in the contest, there is pride and pleasure in it, and the death of the broken corn merchant in his cottage on Egdon Heath is comparable to the death of Ajax, lord of Salamis. The true tragic emotion is ours.

Before such power as this we are made to feel that the ordinary tests which we apply to fiction are futile enough. Do we insist that a great novelist shall be a master of melodious prose? Hardy was no such thing. He feels his way by dint of sagacity and uncompromising sincerity to the phrase he wants, and it is often of unforgettable pungency. Failing it, he will make do with any homely or clumsy or old-fashioned turn of speech, now of the utmost angularity, now of a bookish elaboration. No style in literature, save Scott's, is so difficult to analyse; it is on the face of it so bad, yet it achieves its aim so unmistakably. As well might one attempt to rationalise the charm of a muddy country road, or of a plain field of roots in winter. And then, like Dorsetshire itself, out of these very elements of stiffness and angularity his prose will put on greatness; will roll with a Latin sonority; will shape itself in a massive and monumental symmetry like that of his own bare downs. Then again, do we require that a novelist shall observe the probabilities, and keep close to reality? To find anything approaching the violence and convolution of Hardy's plots one must go back to the Elizabethan drama. Yet we accept his story completely as we read it; more than that, it becomes obvious that his violence and his melodrama, when they are not due to a curious peasant-like love of the monstrous for its own sake, are part of that wild spirit of poetry which saw with intense irony and grimness that no reading of life can possibly outdo the strangeness of life itself, no symbol of caprice and unreason be too extreme to represent the astonishing circumstances of our existence.

But as we consider the great structure of the Wessex novels it seems irrelevant to fasten on little points – this character, that scene, this phrase of deep and poetic beauty. It is something larger that Hardy has bequeathed to us. The Wessex Novels are not one book, but many. They cover an immense stretch; inevitably they are full of imperfections – some are failures, and others exhibit only the wrong side of their maker's genius. But undoubtedly, when we have submitted ourselves fully to them, when we come to take stock of our impressions of the whole, the effect is commanding and satisfactory. We have been freed from the cramp and pettiness imposed by life. Our imaginations have been stretched and heightened; our humour has been made to laugh out; we have drunk deep of the beauty of the earth. Also we have been made to enter the shade of a sorrowful and brooding spirit which, even in its saddest mood, bore itself with a grave uprightness and never, even when most moved to anger, lost its deep compassion for the sufferings of men and women. Thus it is no mere transcript of life at a certain time and place that Hardy has given us. It is a vision of the world and of man's lot as they revealed themselves to a powerful imagination, a profound and poetic genius, a gentle and humane soul.

Source: *The Common Reader: Second Series* (1932; written in 1928) pp. 250–7.

Jean Brooks

THE POETIC STRUCTURE (1971)

The poet's gift has not gone unremarked, but what it means to Hardy's art has not been explored in great detail in the light of modern poetic structure. One could, without much profit, compare some of Hardy's poems with their prosed counterparts to discover the link between poet and poetic novelist. Different kinds of poetry – philosophical, lyrical, elegiac, narrative/dramatic – isolate microscopically various ingredients which unite in the novels to produce the true Hardeian flavour. They crystallize a certain mood or moment of vision which are emotional arias in the novels. 'Beyond the Last Lamp', 'Tess's Lament', 'Proud Songsters', and 'A Light Snow-fall after Frost' (*Tess of the d'Urbervilles*); 'The Pine Planters' and 'In a Wood' (*The Woodlanders*); 'Childhood among the Ferns' and 'Midnight on the Great Western' (*Jude the Obscure*) are fine poems in their own right, because Hardy has added or subtracted features which re-create them in terms of lyric. Usually, however, the prosed poems are more successful in the novels, where they are an organic part of narrative structure and emotional accumulation of detail. To compare 'The Puzzled Game-Birds' with the end of Chapter XLI of *Tess* proves the futility of computer exercises.

The poetic strain is more complex. It is a way of looking at and ordering experience. It includes the ballad qualities of Hardy's narrative, poetic presentation of event and character, his poetic sense of place and history in the re-creation of Wessex, his imaginative blending of new Victorian science and old folk superstition, and the Gothic strangeness of his vision and style. It includes a sensuous apprehension of daily life that embraces the contemplative and metaphysical. Virginia Woolf reminds us ('Impassioned Prose', *T.L.S.* (1926), reprinted in *Granite and Rainbow*, Hogarth Press, 1958) that the novelist has his hands full of the facts of daily living, so 'how can we ask [him] . . . to modulate beautifully off into rhapsodies about Time and Death . . .?' Hardy's achievement of this difficult transition vindicates him as a poetic novelist.

The poetic impulse, expressing the basic but multiple faces of experience, defines the Hardeian quality. He thought of himself as 'an English poet who had written some stories in prose', and in prose tried to preserve the poetry. 'He had mostly aimed at keeping his narratives close to natural life and as near to poetry in their subject as the conditions would allow, and had often regretted that those conditions would not let him keep them nearer still.' (*The Life of Thomas Hardy*, Macmillan, 1930, p. 291.) It reconciles all the seeming contradictions of Hardy's subject, style, and philosophy by giving them equal weight but no synthesis. Hardy anticipates the modern anguish of unresolved tensions in the stylized forms which contain the undirected chaos of life; the traditional character types who reveal Freudian subtleties of psychology; grand gestures punctured by absurd and vulgar intrusions; the dichotomies of common and uncommon, simple and complex, protest and acquiescence. Yeats's definition of the double face of poetry is appropriate to the powerful tensions that constitute the Hardy vision : 'The passion . . . comes from the fact that the speakers are holding down violence or madness – "down Hysterica passio". All depends on the completeness of the holding down, on the stirring of the beast underneath. . . . Without this conflict we have no passion only sentiment and thought.' (Letter to Dorothy Wellesley, 5 August 1936)

The multiple perspective of poetry is more often a strength than a weakness. It gives simultaneously the personal and formal vision; the subjective feel of experience falling on 'all that side of the mind which is exposed in solitude' (Virginia Woolf, 'Impassioned Prose') and the bold epic relief of those characters who 'stand up like lightning conductors to attract the force of the elements' ('The Novels of Thomas Hardy', *The Common Reader*) in their mythopoeic relation to time, death, and fate, both enhanced and diminished by the time-marked Wessex scene that rings their actions. It is the source of Hardy's distinctive ironic tone and structure, his tragi-comedy, his blend of fatalism and belief in the power of chance, and his profound sense of tragedy.

Hardy's ironic mode is the reverse face of his compassion. The pattern of what is runs in tension with the pattern of what ought to be according to human values. Mismatings, mistimings and undesired substitutions for an intended effect point to the 'if only' structure of Hardeian irony. If only Newson had entered the tent a few minutes earlier or later; if only Angel had danced with Tess on the green; if only Tess had not been 'doomed to be seen and coveted that day by the wrong man' instead of by the 'missing counterpart' who 'wandered independently about the earth waiting in crass obtuseness till the late time came'. Hardy's notorious use of coincidence to demonstrate cosmic absurdity is shadowed by its traditional function as an agent of cosmic design. As Barbara Hardy points out in *The Appropriate Form* (Athlone Press, 1964), the use of coincidence in *Jane Eyre* is directed by Charlotte Brontë's belief in Providence; in *Jude the Obscure* by Hardy's belief in the absence of Providence. In Victorian melodrama the 'heroine' of *Tess of the d'Urbervilles* would have been rescued providentially by the 'hero' from the 'villain'. Hardy has neither hero, villain, nor Providence, and the alternative reasons he suggests for Tess's seduction point to the impenetrable mystery of the cosmic scheme.

When passionate personal emotion counterpoints the control of a traditional form, the ironic double vision thus obtained questions the unthinking acceptance of cosmic and social arrangements implied by the patterns Hardy took over from popular narrative and drama. Received morality is shaken and measured by the morality of compassion; poetic and Divine justice by the honesty that allows Arabella and Fitzpiers to flourish while Jude and Winterborne suffer unjustly and die, in a world where personal worth does not decide the issue. The internal tensions between the betrayed-maid archetype of balladry and the fallen woman of Victorian moral literature, set against the intense subjective world of Tess, provoke a complex reaction to her story. The psychological study of a frustrated woman strains against the breathless action of the sensation novel in *Desperate Remedies*. The Golden-Age pastoral exposes the cosmic dissonances of *Far from the Madding Crowd* and *The Woodlanders*. The expected

end of the story in marriage or death takes on a bitter irony in
Jude the Obscure, where the marriage of Sue is more tragic than
the death of Jude. The hymn metres behind some of Hardy's
poetic questionings of the First Cause; the ballad of revenge behind his ballads of generous action; the popular conception of
romantic love behind the cruel, blind, sexual force that sweeps
his characters to ecstasy, madness, suffering, and death, make the
ironic mode of double vision inseparable from style. The puzzled
game-birds in the poem of that name sing their bewilderment
at man's inconsistent cruelty in a graceful triolet. 'The Voice'
sets Hardy's grief for his wife's death to the gay tune of a remembered dance. The harsh physical facts of death deflate the pattern
of the consolation poem in which 'Transformations' is written.
Marsden points out that the beautiful patterns made on the page
by 'The Pedigree' bring out the subtle variations and irregularities
of structure which enact personal defiance of the realization of
heredity to which the poem moves – 'I am merest mimicker and
counterfeit ! – ' (K. Marsden, *The Poems of Thomas Hardy,*
Athlone Press, 1969, p. 120.)

Hardy's multiple vision of experience brings him close to the
modern-Absurdist form of tragi-comedy or comi-tragedy. 'If you
look beneath the surface of any farce you see a tragedy; and,
on the contrary, if you blind yourself to the deeper issues of a
tragedy you see a farce' (*Life*). The comic court-room scene of
The Mayor of Casterbridge in which the furmity hag works
Henchard's downfall, the comic constables who take the foreground while Lucetta lies dying from the shock of the skimmity
ride their incompetence has been unable to prevent; the rustics
who discuss, at length, folklore remedies as Mrs Yeobright lies
mortally wounded from snakebite; the two lovers who quarrel
about their precedence in Elfride's affections when they have
travelled unknowingly with her dead body; the farcical con-
junctions of Ethelberta's three lovers; the love-sick de Stancy's
undignified eavesdropping on Paula's gymnastic exercises in pink
flannel; the Kafka-like distortions of figure or scene, stress the
ironic deflation of romance, heroism, and tragedy by the objective
incursions of absurdity; without, however, denigrating the value
of romance, heroism, and suffering. 'All tragedy is grotesque – if
you allow yourself to see it as such' (*Life*).

In all his work Hardy's personal voice, with its humane values, its Gothic irregularities, its human contradictions and rough edges, its commonness and uncommonness, strains against the rigidities of traditional patterns and expectations. The first two paragraphs of *The Mayor of Casterbridge*, for example, can provide the mixture to be found in all the other novels, *The Dynasts*, and most of the poems – the amalgam of homely simplicity, awkward periphrasis, triteness, and sharp sensuous vision that invests an ordinary scene with the significance of myth and Sophoclean grandeur. The dissonance of the multiple vision dramatically enacts Hardy's metaphysic of man's predicament as a striving, sensitive, imperfect individual in a rigid, non-sentient, absurd cosmos, which rewards him only with eternal death.

The predicament is tragic. A poetic ambiguity of perspective is inherent in the nature of tragedy. It is part of the texture of human hope. 'The end of tragedy . . . is to show the dignity of man for all his helpless littleness in face of the universe, for all his nullity under the blotting hand of time' (Bonamy Dobrée, *The Lamp and the Lute*, Clarendon Press, 1929). In Hardy's tragedy one finds the tragic protagonist, defined for his role by a tragic greatness (not in high estate, as in Sophocles and Shakespeare, but in character alone) that intensifies the sense of life, and flawed by a tragic vulnerability that unfits him for the particular tragic situation he has to face. Jude's sexual and self-degrading impulses are disastrous in view of the obstacles to higher education for working men. Henchard's rash and inflexible temper cannot ride the agricultural changes that overtake Casterbridge. In the tragic universe human errors become tragic errors which co-operate with Fate (those circumstances within and without, which man did not make and cannot unmake, incarnated as natural forces, the clockwork laws of cause and effect, the workings of chance, coincidence, and time, irrational impulses, man-made conventions, and the search for happiness) to bring evil out of his goodness and good intentions, and to bring down on him, and innocent people connected with him, tragic suffering and catastrophe out of all proportion to its cause. The irresponsible sending of a valentine, the concealment of a seduction until the day of the wedding to another man, the careless sealing of love letters and choice of an untrustworthy messenger, release forces of death and destruction which inspire tragic terror at the contemplation of the painful mystery of the workings of inexorable law. Tragic pity is aroused, as Dobrée points out, 'not because someone suffers, but because something fine is bruised and broken' — something too sensitively organized for an insentient world of defect.

But the sense of tragic waste is tempered by tragic joy, because in the tragic confrontation with futility and absurdity Hardy affirms some of the highest values men and women can achieve.

The great writer of tragedy manages to convey that though this be the truth, it is well that men should behave thus and thus; that in spite of all the seeming cruelty and futility of existence, one way of life is better than another; that Orestes is right and Clytemnestra wrong, that Othello is fairer than Iago. Not that fault is to be imputed to the wrongdoer; he also is a pebble of fate, destined to play his part in the eternal drama of good and evil. (Dobrée, *The Lamp and the Lute*)

These values remain unchanged when the people who embodied them are destroyed, and whether the gods are alive or dead. Giles Winterborne's death may contain a criticism of his former backwardness and of Victorian sexual hypocrisy, but in its essence it celebrates the selfless love that can see further than temporary satisfaction of physical desire to the preservation of Grace's image untarnished to posterity. Modern permissiveness cannot change his nobility or the value of his suffering. Giles, Clym, Henchard, Tess, Jude, and Sue are not fulfilled in the eyes of the world. But their tragedy asserts the values for which they suffered (even Eustacia, whose selfishness limits our sympathy, asserts the value of self-assertion), stripped of all recommendations of success.

Hardy's tragic figures, rooted in an unconscious life-process more deterministic than their own, try to mould their lives according to human values, personal will, feeling, and aspiration. Though their self-assertion is overcome by the impersonality of the cosmos, including those instinctive drives they share with the natural world, their endeavour to stamp a humane personal design on cosmic indifference makes them nobler than what destroys them. Hardy had no time for Nietzsche. 'To model our conduct on Nature's apparent conduct, as Nietzsche would have taught, can only bring disaster to humanity' (*Life*). His characters' close and conscious relationship to unconscious nature defines the hope that is contained in the tragic suffering. Hardy's greatest novels are tragic actions which demonstrate the incomplete evolutionary state of man, a throb of the universal pulse, suffering as the pioneer of a more compassionate cosmic awareness – the hope towards which the whole of *The Dynasts* moves. His poems are the cries of tragic love, tragic error, tragic injustice, tragic waste, and tragic awareness with which tragic poets and dramatists from Aeschylus to Beckett have defined the sense of life.

> HAMM : What's he doing? . . .
> CLOV : He's crying. . . .
> HAMM : Then he's living. (Samuel Beckett : *Endgame*)

That Hardy's voice still has the authentic tragic note defines his importance to the modern world. Recent assertions (as in George Steiner's *The Death of Tragedy*) that tragedy died with the gods and an ordered system of Hellenic or Christian values shared by artist and audience, which gave reasons for the suffering and struggle, can hardly stand against the tragic experience of Hardy's work. Hardeian man, sustained only by his own qualities as a human being, defies the chaotic void as Hellenic and Shakespearean man, placed in reference to cosmic myth, defied powers which were, if cruel and unknowable, at least *there* to be defied.

> Then would I bear it, clench myself, and die,
> Steeled by the sense of ire unmerited;
> Half-eased in that a Powerfuller than I
> Had willed and meted me the tears I shed. ('Hap')

A strong plot, 'exceptional enough to justify its telling', explicit in the novels and implicit in many poems, was Hardy's formal correlative for the tragic vision of man confronting his destiny. As Bonamy Dobrée points out, plot ('this is how things happen') is a more important symbol for tragedy than character ('this is what people are like'), 'since the tragic writer is concerned with the littleness of man (even though his greatness in his little-

ness) in the face of unescapable odds'. The hammer strokes of a
clockwork universe on human sensitivity are enacted in a pattern
as rigid as scientific law, likened by Lascelles Abercrombie to a
process of chemistry, in which the elements 'are irresistibly moved
to work towards one another by strong affinity; and the human
molecules in which they are ingredients are dragged along with
them, until the elemental affinity is satisfied, in a sudden flashing
moment of disintegration and re-compounding' (*Thomas Hardy*,
Martin Secker, 1912). There is no inconsistency between Hardy's
determinism and the important role in his works of chance and
coincidence. Chance is direction which we cannot see; but it is
the direction of a blind, groping force, unrelated to anything we
can conceive as conscious purpose. Once more the double perspective of chaos and determinism conjures up a richly complex
poetic response to the fate of living creatures subject to inhuman
cause and effect.

The symmetry and intensity of Hardy's plots, with every link
in the chain of cause and effect made clear, join with his poetic
vision of natural rhythms, and traditional devices of dramatic
development, in a disproportioning of reality to bring out the pattern of the larger forces driving the cosmos and its creatures.
Sensational events, disastrous coincidences, untimely reappear-
ances, overheard or revealed secrets, present a universe where
every action is a hostage to a predetermined and hidden fate.
The supernatural detail, the rural superstition and folk belief,
stand in for the missing Providential direction. Without Providence, everything contributes to the longing for significance. Besides giving the poetic *frisson* at inexplicable mysteries, Hardy's
use of superstition is integral to the characters' relation to fate.
The tragedy of *The Woodlanders* is touched off by old John
South's anthropological involvement with a tree. The primitive
emotion conjured up by the events at the Midsummer Eve 'larries'
lays the foundation of Grace's marriage, her separation, and Mrs
Charmond's death. As J. O. Bailey demonstrates in 'Hardy's
Visions of the Self' (*Studies in Philology*, LVI, 1959) the Hardeian
'ghost' (a walking vision, a dream, a real sight suggesting guilt,
or a mental image presented to the reader) plays the part of a
directing Nemesis in revealing to the character his own inner

nature, causing him to accept responsibility for disasters he had blamed on circumstances, and to take the action that brings the novel to a conclusion.

The characters too have a simple epic and tragic strength. They are types, though not without individuality. All the subtleties of psychology and sociology that might obscure the pattern of their ritual interaction with Fate are stripped away. Life is reduced to its basic elements : birth, mating, death, the weather, man's pain and helplessness in an indifferent universe; the passions and conflicts that spring from an enclosed rural community with its roots in an ancient past and an ancient countryside, its pagan fatalism and ballad values and personal loyalties, being gradually invaded by modern urban restlessness and alienation. The catastrophic passions of the main characters are set off by a peasant chorus quietly enduring the realistic slow trivialities of daily living, which shape human fate by steady accumulation. They are as slow to change as the natural rhythms they are part of. Hardy creates a fundamental persistence from the tension between the two kinds of stability; the eternal recurrence of the natural cycle and the recurrent finiteness of men.

They compose a pool of common wisdom, of common humour, a fund of perpetual life. They comment upon the actions of the hero and heroine, but while Troy or Oak or Fanny or Bathsheba come in and out and pass away, Jan Coggan and Henry [sic] Fray and Joseph Poorgrass remain. They drink by night and they plough the fields by day. They are eternal. We meet them over and over again in the novels, and they always have something typical about them, more of the character that marks a race than of the features which belong to an individual. The peasants are the great sanctuary of sanity, the country the last stronghold of happiness. When they disappear, there is no hope for the race (Virginia Woolf, 'The Novels of Thomas Hardy').

They are equivalent to Camus's nostalgia for a lost paradisal homeland of harmony with things as they are.

The human emotional force of the characters counterpoints the regularity of plot and scientific process; a process which they both obey and defy. Hardy's double vision of man's greatness in values and littleness in the cosmic scheme keeps the tragic balance between fate – the impersonal nature of things – and personal responsibility. When Henchard disregards his wife's last wishes and reads the letter in which she discloses that Elizabeth-Jane is not his child, 'he could not help thinking that the concatenation of events this evening had produced was the scheme of some sinister intelligence bent on punishing him. Yet they had developed naturally. If he had not revealed his past history to Elizabeth he would not have searched the drawer for papers, and so on.' The doubt reflects the painful ambiguity and inscrutability of things; a poetic asset. While it is true that Hardy's poetic pattern stresses the action of fate, it does so to stress too the human responsibility to deflect fate from its path before it is too late. Misery, which teaches Henchard 'nothing more than a defiant endurance of it', teaches Clym to limit his ambitions and Oak to keep one step ahead of an infuriated universe. The adaptive resourcefulness of Farfrae, the loving-kindness of Viviette which triumphs over her sexual passion for Swithin, the determination of Paula to follow her lover through Europe regardless of etiquette, modify a fate that seemed predetermined. Their conscious purpose redefines the concept of fate as what must be *only if no resistance is made*.

In the complexity of things resistance itself has a double edge. The greatest value ephemeral man can find to stand against the threat of meaninglessness is love. It promises to satisfy the thirst for happiness and harmony with cosmic purposes. Hardy's definition of love is unfashionably wide. It includes, as well as the physiological fact and frank relationship between the sexes which he wanted to show his Victorian readers, Viviette's sublimated maternal love for her young lover Swithin, Mr Melbury's for his daughter and Mrs Yeobright's for her son, Henchard's for Farfrae and the girl who is not his daughter. Charley's idealized love for his mistress Eustacia, Clym's for suffering mankind, and the life-loyalties of the interrelated Hintock community. But because its roots are in the impersonal sexual impulses that drive the natural world, love contributes to the tragedy of human consciousness. Respect for the real being of the beloved is lost in illusory wish-projections which cause suffering when they clash with reality. Angel's image of Tess as an inhumanly pure woman, Clym's vision of Eustacia as a school matron and Eustacia's of

Clym as a gay Parisian escort, Bathsheba's defence of Troy as a regular churchgoer, Jude's intermittent treatment of Sue as the 'average' woman, are nature's devices, working on the human tendency to idealization, to accomplish the mating process. The projection causes pain when it moves from lover to lover; love rarely ceases for both at the same moment. But though agony is the inevitable corollary of ecstasy, the pain affirms the life-enhancing quality of love. The caprice it inspires in women – a type of the cosmic caprice of fate – is also a measure of their vitality and truth to life. The will to enjoy, inseparably bound up with the opposing will to suffer (part of 'the circumstantial will against enjoyment'); the instinctive zest for existence modified by the modern view of life as a thing to be put up with, can bring maturity and even happiness. Bathsheba attains maturity and a realistic appraisal of Oak's controlled fidelity. Even Tess is only robbed of the purely human Paradise promised in Talbothays by the inhumanity of man.

Virginia Woolf accepts the great emotional crises as part of Hardy's poetic pattern. 'In all the books love is one of the great facts that mould human life. But it is a catastrophe; it happens suddenly and overwhelmingly, and there is little to be said about it' ('The Novels of Thomas Hardy').

T. S. Eliot, on the other hand, attacks the 'emotional paroxysms' which seem to him a 'symptom of decadence' expressing 'a powerful personality uncurbed by any institutional attachment or by submission to any objective beliefs. . . . He seems to me to have written as nearly for the sake of "self-expression" as a man well can; and the self which he had to express does not strike me as a particularly wholesome or edifying matter of communication . . .' (*After Strange Gods*, Harcourt Brace & Co., 1934). His criticism suggests the distrust of someone who feels the meaning of orthodox allegiances threatened by the affirmation of a life without God or ultimate purpose. But in a world where Eliot's own poetry has revealed the dehumanization of hollow men living in an emotionless waste land, the intense emotion of Hardy's characters and Hardy's personal voice affirm the response of living passion to the human predicament. 'The function of the artist is to justify life by feeling it intensely' (J. E. Barton, 'The Poetry of Thomas

Hardy'). Far from robbing the characters of their human individuality, as Eliot claims, heightened emotion stresses both their
basic humanness and the resistance of the unique personality to
the habit of despair which Camus found worse than despair itself ('None of us was capable any longer of an exalted emotion;
all had trite, monotonous feelings' – *The Plague*), and which
Matthew Arnold had defined in a letter to Clough (14 December
1852) as 'the modern situation in its true *blankness* and *barrenness*,
and *unpoetrylessness*'.

Hardy's poetic persona is untouched by the modern taboo on
tenderness and top notes, though the understatement of deep
feeling also forms part of his vision. His emotional scenes are
operatic rather than melodramatic; arias which reveal the inner
quality of life, with all its dissonant primary passions reconciled
in the musico-poetic form, while the outer action is suspended.
The effect of Boldwood's final gesture, with its poignant return
of his old courtesy, 'Then he broke from Samway, crossed the
room to Bathsheba, and kissed her hand', in the context of his
murder of Troy, can only be compared with the return of the love
leitmotif at the end of Verdi's *Otello*. (The *Life* proves that Verdi
was a composer with whom Hardy felt some affinity.) As the
emotional persuasiveness of music suspends disbelief in what
would be absurd in spoken drama, Hardy's poetic heightening
carries him through operatic implausibilities of action and clumsi-
nesses of style. The unrealistic 'libretto' of the quarrel between
Clym and Eustacia, reminiscent of the quarrel of Brachiano and
Vittoria in *The White Devil*, directs attention away from the
technicalities of expression to the white-hot emotion underneath
that compels the jerky speech rhythms, the trembling of Eustacia's
hands, and the agony of a man still in love with the wife he is
rejecting on principle, who while he ties her bonnet strings for her,
'turned his eyes aside, that he might not be tempted to softness'.

It is the emotion of Hardy's work which one remembers. It
expresses the whole of his many-sided personality, spilling over the
barriers of artistic form to make his work an experience which is
musical and artistic as well as literary. Virginia Woolf's definition
of the special quality of Hardy's characters – 'We recall their
passions. We remember how deeply they have loved each other

and often with what tragic results. . . . But we do not remember how they have loved. We do not remember how they talked and changed and got to know each other, finely, gradually, from step to step and from stage to stage. . . .' ('The Novels of Thomas Hardy') – places his work with those sister arts (in which Hardy was a competent practitioner) which create a universal image of the essence of things to transcend the personal and local details that gave it birth. As W. H. Auden remarked about his experience of writing opera libretti (the T. S. Eliot Memorial lectures given at the University of Kent at Canterbury, 1967): 'Music can, I believe, express the equivalent of *I love*, but it is incapable of saying whom or what I love, you, God, or the decimal system.' In the extraordinary states of violent emotion that distinguish the operatic mode, all differences in social standing, sex, and age are abolished, so that even in a foreign language one can tell the emotion that is being expressed.

Hardy's equivalent for the operatic state often takes a form that is both musical and pictorial. Dance and song are linked with ritual survivals of fertility rites that are an 'irresistible attack upon . . . social order', as in the village gipsying on Egdon and the dance that inspires the change of marriage partners in 'The History of the Hardcomes'. The folk or church music that was part of Hardy's heritage often moves a sexual or compassionate emotion that precipitates a definite step in the story. The step is not always disastrous. The sound of children's voices singing 'Lead kindly Light' re-establishes Bathsheba's relationship with Oak after her tragedy; Farfrae's song stops Henchard from killing him in the loft. Boldwood feels encouraged to consider himself as good as engaged to Bathsheba after their exhibition of harmony at the shearing supper. Wildeve feels there is nothing else to do but marry Tamsin after they have been celebrated by Grandfer's crew as a married couple. Farfrae's modest dance with Elizabeth-Jane at his entertainment precipitates a half-declaration of love. Tess's interest in Angel's music rivets his attention on this unusual milkmaid, whose 'fluty' tones had interrupted his meditations on a music score. The hymn tune of the Wessex composer, which made Sue and Jude clasp hands by an 'unpremeditated instinct', gives rise to her confession of an 'incomplete' marriage with

Phillotson, and points to her search for spiritual harmony with Jude. Even Melbury's irritation at Cawtree's low ballad, which contributes to his rejection of Giles as a suitable mate for his daughter, is a refusal to recognize the primitive side of Grace's nature which is in harmony with the sentiments of the song and the simple woodland company who sang it. The effect of ritual music becomes a correlative for the operations of the Immanent Will, moving people through their emotions to obey its own inscrutable purposes.

Ritual itself is, in modern terms, total theatre. The ritual character of Hardy's operatic scenes – the village gipsying, the skimmity ride, the Egdon bonfires, the arrest at Stonehenge – is stressed by his balletic groupings and his description of scene and characters in terms of the strong contrast of light and shade. This pictorial treatment abstracts personality from the actors and leaves their faces mask-like, with no 'permanent moral expression'. The silhouette, employed most frequently in descriptions of the rustic chorus, expresses a communal emotion rather than individual idiosyncrasy. The figure defined in sharp relief against a dun background, like Clym against the settle or Mrs Yeobright against the heath, or suddenly illuminated, Rembrandt-fashion, in a long shaft of light (Marty at the window, Eustacia in the light from Susan Nunsuch's cottage), suddenly fixes the moving characters through the distancing of pictorial art as eternal tableaux of the littleness of conscious human experience in the surrounding darkness. (Alastair Smart, 'Pictorial Imagery in the Novels of Thomas Hardy', *Review of English Studies*, xII, 1961.) As Cytherea's father falls to his death from the tower, shafts of light falling across the room become for her an objective correlative of tragedy. The essential nature of Arabella and her opposite Sue Bridehead is caught in the framed picture of Delilah and the comparison of Sue to a Parthenon frieze. When the heart and inner meaning has thus been established in a frozen image, it dissolves once more into the drama of people in motion acting out that reality, leaving the reader with a new perspective of their place in the cosmic scheme. . . .

Source: *Thomas Hardy: The Poetic Structure* (1971) pp 10–23.

Raymond Williams

'THE EDUCATED OBSERVER AND THE
PASSIONATE PARTICIPANT' (1970)

The Hardy country is of course Wessex: that is to say mainly
Dorset and its neighbouring counties. But the real Hardy country,
I feel more and more, is that border country so many of us have
been living in: between custom and education, between work
and ideas, between love of place and an experience of change.
This has a special importance to a particular generation, who
have gone to the university from ordinary families and have to
discover, through a life, what that experience means. But it has
also a much more general importance; for in Britain generally
this is what has been happening: a moving out from old ways
and places and ideas and feelings; a discovery in the new of
certain unlooked-for problems, unexpected and very sharp crises,
conflicts of desire and possibility.

In this characteristic world, rooted and mobile, familiar yet
newly conscious and self-conscious, the figure of Hardy stands
like a landmark. It is not from an old rural world or from a
remote region that Hardy now speaks to us; but from the heart
of a still active experience, of the familiar and the changing,
which we can know as an idea but which is important finally in
what seem the personal pressures – the making and failing of
relationships, the crises of physical and mental personality – which
Hardy as a novelist at once describes and enacts.

But of course we miss all this, or finding it we do not know how
to speak of it and value it, if we have picked up, here and there,
the tone of belittling Hardy.

I want to bring this into the open. Imagine if you will the
appearance and the character of the man who wrote this: 'When
the ladies retired to the drawing-room I found myself sitting next

to Thomas Hardy. I remember a little man with an earthy face. In his evening clothes, with his boiled shirt and high collar, he had still a strange look of the soil.' Not the appearance and the character of Thomas Hardy; but of the man who could write that about him, that confidently, that sure of his readers, in just those words.

It is of course Somerset Maugham, with one of his character-istic tales after dinner. It is a world, one may think, Hardy should never have got near; never have let himself be exposed to. But it is characteristic and important, all the way from that dinner-table and that drawing-room to the 'look of the soil', in that rural distance. All the way to the land, the work, that comes up in silver as vegetables, or to the labour that enters that company – that customary civilised company – with what is seen as an earthy face.

In fact I remember Maugham, remember his tone, when I read Henry James on 'the good little Thomas Hardy', or F. R. Leavis saying that *Jude the Obscure* is impressive 'in its clumsy way'. For in several ways, some of them unexpected, we have arrived at that place where custom and education, one way of life and another, are in the most direct and interesting and I'd say necessary conflict.

The tone of social patronage, that is to say, supported by crude and direct suppositions about origin, connects interestingly with a tone of literary patronage and in ways meant to be damaging with a strong and directing supposition about the substance of Hardy's fiction. If he was a countryman, a peasant, a man with the look of the soil, then this is the point of view, the essential literary standpoint, of the novels. That is to say the fiction is not only about Wessex peasants, it is by one of them, who of course had managed to get a little (though hardly enough) education. Some discriminations of tone and fact have then to be made.

First, we had better drop 'peasant' altogether. Where Hardy lived and worked, as in most other parts of England, there were virtually no peasants, although 'peasantry' as a generic word for country people was still used by writers. The actual country people were landowners, tenant farmers, dealers, craftsmen and labourers, and that social structure – the actual material, in a social sense, of the novels – is radically different, in its variety, its shading, and many of its basic human attitudes from the structure of a peasantry. Secondly, Hardy is none of these people. Outside his writing he was one of the many professional men who worked within this structure, often with uncertainty about where they really belonged in it. A slow gradation of classes is characteristic of capitalism anywhere, and of rural capitalism very clearly. Hardy's father was a builder who employed six or seven work-men. Hardy did not like to hear their house referred to as a cottage, because he was aware of this employing situation. The house is indeed quite small but there is a little window at the back through which the men were paid, and the cottages down the lane are certainly smaller. At the same time, on his walk to school, he would see the mansion of Kingston Maurward (now happily an agricultural college) on which his father did some of the estate work, and this showed a sudden difference of degree which made the other distinction comparatively small though still not unim-portant. In becoming an architect and a friend of the family of a vicar (the kind of family, also, from which his wife came) Hardy moved to a different point in the social structure, with connections to the educated but not the owning class, and yet also with connections through his family to that shifting body of small em-ployers, dealers, craftsmen and cottagers who were themselves never wholly distinct, in family, from the labourers. Within his writing his position is similar. He is neither owner nor tenant, dealer nor labourer, but an observer and chronicler, often again with uncertainty about his actual relation. Moreover he was not writing for them, but about them, to a mainly metropolitan and unconnected literary public. The effect of these two points is to return attention to where it properly belongs, which is Hardy's attempt to describe and value a way of life with which he was closely yet uncertainly connected, and the literary methods which follow from the nature of this attempt. And so often when the cur-rent social stereotypes are removed the critical problem becomes clear in a new way.

It is the critical problem of so much of English fiction, since the actual yet incomplete and ambiguous social mobility of the nineteenth century. And it is a question of substance as much as of method. It is common to reduce Hardy's fiction to the impact of an urban alien on the 'timeless pattern' of English rural life. Yet though this is sometimes there the more common pattern is the relation between the changing nature of country living, determined as much by its own pressures as by pressures from 'outside', and one or more characters who have become in some degree separated from it yet who remain by some tie of family inescapably involved. It is here that the social values are dramatised in a very complex way and it is here that most of the problems of Hardy's actual writing seem to arise.

One small and one larger point may illustrate this argument, in a preliminary way. Nearly everyone seems to treat Tess as simply the passionate peasant girl seduced from outside, and it is then surprising to read quite early in the novel one of the clearest statements of what has become a classical experience of mobility : 'Mrs. Durbeyfield habitually spoke the dialect; her daughter, who had passed the Sixth Standard in the National School under a London-trained mistress, spoke two languages : the dialect at home, more or less; ordinary English abroad and to persons of quality.' Grace in *The Woodlanders*, Clym in *The Return of the Native* represent this experience more completely, but it is in any case a continuing theme, at a level much more important than the trivialities of accent. And when we see this we need not be tempted, as so often and so significantly in recent criticism, to detach *Jude the Obscure* as a quite separate kind of novel.

A more remarkable example of what this kind of separation means and involves is a description of Clym in *The Return of the Native* which belongs in a quite central way to the argument I traced in *Culture and Society* : 'Yeobright loved his kind. He had a conviction that the want of most men was knowledge of a sort which brings wisdom rather than affluence. He wished to raise the class at the expense of individuals rather than individuals at the expense of the class. What was more, he was ready at once to be the first unit sacrificed.' The idea of sacrifice relates in the whole action to the familiar theme of a vocation thwarted or damaged by a mistaken marriage, and we shall have to look again at this characteristic Hardy deadlock. But it relates also to the general action of change which is a persistent social theme. As in all

H.T.T.N.—D

major realist fiction the quality and destiny of persons and the quality and destiny of a whole way of life are seen in the same dimension and not as separable issues. It is Hardy the observer who sets this context for personal failure :

In passing from the bucolic to the intellectual life the intermediate stages are usually two at least, frequently many more; and one of these stages is sure to be worldly advance. We can hardly imagine bucolic placidity quickening to intellectual aims without imagining social aims as the transitional phase. Yeobright's local peculiarity was that in striving at high thinking he still cleaved to plain living – nay, wild and meagre living in many respects, and brotherliness with clowns. He was a John the Baptist who took ennoblement rather than repentance for his text. Mentally he was in a provincial future, that is, he was in many points abreast with the central town thinkers of his date. . . . In consequence of this relatively advanced position, Yeobright might have been called unfortunate. The rural world was not ripe for him. A man should be only partially before his time; to be completely to the vanward in aspirations is fatal to fame. . . . A man who advocates aesthetic effort and deprecates social effort is only likely to be understood by a class to which social effort has become a stale matter. To argue upon the possibility of culture before luxury to the bucolic world may be to argue truly, but it is an attempt to disturb a sequence to which humanity has been long accustomed.

The subtlety and intelligence of this argument from the late 1870s come from a mind accustomed to relative and historical thinking, not merely in the abstract but in the process of observing a personal experience of mobility. This is not country against town, or even in any simple way custom against conscious intelligence. It is the more complicated and more urgent historical process in which education is tied to social advancement within a class society, so that it is difficult, except by a bizarre personal demonstration, to hold both to education and to social solidarity ('he wished to raise the class'). It is the process also in which culture and affluence come to be recognised as alternative aims, at whatever cost to both, and the wry recognition that the latter will always be the first choice, in any real history (as Morris also observed and indeed welcomed).

The relation between the migrant and his former group is then

exceptionally complicated. His loyalty drives him to actions which
the group can see no sense in, its overt values supporting the
association of education with personal advancement which his
new group has already made but which for that very reason he
cannot accept.

'I am astonished, Clym. How can you want to do better than you've
been doing?'

'But I hate that business of mine. . . . I want to do some worthy
things before I die.'

'After all the trouble that has been taken to give you a start, and
when there is nothing to do but keep straight on towards affluence,
you say you . . . it disturbs me, Clym, to find you have come home
with such thoughts. . . . I hadn't the least idea you meant to go back-
ward in the world by your own free choice. . . .'

'I cannot help it,' said Clym, in a troubled tone.

'Why can't you do . . . as well as others?'

'I don't know, except that there are many things other people
care for which I don't. . . .'

'And yet you might have been a wealthy man if you had only
persevered. . . . I suppose you will be like your father. Like him, you
are getting weary of doing well.'

'Mother, what is doing well?'

The question is familiar but still after all these years no question
is more relevant or more radical. Within these complex pressures
the return of the native has a certain inevitable nullity, and his
only possible overt actions can come to seem merely perverse.
Thus the need for social identification with the labourers produces
Clym's characteristic negative identification with them; becoming
a labourer himself and making his original enterprise that much
more difficult: 'the monotony of his occupation soothed him,
and was in itself a pleasure'.

All this is understood and controlled by Hardy but the pressure
has further and less conscious effects. Levin's choice of physical
labour, in *Anna Karenina*, includes some of the same motives
but in the end is a choosing of people rather than a choosing of
an abstract Nature – a choice of men to work with rather than a
natural force in which to get lost. This crucial point is obscured
by the ordinary discussion of Hardy's attachment to country life,

which would run together the 'timeless' heaths or woods and the
men working together on them. The original humanist impulse –
'he loved his kind' – can indeed become anti-human : men can
be seen as creatures crawling on this timeless expanse, as the imagery of the heath and Clym's work on it so powerfully suggests.
It is a very common transition in the literature of that period
but Hardy is never very comfortable with it, and the original
impulse, as in *Jude the Obscure*, keeps coming back and making
more precise identifications.

At the same time the separation of the returned native is not
only a separation from the standards of the educated and affluent
world 'outside'. It is also to some degree inevitably from the
people who have not made his journey; or more often a separation
which can mask itself as a romantic attachment to a way of life
in which the people are merely instrumental : figures in a landscape or when the literary tone fails in a ballad. It is then easy, in
an apparently warm-hearted way, to observe for the benefit of
others the crudity and limitations but also the picturesqueness,
the rough humour, the smocked innocence of 'the bucolic'. The
complexity of Hardy's fiction shows in nothing more than this :
that he runs the whole gamut from an external observation of
customs and quaintnesses, modulated by a distinctly patronising
affection (as in *Under the Greenwood Tree*), through a very positive identification of intuitions of nature and the values of shared
work with human depth and fidelity (as in *The Woodlanders*), to
the much more impressive but also much more difficult humane
perception of limitations, which cannot be resolved by nostalgia
or charm or an approach to mysticism, but which are lived through
by all the characters, in the real life to which all belong, the limitations of the educated and the affluent bearing an organic relation
to the limitations of the ignorant and the poor (as in parts of
Return of the Native and in *Tess* and *Jude*). But to make these
distinctions and to see the variations of response with the necessary
clarity we have to get beyond the stereotypes of the autodidact
and the countryman and see Hardy in his real identity : both the
educated observer and the passionate participant, in a period of
general and radical change. . . .

*   *   *

The complication is that this is a very difficult and exposed position for Hardy to maintain. Without the insights of consciously learned history and of the educated understanding of nature and behaviour he cannot really observe at all, at a level of extended human respect. Even the sense of what is now called the 'timeless' – in fact the sense of history, of the barrows, the Roman remains, the rise and fall of families, the tablets and monuments in the churches – is a function of education. That real perception of tradition is available only to the man who has read about it, though what he then sees through it is his native country, to which he is already deeply bound by memory and experience of another kind : a family and a childhood; an intense association of people and places, which has been his own history. To see tradition in both ways is indeed Hardy's special gift : the native place and experience but also the education, the conscious inquiry. Yet then to see living people, within this complicated sense of past and present, is another problem again. He sees as a participant who is also an observer; this is the source of the strain. For the process which allows him to observe is very clearly in Hardy's time one which includes, in its attachment to class feelings and class separations a decisive alienation.

If these two noticed Angel's growing social ineptness, he noticed their growing mental limitations. Felix seemed to him all Church; Cuthbert all College. His Diocesan Synod and Visitations were the mainsprings of the world to the one; Cambridge to the other. Each brother candidly recognized that there were a few unimportant scores of millions of outsiders in civilized society, persons who were neither University men nor Churchmen; but they were to be tolerated rather than reckoned with and respected.

This is what is sometimes called Hardy's bitterness, but in fact it is only sober and just observation. What Hardy sees and feels about the educated world of his day, locked in its deep social prejudices and in its consequent human alienation, is so clearly true that the only surprise is why critics now should still feel sufficiently identified with that world – the world which coarsely and coldly dismissed Jude and millions of other men – to be willing to perform the literary equivalent of that stalest of political tactics : the transfer of bitterness, of a merely class way of thinking, from those who exclude to those who protest. We did not after all have to wait for Lawrence to be shown the human nullity of that apparently articulate world. Hardy shows it convincingly again and again. But the isolation which then follows, while the observer holds to educated procedures but is unable to feel with the existing educated class, is severe. It is not the countryman awkward in his town clothes but the more significant tension – of course with its awkwardness and its spurts of bitterness and nostalgia – of the man caught by his personal history in the general structure and crisis of the relations between education and class, relations which in practice are between intelligence and fellow-feeling. Hardy could not take the James way out, telling his story in a 'spirit of intellectual superiority' to the 'elementary passions'. As he observes again of the Clare brothers : 'Perhaps, as with many men, their opportunities of observation were not so good as their opportunities of expression.' That after all is the nullity, in a time in which education is used to train members of a class and to divide them from other men as surely as from their own passions (for the two processes are deeply connected). And yet there could be no simple going back.

They had planted together, and together they had felled ; together they had, with the run of the years, mentally collected those remoter signs and symbols which seen in few are of runic obscurity, but all together made an alphabet. From the light lashing of the twigs upon their faces when brushing through them in the dark, they could pronounce upon the species of tree whence they stretched ; from the quality of the wind's murmur through a bough, they could in like manner name its sort afar off.

This is the language of the immediate apprehension of 'nature', for in that form, always, Hardy could retain a directness of communication. But it is also more specifically the language of shared work, in 'the run of the years', and while it is available as a memory, the world which made it possible is, for Hardy, at a distance which is already enough to detach him : a closeness, paradoxically, that he is still involved with but must also observe and 'pronounce upon'. It is in this sense finally that we must consider Hardy's fundamental attitudes to the country world he was writing about. The tension is not between rural and urban, in the ordinary senses, nor between an abstracted intuition and an abstracted intelligence. The tension, rather, is in his own position, his own lived history, within a general process ·of change which could come clear and alive in him because it was not only general but in every detail of his feeling observation and writing immediate and particular.

Every attempt has of course been made to reduce the social crisis in which Hardy lived to the more negotiable and detachable forms of the disturbance of a 'timeless order'. But there was nothing timeless about nineteenth-century rural England. It was changing constantly in Hardy's lifetime and before it. It is not only that the next village to Puddletown is Tolpuddle, where you can look from the Martyrs' Tree back to what we know through Hardy as Egdon Heath. It is also that in the 1860s and 1870s, when Hardy was starting to write, it was what he himself described as 'a modern Wessex of railways, the penny post, mowing and reaping machines, union workhouses, lucifer matches, labourers who could read and write, and National school children'. Virtually every feature of this modernity preceded Hardy's own life (the railway came to Dorchester when he was a child of seven). The effects of the changes of course continued. The country was not timeless but it was not static either; indeed, it is because the change was long (and Hardy knew it was long) that the crisis took its particular forms.

We then miss most of what Hardy has to show us if we impose on the actual relationships he describes a pastoral convention of the countryman as an age-old figure, or a vision of a prospering countryside being disintegrated by Corn Law repeal or the railways or agricultural machinery. It is not only that Corn Law repeal and the cheap imports of grain made less difference to Dorset : a county mainly of grazing and mixed farming in which the coming of the railway gave a direct commercial advantage in the supply of milk to London : the economic process described with Hardy's characteristic accuracy in *Tess* :

They reached the feeble light, which came from the smoky lamp of a little railway station; a poor enough terrestrial star, yet in one sense of more importance to Talbothays Dairy and mankind than the celestial ones to which it stood in such humiliating contrast. The cans of new milk were unladen in the rain, Tess getting a little shelter from a neighbouring holly tree....

. . . 'Londoners will drink it at their breakfasts tomorrow, won't they?' she asked. 'Strange people that we have never seen . . . who don't know anything of us, and where it comes from; or think how we two drove miles across the moor tonight in the rain that it might reach 'em in time?'

It is also that the social forces within his fiction are deeply based in the rural economy itself: in a system of rent and trade; in the hazards of ownership and tenancy; in the differing conditions of labour on good and bad land and in socially different villages (as in the contrast between Talbothays and Flintcomb Ash); in what happens to people and to families in the interaction between general forces and personal histories – that complex area of ruin or survival, exposure or continuity. This is his actual society, and we cannot suppress it in favour of an external view of a seamless abstracted country 'way of life'.

It is true that there are continuities beyond a dominant social situation in the lives of a particular community (though two or three generations, in a still partly oral culture, can often sustain an illusion of timelessness). It is also obvious that in most rural landscapes there are very old and often unaltered physical features, which sustain a quite different time-scale. Hardy gives great importance to these, and this is not really surprising when we consider his whole structure of feeling. But all these elements are overridden, as for a novelist they must be, by the immediate and actual relationships between people, which occur within existing contemporary pressures and are at most modulated and interpreted by the available continuities.

The pressures to which Hardy's characters are subjected are then pressures from within the system of living, not from outside it. It is not urbanism but the hazard of small-capital farming that changes Gabriel Oak from an independent farmer to a hired labourer and then a bailiff. Henchard is not destroyed by a new and alien kind of dealing but by a development of his own trade which he has himself invited. It is Henchard in Casterbridge who speculates in grain as he had speculated in people; who is in every sense, within an observed way of life, a dealer and a destructive one; his strength compromised by that. Grace Melbury is not a country girl 'lured' by the fashionable world but the daughter of a successful timber merchant whose own social expectations, at this point of his success, include a fashionable education for his daughter. Tess is not a peasant girl seduced by the squire; she is the daughter of a lifeholder and small dealer who is seduced by the son of a retired manufacturer. The latter buys his way into a country house and an old name. Tess's father and, under pressure, Tess herself, are damaged by a similar process, in which an old name and pride are one side of the coin and the exposure of those subject to them the other. That one family fell and one rose is the common and damaging history of what had been happening, for centuries, to ownership and to its consequences in those subject to it. The Lady Day migrations, the hiring fairs, the intellectually arrogant parson, the casual gentleman farmer, the landowner spending her substance elsewhere: all these are as much parts of the country 'way of life' as the dedicated craftsman, the group of labourers and the dances on the green. It is not only that Hardy sees the realities of labouring work, as in Marty South's hands on the spars and Tess in the swede field. It is also that he sees the harshness of economic processes, in inheritance, capital, rent and trade, within the continuity of the natural processes and persistently cutting across them. The social process created in this interaction is one of class and separation, as well as of chronic insecurity, as this capitalist farming and dealing takes its course. The profound disturbances that Hardy records cannot then be seen in the sentimental terms of a pastoral: the contrast between country and town. The exposed and separated individuals, whom Hardy puts at the centre of his fiction, are only the most developed cases of a general exposure and separation. Yet they are never merely illustrations of this change in a way of life. Each has a dominant personal history, which in psychological terms bears a direct relation to the social character of the change.

S o u r c e : *The English Novel from Dickens to Lawrence* (1970) pp. 98–106, 109–15.

PART THREE

Modern Studies on Individual Novels

I *The Return of the Native*

John Paterson

AN ATTEMPT AT GRAND TRAGEDY
(1966)

The Return of the Native has been ranked by some indulgent
readers with *The Mayor of Casterbridge* and *Tess of the d'Urbervilles* and *Jude the Obscure*; but, for all its superficial impressive-
ness, it doesn't really belong in their distinguished company. Too
studied and self-conscious an imitation of classical tragedy, it
doesn't have their immediate reality, their powerful authenticity.
In the ceremonial chapters of Egdon Heath and Eustacia Vye,
in the set speeches and soliloquies of the heroine, in the novel's
conscientious observation of the unities of time and space, in its
organization (as originally planned) in terms of the five parts
or 'acts' of traditional tragedy, *The Return of the Native* was
meant to recall the immensities of Sophocles and Shakespeare.
But the facts of its fiction simply do not justify the application
of so grand, so grandiose, a machinery. Its men and women are
seldom equal after all to the sublime world they are asked to
occupy. In the Vyes and the Yeobrights, Hardy evidently intended a little aristocracy fit to bear the solemn burdens of tragedy.
But they remain a species of stuffy local gentility and as such
incapable of heroic transformations. Eustacia may justify the
formidable frame of reference in which she is set, but to associate
Clym, the translated shopkeeper, with the likes of Oedipus and
Aeneas is to emphasize how far short of them he really falls. Mrs.
Yeobright's identification with Lear – in her final agony she is
equipped with a heath, a hovel and a fool – is perhaps more deserved, but it shows too visibly and seems only slightly less wilful

than Clym's identification with heroes of classical fame. In the
unfolding of her fate, money, her collection of precious guineas,
surely plays a more crucial part than should consist with an action
of Sophoclean or Shakespearean size. Even the death of the splendid Eustacia is in part determined by a shortage of funds.

The plot of the novel, then, lacks the terrific and terrifying
logic of cause and effect that marks the plots of the greatest
exercises in this line. That it operates the way it does is more
accidental than necessary. If Diggory had known that half the
guineas belonged to Clym, if Mrs. Yeobright's arrival at her
son's house had not coincided with Wildeve's, if Eustacia had
not mistakenly thought her husband awake, if she had received
his letter or had had a few more pence in her purse, then the tragic
disaster would not have taken place at all. The presence of the
fateful and the inevitable is felt as little in the 'action' of the
characters as in the action of the plot. Their motives for doing
what they do, for contriving their own undoing, are often only
specious and arbitrary and seem determined by the needs of a
tyrannical plot. Diggory's sentimental motive for haunting the
heath speaks well for his heart but may impress the reader as odd
and even gratuitous. Eustacia's reasons for not at once opening
the door to Mrs. Yeobright seem strained and dubious and even
her reasons for doing herself in at the end are not wholly con-
vincing. Hardy does manage on the whole to bring these things off,
but not without arousing in the reader the uneasy sensation that
he has had the narrowest of escapes, that all the time he has been
skating on the thinnest of ice. The inexorability of its tragic development has seemed too often to express, in short, not the natural
needs or necessities of the novel but the applied will or wilfulness
of the author. . . .

But *The Return of the Native* is better than its defects; it
breathes a reality that its very manifest weaknesses are powerless to explain or explain away. The sources of this reality are
not easily identifiable. That they don't exist in Hardy's conceptions that are usually trite or clumsy or obvious is clear enough.
That they don't exist in the raw materials he worked with, in
that traditional stockpile of ruined maids, mysterious strangers,
dashing soldiers and sailors, lovers faithful or faithless, dark-

dyed villains, etc., is equally clear. Few readers briefed in advance on the plots and characters of *Far From the Madding Crowd, The Woodlanders, Tess of the d'Urbervilles, The Return of the Native,* would think them worth the trouble of a further exploration. Their matter would seem too thin or too poor or too simple-minded for artistic conversion. It is just here, though, that the sources of Hardy's power to chasten and subdue disclose themselves. It was in the life and imagination he brought with so much simple faith and fervor to his large but crude conceptions, to his rude but primitive images, that his power to persuade resides. In spite of the many excellent and obvious reasons for not believing in the experience of the novel, we do in the end believe in it because Hardy himself did. He wins our consent because what he records has been both closely observed and deeply felt. . . .

In the end, however, the novel derives more from Hardy's imagination than from his observation and experience, so that the detail that provides its intensest and most vivid pages is better described as poetic than as realistic. Like Wordsworth, Hardy worked to transfigure the trivial and the commonplace, to make the ordinary extraordinary. The business of the artist was, he said, to make Nature's defects 'the basis of a hitherto unperceived beauty, by irradiating them with "the light that never was" . . .'. As the creatures of a tragic or symbolic or conceptual machinery, Hardy's people may sometimes fail at the purely realistic level, but because they are made to move as often as they are in an ambience of poetic beauty and wonder, these intermittent failures are not decisive. Images like Thomasin gathering holly boughs 'amid the glistening green and scarlet masses of the tree' or Eustacia unclosing her lips in a laugh 'so that the sun shone into her mouth as into a tulip and lent it a similar scarlet fire' exercise a chemical influence out of all proportion to their mass or quantity and have the effect of compensating for the novel's many flat and sandy moments. Even a character as tenuous and abstract as Clym can be quickened into vital life on occasion by the magic of Hardy's incandescent imagination as when 'the eclipsed moonlight shines upon [his] face with a strange foreign colour, and shows its shape as if it were cut out of gold'. The same transfiguring force enters the novel's individual scenes and epi-

sodes. Eustacia's voyage across the moonlit heath with the mummers, the weird nocturnal game of dice between Wildeve and
the reddleman, the unearthly trancelike dance on the green at
East Egdon – such radiant scenes as these have the power to
cancel out the occasional lapses in the novel's plotting or causa-
tion. It was this power to change the ordinary stuff of reality into
something rich and strange, this power to discover beneath the
surface of ordinary life and being rare and mysterious states of
life and being, that led D. H. Lawrence to discover in Hardy a
brother under the skin.[1]

The same powerful imagination everywhere informs and transforms the novel. *The Return of the Native* can survive the defects
of its plot because the plot as such all but disappears in the greater
and more inclusive music of theme and imagery. Though its
action scarcely qualifies as a tragic action, the novel does evoke,
in its accumulating allusions to the geography, history and literature of classical antiquity, the heroic world out of which tragedy
came and to this extent places the otherwise purely local or
domestic action in a context that enlarges and enrichens. Variously
described as the home of the Titans, as Dante's Limbo, as 'Homer's
Cimmerian land', Egdon Heath can suggest the lightless under-
world of the ancients. Representing the diminished consciousness
of modern times, Clym's is explicitly contrasted with the heroic
consciousness of Hardy's prelapsarian Greeks. Persistently identified with the legend and literature of antiquity, Eustacia, on
the other hand, suggests the anachronistic and hence foredoomed
revival of that consciousness. Her profile compares with Sappho's;
she 'can utter oracles of Delphian ambiguity'; her dream has 'as
many ramifications as the Cretan labyrinth'. In the most dazzling
of her Mediterranean associations, she is established as the lineal
descendant of Homeric kings, as the last of the house of Phaeacia's
princely Alcinous.

What most energetically enters and irradiates the matter of
The Return of the Native, however, is its Promethean theme
and imagery. Clym and his Egdon Heath are specifically affiliated
with the banished Titan, with the fallen benefactor of mankind;
but it is the novel's fire imagery, by inference Promethean, that
most fully asserts this primary motif. The darkness of the heath is

thus disturbed, early in the novel, by fires that mark the anniversary of the Gunpowder Plot. Wildeve makes his presence known by releasing at Eustacia's window a moth that perishes in the flames of her candle. On the day Mrs. Yeobright dies, the universe of Egdon is imagined as almost literally in flames and her death is a symbolic death-by-fire : 'The sun . . . stood directly in her face, like some merciless incendiary, brand in hand, waiting to consume her.' Eustacia herself will perish in the same fatal flames : burned in effigy by Susan Nunsuch and acting out the parable of Wildeve's moth-signal, she will hurl herself into 'the boiling caldron' of the weir. This theme affects not only the major imagery of action and setting but also the minor imagery of word and phrase. In Eustacia's presence, 'the revived embers of an old passion glowed clearly in Wildeve', who fancies himself victimized by 'the curse of inflammability'. 'A blaze of love, and extinction' Eustacia herself prefers characteristically to 'a lantern glimmer of the same'. After first meeting Clym she is 'warmed with an inner fire' and she will later denounce Mrs. Yeobright 'with a smothered fire of feeling' and with 'scalding tears' trickling from her eyes.

At the very last, however, the source of the novel's 'felt' life or power is much more elusive, less accessible, than the chemistry of its language and imagery. That ultimate source can only aproximately be identified as what Francis Fergusson would call its 'action', the sensitive inner movement or motion of its feeling. It may be difficult to accept, to believe in, the novel's rickety and arbitrarily directed plot; but it is not at all difficult to accept and believe in its 'action', the curve of the emotion that animates it and is the true shape of its 'felt' life. What eventually overcomes us is the tragic rhythm of the action as it moves in the experience of the chief characters through the phases first of purpose or will or desire, then of passion or suffering as what the characters intend or desire is resisted and defeated, and finally of perception or knowledge as they recognize the limits of their world and of their power to change it. If *The Return of the Native* does not rank with the greatest novels, it is because it fails, in the imagery of character and plot, to enact with full and confident power this tragic rhythm of action. But if it remains a good or nearly great

novel, it is because it does enact, however imperfectly, this powerful and profoundly felt rhythm. . . .

The novel as Hardy initially conceived it was a very different
novel from the one we now have. Now Mrs. Yeobright's niece
and Clym's cousin, Thomasin was originally conceived as Mrs.
Yeobright's daughter and Clym's sister. Now a witch in only the
metaphorical sense, Eustacia was at first imagined as a witch in
the more literal sense and, as such, was more malevolently the
persecutor of a helpless Thomasin Yeobright than she now is. In
the novel's present form, Thomasin leaves one morning with Wildeve to be married but returns that evening alone, hysterical and
unmarried because the license produced by her husband-to-be
has proved invalid. According to the original or provisional terms
of the novel, however, Thomasin was to have lived with Wildeve
for a week before discovering that the marriage ceremony, perhaps by her paramour's wilful and malicious design, had been
illegal. Hardy's decision to abandon the original program of the
novel was doubtless determined by editorial pressure, a pressure
emanating probably from the offices of the *Cornhill Magazine* to
whose editor, Leslie Stephen, it was first shown. Responsible for
the serial publication of *Far From the Madding Crowd* and *The
Hand of Ethelberta*, Stephen had had already in the past to
restrain Hardy's difficult and dangerous imagination. 'I may be
over particular,' he wrote in connection with *The Hand of Ethelberta*, 'but I don't like the suggestion of the very close embrace
in the London churchyard.' Now presented with *The Return of
the Native* in an evidently embryonic form, the editor felt called
upon again to correct and control his client. 'Though he liked the
opening,' Hardy reported, 'he feared that the relations between
Eustacia, Wildeve and Thomasin might develop into something
"dangerous" for a family magazine, and he refused to have anything to do with it unless he could see the whole.' Although *The
Return of the Native* was eventually serialized in *Belgravia*, not in
the *Cornhill*, the anxious author was evidently inspired by
Stephen's serious misgivings to subject the novel in its germinal
form to the radical revision that resulted in the version we now
have.

The history of the novel's distortion under editorial pressure was not to end with Hardy's separation from Stephen and the *Cornhill*. His employers on the board of *Belgravia* could have been no more liberal than his old employers had been. Though the opposition between Christian and pre-Christian values is vital to the novel's total effect, no specific denigration of the Christian religion was permitted to enter the text. In such outlandish spots as Egdon, Hardy planned to say, 'homage to nature, self-adoration, frantic gaieties, fragments of Teutonic rites to divinities whose names are forgotten, have in some way or other survived medieval Christianity'. Editorial tact prevailed, however, and the phrase 'medieval Christianity' was subsequently neutralized to 'medieval doctrine'. Even more damaging to the novel's free imaginative development was the suppression of all references to lips and legs and bodies. Though the force that brings Wildeve and Eustacia together is manifestly other than spiritual or sentimental, no explicit indication of its sexual character was permitted. These wicked lovers were not to be granted even the small freedom of a kiss. 'You are a pleasant lady to know,' Wildeve was at one time permitted to say, 'and I daresay as sweet [to kiss] as ever – almost.' The dangerous infinitive was rigorously removed, however, from the text of the manuscript. Just as tyrannical was the public passion for the happy ending. Hardy had intended, as he confessed in a footnote on page 473 of the definitive edition of 1912, to conclude *The Return of the Native* with the fifth book : with the deaths of Wildeve and Eustacia, with the widowhood of Thomasin and the disappearance of the reddleman. He was forced by editorial policy, however, to add a sixth book : to arrange the marriage of a reconstructed reddleman and a rehabilitated widow and thus to dishonor his original intention. . . .

[But, Paterson says, it would be a mistake to exaggerate the effect of Hardy's "exposure to a prudential editorial policy"; and he goes on to say :]

There's even a question whether the energetic moral censorship of the time really affected more than the superficies of the novel. It did make it difficult for Hardy to represent his men and women as sexual as well as social creatures. But it didn't prevent him from forcibly expressing the novel's crucial criticism

of Christianity. No explicit condemnation of the religious estab-
lishment was, of course, permitted to appear at the surface of the
novel. But the condemnation is not the less a condemnation because it is not explicit. Indeed, much of its power may derive
from the accident that it was driven underground, that Hardy was
compelled by the nature of the circumstances to dramatize indirectly, at the level of artistic suggestion, what he couldn't
plainly say. Identified with a world not yet touched by the spec-
tral hand of Christianity, Eustacia Vye reincarnated on the
withered parish of Egdon Heath the larger and braver vision of
the ancient Greeks. In her suffering and death she dramatizes the
tragic humiliation, in a diminished world, of the heroic pre-
Christian understanding of things. It doesn't surprise us, therefore,
that though no longer literally the witch, that immemorial an-
tagonist of the Christian faith, she remains that black creature in
the figurative sense at least. Nor does it surprise that of all the
parts in the mummers' play, she should draw precisely that of the
antichrist, the Turkish Knight, who must, with ritual inexorability, suffer defeat and death at the hands of the Christian
champion.

Eustacia stands in this in opposition to her husband, whose
allegedly advanced views only thinly disguise the Christian champion. For if Clym consistently deceives himself and sometimes
his creator, he doesn't deceive his mother, who correctly under-
stands him as a missionary in disguise, or his wife, who associates
him half-satirically with the Apostle Paul. Nor does he always
deceive Hardy *either*, who sometimes exposes him to the most
damaging ironies. Clym's theoretical and pious intelligence suffers,
for example, when contrasted with the practical and instinctive
intelligence of a still-unchristened peasant community very properly skeptical of his plans to improve it. ' 'Tis good-hearted of
the young man', says one member of that community with a
condescension that events will justify. 'But, for my part, I think
he had better mind his own business.' The ironies at Clym's expense are especially trenchant at the novel's end where his denial
of life in a spirit of Christian self-renunciation contrasts dramatically with the life-renewing rites both of Maypole-day and of
Thomasin's marriage. Whether Hardy intended it or not – and

it's hard to believe he didn't – Clym's theatrical conversion is reduced by the savage rites of spring and marriage to ludicrous
terms.

As the unreconstructed reddleman, Diggory Venn was evidently
meant to honor the stoic and realistic values of a pre-Christian
way of life and, tacitly at least, to criticize the nicer, less permissive,
values that come in with Christianity. Originally meant 'to have
retained his isolated and weird character to the last, and to have
disappeared mysteriously from his heath', he was to have sym-
bolized the displacement by the Christian dispensation of that
elusive and nearly demoniacal spirit of fen and forest that had
found its last resting place on Egdon. Identified with Cain, with
Ishmael, with Mephistopheles, he was to have stood with Eustacia
Vye, and to a certain extent still stands with her, outside the pale
of Christian salvation. For the novel's anti-Christian character,
however, the members of the peasant community with their
hearty celebration of the natural life and their instinctive distrust of the church are mainly responsible. Their performances
derive, that is, from levels of thinking and feeling older than and
antagonistic to the innovations of Christianity. The bonfires they
build in their first appearance have their antecedents in a barbaric
Druidical and Anglo-Saxon past. As mummers they reenact the
old folk-play, the St. George play, whose Christian veneer scarcely conceals the pre-Christian fertility rite. As participants in
the ancient ritual of Maypole-day, they celebrate a vitality older
and stronger than Christianity. 'In name they were parishioners,'
Hardy notes with evident satisfaction, 'but virtually they belonged
to no parish at all.' Hardy's denigration of Christianity is perhaps
most explicit in the ludicrous figure of Christian Cantle, the caricature of the Christian man. Dissociated from the pagan community with its profane celebration of natural joy and virtue, the
pious Christian alone refrains from joining the mad, demoniacal
measure about the Promethean bonfire of November 5. His physical decrepitude and sexual impotence – he's the man no woman
will marry – stand out beside the life-worshiping vitality of Grandfer and Timothy and the rest of that lusty crew. And where he
lives in constant terror of the sights and sounds of the savage
heath, they, complete pagans that they are, feel perfectly at home

in this grimmest of all possible worlds. Though the subversive, anti-Christian argument of *The Return of the Native* could not openly be asserted, it was and remains everywhere active beneath the novel's unassuming surface. Hardy may have been hampered in the exercise of his artistic will by the virulent censorship of the time, but he couldn't, it's clear, be stopped by it. If his strong and stubborn imagination couldn't have its will one way, it would have it another. . . .

S o u r c e : from the Introduction to *The Return of the Native* (Harper & Row edition, 1966), reprinted here under the title 'An Attempt at Grand Tragedy'.

NOTE

1. D. H. Lawrence, 'Study of Thomas Hardy', in *Phoenix; The Posthumous Papers of D. H. Lawrence* (New York, 1936).

Leonard W. Deen

HEROISM AND PATHOS IN
THE RETURN OF THE NATIVE (1960)

Of all Hardy's novels, *The Return of the Native* is the one which most invites comparison with grand tragedy. It is full of elevating and sobering allusions to such tragic and heroic figures as Aeneas, Oedipus, Lear, and Cleopatra. Eustacia Vye, more than any other of Hardy's protagonists, seems intended to be grandly heroic, to exist on a higher level of significance than the other characters in the novel. She is alone, rebellious, even powerful – and so little explicable that she can be taken for a witch by the superstitious. Eustacia's state of heroic isolation is emphasized by a tragic chorus of country folk clearly set off from the actors in the drama. They provide a Shakespearean (grave diggers and porter) comic change-of-pace as well as a contrast of styles and levels of seriousness; and, functioning as Greek chorus, from a position of sanity and safety they comment on the illusion, ambition, or *hubris* of the antagonists. But for all these approaches to the heroic style, Hardy seems curiously uncertain whether his story constitutes high tragedy. *The Return of the Native* begins heroically, but slips more and more into the diminishing ironic and pathetic mode which characterizes Hardy's later tragedies.

Eustacia Vye is a young woman with romantic dreams of heroic love and social brilliance, who marries under the illusion that her husband, Clym Yeobright, will fulfill her dreams, and help her to escape her remote and isolated life on Egdon Heath. Disillusionment, conflict with her mother-in-law, and a violent quarrel with her husband lead her to attempt a desperate flight with a former lover, Damon Wildeve. On her way to meet him, she drowns, and Wildeve drowns in an attempt to rescue her. Hardy never tells us whether Eustacia's drowning is accident or suicide, but suicide is the inevitable explanation, since she considers herself trapped between the intolerable alternatives of staying on Egdon Heath or living with a lover she thinks vastly inferior to herself.

Given a bare synopsis of the plot, one is scarcely prepared for the Eustacia of the novel. At one time or another, Hardy suggests that she is a goddess (Aphrodite probably) in her power and capriciousness, a Titaness in her rebelliousness, a witch in her solitude and mystery, a *femme fatale* in her power to arouse passion in others, and a Cleopatra in her pride, her passion, and her scorn of consequences. Hardy is perhaps aiming at infinite variety, but his efforts in this kind are largely self-defeating. For one thing, his descriptions of Eustacia so complicate our impressions of her that it is almost impossible to form a consistent image of her, except that she is meant to be awe-inspiring. For another, he makes her more impressive than she has a right to be, considering her age and sex and the apparently frivolous nature of her desires. She does little to demonstrate or to justify the dazzling array of qualities Hardy ascribes to her.

Eustacia can remain mysterious and fatal only as long as our view of her is external and relatively long range, as it is at her first appearance. She is standing on an ancient grave on the summit of Rainbarrow, the highest hill in Egdon.

There the form stood, motionless as the hill beneath. Above the plain rose the hill, above the hill rose the barrow, and above the barrow rose the figure. Above the figure was nothing that could be mapped elsewhere than on a celestial globe. . . . The scene was strangely homogeneous, in that the vale, the upland, the barrow, and the figure above it amounted only to unity. Looking at this or that member of the group was not observing a complete thing, but a fraction of the thing.[1]

At the approach of others Eustacia (whom Hardy has not yet identified) leaves.

The imagination of the observer clung by preference to that vanished, solitary figure, as to something more interesting, more important, more likely to have a history worth knowing than these newcomers, and unconsciously regarded them as intruders. But they remained, and established themselves; and the lonely person who hitherto had been queen of the solitude did not at present seem likely to return (p. 14).

Silhouetted against the sky, Eustacia seems almost to have risen from the earth on which she stands. She is 'queen of the solitude', quite literally elevated, and she is 'discovered' standing on a grave, with which she is persistently associated throughout the novel. The scene is carefully composed for its heroic-tragic implications.

The heath on which Eustacia is first seen provides an index for all the other characters as well. As a symbol of man's unchangeable place in nature, and of his endurance, it measures each character's acceptance of his earthly fate. Clym, the native returned, as furze cutter symbolically submerges himself in the life of the heath; Thomasin Yeobright (his cousin) considers the heath her natural and appropriate environment. They have chosen the safer and more reasonable part, and thus, in the logic of the novel, they can be neither heroic nor tragic. Wildeve attempts to evade the heath; he loses his life, and Hardy intends his death to give him a certain dignity which he did not have alive. Mrs. Yeobright, who has more force than Wildeve, and whose death is considerably more significant than his, is only less unreconciled to her existence than Eustacia. Just before her death she has a vision of an intensely desired escape :

She leant back to obtain more thorough rest, and the soft eastern portion of the sky was as great a relief to her eyes as the thyme was to her head. While she looked a heron arose on that side of the sky and flew on with his face towards the sun. He had come dripping wet from some pool in the valleys, and as he flew the edges and linings of his wings, his thighs, and his breast were so caught by the bright sunbeams that he appeared as if formed of burnished silver. Up in the zenith where he was seemed a free and happy place, away from all contact with the earthly ball to which she was pinioned; and she wished that she could arise uncrushed from its surface and fly as he flew then (p. 343).

Death is of course the only escape possible. The human involve-

ment in the round of existence is inexorable, and all visions of
freedom or of paradise are denied.

More proudly and intransigently than anyone else, Eustacia re-
bels against the heath. For Hardy this rebellion makes her not
only tragic but heroic, though her situation as goddess misplaced
in this sublunary world (she is repeatedly associated with the
moon) is not without its irony :

But celestial imperiousness, love, wrath, and fervour had proved
to be somewhat thrown away on netherward Egdon. Her power was
limited, and the consciousness of this limitation had biassed her development. Egdon was her Hades, and since coming there she had
imbibed much of what was dark in its tone, though inwardly and
eternally unreconciled thereto. Her appearance accorded well with
this smouldering rebelliousness, and the shady splendour of her beauty
was the real surface of the sad and stifled warmth within her. A true
Tartarean dignity sat upon her brow, and not factitiously or with
marks of constraint, for it had grown in her with years (p. 77).

The heath mirrors the minds of its inhabitants, and for Eustacia
it is hell. She is not the initially triumphant hero, Oedipus or
Agamemnon, but the bitterly enduring hero, Milton's Satan or
Shelley's Prometheus. She is a romantic (she is a whole history of
romanticism) seen romantically. She is emblematic of the feeling
and infinite desire which rebel against inevitable limitation, and
thus is the supremely tragic figure of the novel.

These early scenes have shown us Eustacia's outer character,
built up by allusion and external description and the implications
of setting. So far as her tragic heroism is evoked by these means,
the tragic conception of *Return* is static; it consists mostly in the
mysterious and superior isolation of the heroine, her singularity.
It seems a tragedy of portentous mood and circumstance; Eustacia
looks tragic and acts tragic in a quite theatrical way. What James
would presumably call tragic drama – action rendered by dialogue and dramatic confrontation – is often obscured by tragic
scene or tableau, the trappings and the suits of woe.

What keeps external and scenic portent from swallowing the
novel is the fact that it is excessive only in the opening scenes. It
soon retires into the background (where it belongs of course), and
the foreground is occupied by a tragic action which proceeds

mainly on two levels – that of overt purpose, conflict, and misunderstanding, and that of symbolic and ritual revelation of Eustacia's inner life and character. The revelatory action presents
a different Eustacia from the one we see first. She remains the
central figure of a tragedy, but she is not so exaggeratedly heroic
as she seems from outside.

The ritual or symbolic action begins with a dream which
Eustacia has shortly after Clym's return, and before she has seen
him (though she has heard his voice, and has fallen in love with
him sight unseen). In her dream she finds herself ecstatically dancing with a helmeted knight. Suddenly they dive into a pool, and
come out on the other side into a kind of 'iridescent' paradise.
They kiss, and he crumbles like a pack of cards, without her having identified him. The dream, of course, is a prevision of Eustacia's drowning at the weir; what she interprets as a promise of
ideally romantic love is instead a promise of death.

The symbolic action of the dream is bit by bit 'realized' in
later scenes of the novel. In the first scene, Eustacia decides to
join a party of mummers who are to present 'the well-known play
of St. George' at a Christmas party of the Yeobrights'. Disguised
by hanging ribbons which represent the vizor of her helmet,
Eustacia plays the part of the Turkish knight. In doing so, she
seems both to take the role of the helmeted knight of the dream,
and to undergo a ritual death at the hands of another helmeted
knight, St. George. Eustacia has two purposes in becoming a
mummer – one recognized and the other buried. Driven by boredom and the hope that he might be the means of rescuing her
from the heath, she is desperately anxious to meet Clym, who has
just returned from Paris, the heart of the romantic and fashionable world. Although she does not dance with Clym, she hopes
that he 'is' the knight of her dream. In the mumming scene
Eustacia also reveals a second desire, a more destructive one, of
which she is not conscious. As Hardy is careful to emphasize, in
becoming a mummer Eustacia 'changes sex', and the whole episode is an adventure on the outer limits of female respectability.
What is suggested elsewhere in the novel is clearly revealed here.
Eustacia in the mumming assumes the heroic masculine role to
which she is always aspiring. She wants to alter her essential

human condition, to change her sex. A dissatisfaction so thorough-going amounts to a denial of life itself.

The second scene which carries out in reality the events of Eustacia's dream takes place after her marriage to Clym Yeo-bright. In it she dances, by moonlight, with Wildeve. She is again disguised, this time by a veil, and the dance is a 'pagan' throwing off of restraint, a celebration of the 'pride of life', and a ritual of passionate unreason which 'drives the emotions to rankness'. It is a 'riding upon the whirlwind' which deadens conscious con-trol: 'her soul had passed away from and forgotten her features, which were left empty and quiescent, as they always are when feeling goes beyond their register' (p. 310). Wildeve's response is equally abandoned. He is repeatedly associated with the moth who immolates himself in the flame, and he is here seen taking fire from Eustacia. Furthermore, the dance identifies Wildeve as the partner with whom Eustacia dances in the dream, and who dives with her into the pool – that is, the fellow-victim of her drowning. For both Eustacia and Wildeve the dance is not only a sublimation of more specifically sexual desires (the symbolic sexuality of the dances which occur in Hardy's novels scarcely needs to be pointed out): it is also a ritual embracing of oblivion and death. Wildeve had earlier ratified his own death, in the alien and overwhelming presence of the heath, by an unlucky cast of the dice – which are 'powerful rulers of us all, and yet at my command', as Christian Cantle affirms.

The dream and the later scenes which are linked to it operate not only as tragic portents, but as oblique revelations of weakness in the self. Eustacia assumes in them two 'roles' – the conscious self which, desiring passionate love above all things, nevertheless keeps this desire under reasonable control, and the vizored knight, or its other manifestation, the veiled dancer. The knight and the dancer reveal a tragic and sometimes Dionysian self-destructive-ness in Eustacia. The two dances, the dream dance and the dance on the heath, have the significance Hardy ascribed to the mum-ming, itself a kind of dance: they are all rites in which 'the agents seem moved by an inner compulsion to say and do their allotted parts whether they will or no' (p. 144). They are all rituals of which Eustacia's story is the mythical development. Her buried self takes control of her and destroys her. Her abandonment to it makes her death 'necessary', the fruit of her character as much as of her circumstances and her luck. Beneath her external and superhuman mask as *femme fatale* or goddess of love, Eustacia is an all too human victim of her own nature.

But the irony implicit in our double vision of Eustacia's role and personality is not firmly controlled. Hardy has implicated himself too deeply in her appearance of being larger than life to be able to detach himself from it. It has been clear throughout the novel that Eustacia acquiesces in illusion. Her life is primarily nocturnal, a moonlight existence. While she recognizes what she calls the 'mendacity of the imagination', she yields to its deception. 'Let us only look at what seems', she says, and she has no patience with fact that conflicts with desire. Her reason tells her that Wildeve is unworthy of her, that Clym's aims are inconsistent with her own, and that his personality fails to satisfy her dreams of the heroic; yet she succeeds, at different times, in altering both Clym and Wildeve to something sufficiently like the image of her desire. Hardy insists that this failing makes her more admirable. He remarks of her falling in love with Clym before she has met him, 'The fantastic nature of her passion, which lowered her as an intellect, raised her as a soul' (p. 139). The fantastic nature of her passion does not exalt her, though it is not incompatible with tragedy. In the overwhelming of her reason by her passions there is an imbalance, a simultaneous strength and weakness, to which admiration or condemnation is equally irrelevant. This self-destructive excess in Eustacia is tragic, but it is sometimes falsified by Hardy's explanatory comments and by a rhetoric which inflates Eustacia's 'real' character, the one revealed to us by the logic of actions and events.

The ritual scenes I have described establish the necessity of the catastrophe primarily by revealing Eustacia as a tragic type. In them she wordlessly acts out her character and fate. The more immediate causes of her death, of course, are in her conflicts with and misunderstandings of other characters. But the two levels of action illuminate each other by their interconnections. Running parallel to but ahead of the external drama, the submerged action gives the external events a deep resonance of dramatic irony.

The overt action turns largely on the forces which destroy Eus-

tacia's and Clym's excessively romantic and illusory married happiness. (As the titles of Books III and V indicate, first comes the
'Fascination', then the 'Discovery'.) One of the essential destructive forces is, of course, their emotional and intellectual incompatibility. Hardy seems to have conceived Clym, at least in the
beginning, as a kind of Hamlet – a superior mind and sensibility
ravaged by that disease, thought, and misunderstood by the cruder
world. Clym also has strong suggestions of the prophet who retires from a luxurious and self-indulgent society in order to criticize and to reform it; he intends to begin in the wilderness of the
heath. His force as prophet is considerably weakened, however,
by his becoming the inevitable victim of a world whose worldliness
he does not comprehend. He is a prophet of the future who fails
to see how intractably primitive the world of Egdon Heath is. And
as overspiritualized modern man he is equally blind to Eustacia's
primitiveness. She is all pagan self-assertion and passion; he has
chosen the different way of self-denial and devotion to the good
of others. The two almost become figures in an allegory of flesh
and spirit, like the abstractly patterned interplay of flesh and
spirit (or perverse spirit) in *Jude the Obscure*. Eustacia is not only
less spiritually pure than Clym; she has many of the masculine
qualities – energy, aggressiveness, ambition, and Promethean rebellion – which he lacks. If Eustacia is too fervid, Clym is too
idealistic for life on earth, and suffers from blindness to the way
of the world. He is, in fact, symbolically stricken with blindness
shortly after his marriage to Eustacia, and Hardy, perhaps too
obviously, murmurs 'Oedipus'.

The primal flaw in Eustacia's and Clym's marriage is increased
by the earlier conflicting but ineradicable emotional commitments each has made. Eustacia is unable to escape Wildeve's
hold on her. Clym cannot free himself from his mother, and considers Eustacia his 'mother's supplanter'. The intentional conflict
is between Eustacia and her mother-in-law, who end by destroying one another. Clym seems to exist primarily to define this conflict, as the rather passive and uncomprehending prize of the
struggle between the two women. (Eustacia's and Mrs. Yeobright's mutual distrust and dislike is well established in Book I,
'The Three Women', before Clym even appears.) The crisis of the

struggle is the 'Closed Door' episode in which Eustacia, Wildeve, Clym, and Mrs. Yeobright are involved. It is an implausible but expressionistically powerful scene which freezes all the actors in positions which expose their essential relations to one another. Clym is characteristically unaware of anything – in a more than natural sleep on the floor. Wildeve, innocently and yet not innocently, is talking to Eustacia, showing his regret at not having married her. As always, he plays the role of feckless catalyst of catastrophe : it is his presence which causes Eustacia, when she hears the knock at the door, to decide on the very measures which increase her apparent guilt. She looks out of the window, is seen by Mrs. Yeobright, but does not open the door. She assumes that Clym will open it. The destructive moment for us is pure vision; for Mrs. Yeobright it is fatefully ambiguous. To her Eustacia's action has the appearance of a deliberate and hateful denial, and Clym seems equally implicated in it. This shocking rejection, with unnecessary assistance from the heath, ends by killing Mrs. Yeobright before she can reach home.

After his mother's death, the struggle between Eustacia and Mrs. Yeobright continues within Clym, and the victory, such as it is, goes to Mrs. Yeobright, who achieves it from beyond the grave. Playing out his role as Oedipus, Clym determinedly pursues his search into the mystery of his mother's death until he succeeds in destroying his own happiness, and Eustacia's as well. But not by learning the truth, as Oedipus does; he only exchanges ignorance for misinterpretation, for the deceptive outside view of Johnny Nunsuch and Mrs. Yeobright. Deceived by the apparent meaning of Wildeve's presence and Eustacia's 'refusal' to open the door, he accuses Eustacia of infidelity and of causing his mother's death. Eustacia, who considers herself innocent (though guilty of having been afraid to tell Clym of the incident), is too proud to stoop to explanations, and after a violent quarrel with Clym she leaves the house. Her attempt at an escape with Wildeve, leading to the death of both, follows.

The last book, 'Aftercourses', is a descent from their stormy deaths to a spectacle of bitter suffering in which Clym takes the center of the stage, and the tragedy, or pathos, becomes his. After Eustacia's death the guilt with which he had responded to his mother's death is doubled: 'I spoke cruel words to her, and she left my house. I did not invite her back till it was too late. It is I who ought to have drowned myself. It would have been a charity to the living had the river overwhelmed me and borne her up. But I cannot die. Those who ought to have lived lie dead; and here am I alive!' (p. 449). To this Diggory Venn replies, 'You may as well say that the parents be the cause of a murder by the child, for without the parents the child would never have been begot'. Nevertheless, Clym's 'great regret' remains that 'for what I have done no man or law can punish me' (p. 449).

Hardy means us to see Clym's sense of guilt as excessive. Clym had sent the letter of reconciliation to Eustacia in time to prevent her flight, but it never reached her. As usual in Hardy's novels, at the crisis the physical context of human action asserts itself abstractly and symbolically as the mischances of time and space – misplacing and mistiming. The effect is that of a hair-breadth rescue which at the last minute turns a happy ending into a catastrophe. But this effect does not bear analysis. The complicated series of thwarting mischances which causes Eustacia to miss the letter is clearly unnecessary to explain her death, nor would such a rescue have been very efficacious, given Eustacia's and Clym's deep incompatibility and Eustacia's reckless and despairing self-destructiveness. What Hardy intends, clearly, is an ironic parody of Providence. The pattern of events preceding Eustacia's death (including Susan Nunsuch's magical operations upon Eustacia's effigy) reveals a sinister and demonic 'providence' which, instead of saving, destroys. But the effective causes of the tragedy are of course deeper – in Clym's and Eustacia's inability to conceive one another, in the uncontrolled play of irrational forces in Eustacia, in past choices which prove to be irrevocable, and in the bitter enmity between Eustacia and Mrs. Yeobright. Hardy's concatenation of last-minute unlucky events has the effect of doubly reinforcing a tragedy which is already necessary. This supererogation of tragic effects blurs the psychological and dramatic structure of the action in the interests of a 'philosophic' comment – an effort to indict the universe. The irony of the missed letter is excessively underlined, and as so often happens in Hardy's novels (and his poetry) the final effect of the irony is pathos. The episode tends to absolve both Eustacia and Clym of responsibility, and to make both appear to be the innocent victims of a malignant fate.

Irony and pathos dominate the last scenes of the novel. In the final scene, Clym becomes a lay preacher, or rather 'moral lecturer' who takes his texts from 'all kinds of books', delivers a discourse from the summit of Rainbarrow, on the following dutifully filial text (1 Kings, 2 : 19) :

'And the king rose up to meet her, and bowed himself unto her, and sat down on his throne, and caused a seat to be set for the king's mother; and she sat on his right hand. Then she said, I desire one small petition of thee; I pray thee say me not nay. And the king said unto her, Ask on, my mother : for I will not say thee nay' (pp. 484–5).

Towards Clym as 'lecturer on morally unimpeachable subjects' Hardy's attitude is ambiguous. Viewed sympathetically, Clym can be seen as cruelly misunderstood by an uncomprehending world. But from a more practical point of view, he is simply incapacitated for effective existence in the world.

Some believed him, and some believed not; some said that his words were commonplace, others complained of his want of theological doctrine; while others again remarked that it was well enough for a man to take to preaching who could not see to do anything else. But everywhere he was kindly received, for the story of his life had become generally known (p. 485).

At the end of the novel Clym remains emptied of his force, a diminished and pathetic victim.

Clym is much more typical of the tragic heroes of Hardy's later novels than Eustacia in her heroic aspects is. The two together, however, share the essential characteristics of Hardy's later protagonists. Eustacia has their self-destructiveness (disguised as rebellion against fate), and, finally, their pathos. Clym has both their pathos and their overgrown guilt and self-accusation. Michael Henchard, Tess Durbeyfield, Jude Fawley, and Sue Bridehead are all self-destructive, and self-accusation is an essential cause of their suffering. What accuses them, and Clym as well, is not so much conscience as the superego – which defines more exactly Hardy's belief that such tortures result in large part from taking internally and too seriously the external and rigid dictates of the moral codes of society. Partly, Hardy seems to want to exorcise the inflexibility and excess of the Victorian sense of guilt and duty. But his primary interest is in the victims of accusation. Towards them his feeling is excruciatingly sympathetic – so much so that they hover continually on the verge of being entirely pitiful figures. The dense and complex evocation of a culture which occupied the earlier Victorian novelists is missing from Hardy's novels. More accurately, when it exists, it does so peripherally, as a frame – as in the folk who act as chorus in *Return*. Hardy's attention is lyric and in-driving, towards the inmost emotional and suffering vulnerability of single figures isolated from one another and from the society which surrounds them. In his last novel, *Jude the Obscure*, society has become so internalized that the outer social world appears almost entirely as a reflected and distorted image; we see it only as it threatens or exiles his isolated heroes; and we see it less in its action than in their reaction. *Jude* is the logical development of a tendency towards the pathos of isolation and self-inflicted punishment clearly visible at least as early as *Return of the Native*.

The action of Hardy's tragedies is almost always the doomed struggle against isolation – the struggle towards a common world. Eustacia Vye is typical of all Hardy's tragic victims in finding it impossible to harmonize the outer world (both social and physical) with her inner world of feeling, and in dissipating her life in the struggle. The real struggle, or ironic discrepancy rather, is between hopes or dreams and the immovable and incalculable circumstances which frustrate them. The discovery is usually the characters' realization of the inevitability of frustration, and it is generalized as a recognition of their hopeless plight as sensitive and emotionally vulnerable beings in an unconscious and indifferent but seemingly malignant universe. Eustacia's last soliloquy has its parallel in almost all Hardy's tragic novels : 'O, the cruelty of putting me into this ill-conceived world! I was capable of much; but I have been injured and blighted and crushed by things beyond my control! O, how hard it is of Heaven to devise such

tortures for me, who have done no harm to Heaven at all!'
(p. 422).

The archetypal figures of Hardy's tragedies are Tantalus
(' "Life offers – to deny!" ')[2] and Job. His characters' response to
the crushing of their hopes, to the withdrawal of life's offering, is
most often Job's: ' "Let the day perish." ' Like Eustacia, they
think themselves the victim of a demonic torturer, as Job is Satan's
victim, and they are denied Job's final revelation. Hardy's tragedies end by revealing a gigantic flaw in the very conditions of life
– in the discrepancy between personality and environment, sensibility and circumstance. There is no remedy for this flaw. One can
only stoically adapt himself to it, as the animal who survives in the
struggle for existence must adapt himself to his environment. In
Hardy's tragedies impulse, energy, *élan* are almost always punished. Like Clym, those who survive learn (or try to learn) what
to make of a diminished thing. The effect is pathos emphasized
and underlined.

In spite of its elements of heroic tragedy *The Return of the
Native* expresses essentially the same disillusioned-ironic tragic
attitude that the later tragedies – *The Mayor of Casterbridge,
Tess of the d'Urbervilles*, and *Jude the Obscure* – do. Because
of their emphasis on pathos and irony, their reduction of the tragic
figure to a pitiable one, some critics would deny that these novels
(particularly *Tess* and *Jude*) are tragic at all. Perhaps Hardy's
attempt to elevate Eustacia to the heroic level betrays the same
doubt in his mind. Whether or not the novels are legitimate and
perhaps peripheral modes of tragedy I am not prepared to argue.
What is important to recognize, I think, is their disillusioned
skepticism as to the possibility of romance and heroism, their
concentrated drama and bold symbolism of the inner life, and their
protagonists' acute sense of isolation in an alien society and in a
universe abandoned or forgotten by a god who is after all only a
fiction. In these elements they set the pattern for one of the dominant traditions of the modern novel.

S o u r c e : *Nineteenth-Century Fiction*, vol. 15 (1960–1) pp.
207–19.

NOTES

1. *The Return of the Native*, p. 13. All quotations from *The Return of the Native* are from the Macmillan edition of *The Works of Thomas Hardy in Prose and Verse*, 23 vols (London, 1912–26) vol. IV.

2. 'Yell'ham-Wood's Story', *Collected Poems of Thomas Hardy* (New York, 1940) p. 280.

II *The Mayor of Casterbridge*

Robert C. Schweik

CHARACTER AND FATE IN
THE MAYOR OF CASTERBRIDGE (1966)

Perhaps the most compelling evidence of really fundamental
inconsistencies in *The Mayor of Casterbridge* is to be found, not in
those analyses intended to show that the novel is seriously flawed,[1]
but in the startlingly divergent interpretations proposed by critics
who have attempted to discover some underlying consistency in
Hardy's treatment of the relationship of Henchard's character to
his fate. Two recent discussions of *The Mayor of Casterbridge*
exemplify the almost polar extremes to which this divergence can
tend : as John Paterson has interpreted the novel, Henchard is a
man guilty of having violated a moral order in the world and thus
brings upon himself a retribution for his crime; but, on the other
hand, as *The Mayor of Casterbridge* has been explicated by Frederick Karl, Henchard is an essentially good man who is destroyed
by the chance forces of a morally indifferent world upon which
he has obsessively attempted to impose his will.[2] The fact is that
The Mayor of Casterbridge is capable of supporting a variety of
such conflicting assessments both of Henchard's character and of
the world he inhabits, and further discussion of the novel must
proceed, I think, by giving this fact more serious attention. Hardy
strenuously insisted that both as novelist and as poet he dealt with
'impressions' and made no attempt at complete consistency;[3]
what is worth considering is whether or not Hardy put his inconsistency to any use and what, if any, advantage he may have
gained by doing so.

The sacrifice of simple consistency in fiction can yield some important compensations, particularly in the freedom it allows a novelist to manipulate detail and aspect as a means of controlling and shifting reader attitude as the work progresses. It is possible to make a rhetorical use of elements whose implications will not add up to a logically consistent whole. Clearly such a rhetoric can serve the imaginative purpose of the novel if it is arranged to generate an initial image of life which is then altered by subsequent changes in the handling of character and event, and when the progress of the whole is such as to move the reader from one way of looking at things to another less immediately acceptable view of them. A novelist may meet his readers by providing a view of life which is socially orthodox, familiar, and comforting, then more or less deliberately shift his ground and, in effect, undertake to persuade his audience to adjust or abandon that view in order to accommodate some other less familiar or less comforting one. In such cases, it is not in the sum of its particulars but in the organization of their presentation that the novel will have its unity, and this, I believe, is true of the organization of *The Mayor of Casterbridge*.

The largest elements in *The Mayor of Casterbridge* are four relatively self-contained and structurally similar 'movements' of progressively diminishing lengths, roughly comprising chapters I–XXXI, XXXI–XL, XLI–XLIII, and XLIV–XLV. Each provides a variation on a common pattern: an initial situation which seems to offer some hope for Henchard is followed by events which create doubt, fear, and anxious anticipation for an outcome that comes, finally, as a catastrophe. Furthermore, in each of these succeeding movements there is a reduction in the scope of Henchard's expectations and a corresponding increase in the emphasis which Hardy puts both upon Henchard's anxiety for success and upon the acuteness of his subsequent feeling of failure. Much of our response to Hardy's account of Henchard's final withdrawal and lonely death depends, certainly, upon the cumulative impact of these successively foreshortened and intensified movements from hope to catastrophe; but the particular tragic response which *The Mayor of Casterbridge* seems calculated to evoke is also the product of other adjustments in detail and emphasis from movement to movement which have the effect of repeatedly shifting our perception of Henchard's character, of the kind of world he inhabits, and of the meaning of the catastrophes which he suffers.

The first and by far the longest of these movements (slightly more than half of the novel) falls into two almost equal parts. The opening fourteen chapters of *The Mayor of Casterbridge* establish a situation which seems to offer hope for Henchard's success. Following the brief prefatory account of Henchard's economic and moral nadir at Weydon Priors and his resolution to make a 'start in a new direction',[4] Hardy abruptly bridges an intervening eighteen years to reveal the outcome of Henchard's vow; and not only does Henchard reappear transformed into a figure of affluence and social standing, but events now seem to augur his further financial and social success : he gains the commercial support and personal companionship of Farfrae, effects a reconciliation with his lost wife and child, and seems about to find a solution to the awkward aftermath of his affair with Lucetta. Hardy implies, certainly, that Henchard has undergone no equivalent moral transformation; we learn that he is conscientiously abstemious, but is otherwise simply 'matured in shape, stiffened in line, exaggerated in traits; disciplined, thought-marked – in a word, older', and what details contribute to our first impression of the new Henchard – his aloofness, his harsh laugh, the hint of moral callousness in his stiff reply to complaints about his bad wheat – tend to support, as Hardy remarks, 'conjectures of a temperament which would have no pity for weakness, but would be ready to yield ungrudging admiration to greatness and strength. Its producer's personal goodness, if he had any, would be of a very fitful cast – an occasional almost oppressive generosity rather than a mild and constant kindness (v).' Yet, an examination of the following nine chapters will reveal that it is precisely Henchard's fitful personal goodness that Hardy does emphasize. Henchard's consistent if 'rough benignity', his gruff friendliness and frankness with Farfrae, his concern for Lucetta, his efforts to make amends to Susan and Elizabeth Jane, his determination to 'castigate himself with the thorns which these restitutory acts brought in their train', and his humanizing acknowledgments of his own loneliness and need for companionship – these are the most prominent signs of Henchard's character in chapters VI–XIV; they tend to minimize his earlier harshness, so that by chapter xiv, at the high-water mark of Henchard's apparent success. Hardy's bland comment that he was as kind to Susan as 'man, mayor, and church-warden could possibly be' squares so well with the repeated evidences of Henchard's gruff personal goodness in action that it carries little more than a muted suggestion of stiffness and social pride.

The remaining chapters of the first movement (xv–xxxi) then reverse the course of Henchard's fortunes, and as Hardy gradually increases the sharpness of Henchard's disappointments and anxieties, he also arranges the action so that Henchard's frustrated wrath is vented with increasing vehemence and with more obvious moral culpability on persons who appear to deserve it less and who suffer from it more intensely. In short, the 'temperament which would have no pity for weakness' gradually re-emerges, and by the conclusion of the first movement it is again the dominant feature of Henchard's character. The first sign of this progressive deterioration in Henchard – his grotesque attempt to punish Abel Whittle (xv) – is almost immediately countered by a revelation of Henchard's previous charities to Whittle's mother and by the frankness he displays in his reconciliation with Farfrae. But as the action continues Hardy develops situations which manifest more and more clearly the vehemence and injustice of Henchard's conduct. A first petty annoyance at his loss of popularity turns gradually into the more clearly misplaced and unjustly envious anger which prompts Henchard to dismiss Farfrae and to regard him as an 'enemy'. It is in this context that Hardy supplies an often quoted authorial comment which broadly implies a connection between Henchard's moral stature and his fortune : 'character is fate', Hardy reminds his readers, and he pointedly observes that Farfrae prospers like Jacob in Padan-Aram as he blamelessly pursues his 'praiseworthy course', while the gloomy and Faust-like Henchard has 'quitted the ways of vulgar men without light to guide him on a better way' (xvii).

The chapters which follow seem designed to illustrate this point, for as Henchard's harshness and pitilessness become more apparent, his fortunes decline. What begins in Henchard's impulsive desire for a 'tussle . . . at fair buying and selling' (xvii) develops into his more desperately planned and culpably savage effort to destroy Farfrae's career, 'grind him into the ground', and 'starve him out' (xxvi). Henchard's turning on Farfrae is followed by his more cruelly felt coldness to the unsuspecting Elizabeth Jane, who is the innocent victim of Henchard's anger over the ironic turn of events by which he has discovered the secret of her parentage. And, finally, in his last exasperated effort to best Farfrae, Henchard takes the still more obviously vicious course of wringing an unwilling promise of marriage from Lucetta by mercilessly threatening to reveal their former relations (xxvii). At this point in the action, Hardy reintroduces the furmity woman, whose public exposure of Henchard's past wrong to his wife not only helps to bring about Henchard's fall but also serves to reinforce momentarily the sinister aspect of his character which the previous chapters have made increasingly evident.

Thus, throughout the long first movement of *The Mayor of Casterbridge* Hardy uses both action and authorial comment to shift our impression of Henchard's moral stature in a curve which parallels his economic rise and fall. Nature and chance are repeatedly made to serve what seems to be a larger moral order in the world; Henchard himself comes to feel that some intelligent power is 'bent on punishing him' (xix) and is 'working against him' (xxvii); and the course of Henchard's career might stand as testimony for the familiar and comforting belief that the wise and good shall prosper and the wicked and rash shall fail. Certainly there is almost a fable-like congruity in the sequence by which Hardy gradually brings Henchard back to something like his moral nadir at Weydon Priors just before public disgrace and bankruptcy come like a retribution and precipitate him to social and economic ruin. Hence, in spite of its really complex and ambiguous cause and effect relationships,[5] the first movement of *The Mayor of Casterbridge* does seem to exemplify the dictum that 'character is fate'; it does so largely because Hardy maintains a general correspondence between the changes in Henchard's apparent moral stature and the changes in his fortunes.

Henchard's fall marks, however, the beginning of another tragic cycle in the novel – a second movement which again opens on a note of rising hope that is followed by a reversal and a falling action which terminates in catastrophe. Hardy clearly intends to leave no doubt about Henchard's fate after the furmity woman has revealed his past: 'On that day – almost at that minute – he passed the ridge of prosperity and honour, and began to descend rapidly on the other side' (xxxi). But having predicted the imminent collapse of Henchard's fortunes, Hardy once more shifts the aspect in which he presents Henchard's character and career; and out of his account of Henchard's failure he contrives to establish a situation which seems to offer renewed hope. Thus he makes the court incident an occasion for a comment which puts Henchard's career in a more favorable light :

The amends he had made in after life were lost sight of in the dramatic glare of the original act. Had the incident been well-known of old and always, it might by this time have grown to be lightly regarded as the rather tall wild oat, but well-nigh the single one, of a young man with whom the steady and mature (if somewhat headstrong) burgher of today had scarcely a point in common (xxxi).

Thereafter, Hardy stresses Henchard's generosity and integrity. We learn that it was the failure of a debtor whom Henchard had 'trusted generously' which brought about the final collapse of his fortunes, and the bankruptcy proceedings themselves serve to dramatize Henchard's scrupulous integrity as well as the finer instinct for justice which prompts him to sell his watch in order to repay a needy cottager. In short, Henchard now begins to appear in a character which seems worthy of the general approval of his creditors and the renewed sympathies of his townsmen, who, we are told, come to regret his fall when they have perceived how 'admirably' he had used his energy (xxxi). These signs of a hopeful change in Henchard's public reputation are followed in the next chapter by indications of a corresponding change in his private attitudes. Hardy suggests, first, the possibility of Henchard's reconciliation with Farfrae by a scene in which the kindness of Farfrae prompts Henchard to admit, 'I – sometimes think I've wronged 'ee !' and to depart, after shaking hands, 'as if unwilling to betray himself further'. This is followed by Henchard's reconciliation with Elizabeth Jane, who tends him through a brief illness; and the result, Hardy remarks, is a distinct alteration in Henchard's outlook :

The effect, either of her ministrations or of her mere presence, was a rapid recovery . . . and now things seemed to wear a new colour in his eyes. He no longer thought of emigration, and thought more of Elizabeth. The having nothing to do made him more dreary than any other circumstance; and one day, with better views of Farfrae than he had held for some time, and a sense that honest work was not a thing to be ashamed of, he stoically went down to Farfrae's yard and asked to be taken on as a journeyman hay-trusser. He was engaged at once (XXXII).

Through the space of two chapters, then, Hardy repeatedly presents Henchard in ways which not only emphasize his maturity, integrity, and good sense but also suggest the possibility that he may now successfully accommodate himself to his new situation.

But in the following chapters there is an abrupt reversal, a second descending action, and what at first appears to be a second corresponding degeneration of Henchard's character. In rapid succession we are told that Henchard has undergone a 'moral change' and has returned to his 'old view' of Farfrae as the 'triumphant rival who rode rough-shod over him' (XXXII); that Henchard's drinking has brought on a new 'era of recklessness' (XXXIII); and that 'his sinister qualities, formerly latent' have been 'quickened into life by his buffetings' (XXXIV). Certainly, the series of progressively heightened crises which follow depend upon and repeatedly dramatize Henchard's sinister potential for hatred and violence. But they do so with an important difference : previously Henchard's antagonisms have been checked by external forces; now Hardy emphasizes the internal compulsions toward decency and fairness which at critical moments in the action decisively frustrate Henchard's destructive intent. Thus the crisis which Henchard precipitates by reading Lucetta's letters to Farfrae comes to an unexpected conclusion : 'The truth was that, as may be divined, he had quite intended to effect a grand catastrophe at the end of this drama by reading out the name : he had come to the house with no other thought. But sitting here in cold blood he could not do it. Such a wrecking of hearts appalled even him' (XXXIV). Twice more Henchard brings matters to the brink of violence, and in each case the crisis is resolved when he is prompted by some inner compulsion to desist. In his deter-

mination to defy Farfrae and personally greet the Royal Visitor,
Henchard presses the issue to a point just short of violence, only
to be moved by an 'unaccountable impulse' to respect Farfrae's
command and give way (xxxvii). This incident precipitates Henchard's attack on Farfrae in the hayloft; and once again, at the
moment when Farfrae's life is in his hands, Henchard is so
touched by Farfrae's reproachful accusation that he feels compelled to relent. Instead, he flings himself down on some sacks 'in
the abandonment of remorse' and takes 'his full measure of shame
and self reproach' (xxxviii). What seems central to Hardy's
characterization of Henchard throughout these crises, then, is that
incapacity for callous destructiveness which repeatedly frustrates
his reckless antagonism. Then, as the action continues through the
events which culminate in the death of Lucetta, it is the frustration of Henchard's attempt to redeem himself which brings about
his personal catastrophe. For Henchard is 'possessed by an over-
powering wish . . . to attempt the well-nigh impossible task of
winning pardon for his late mad attack' (xxxviii): he vainly
attempts to save Lucetta's life, and finding himself unable to persuade Farfrae to return to his wife, he is brought, finally, to the
point of despair : 'The gig and its driver lessened against the sky in
Henchard's eyes; his exertions for Farfrae's good had been in vain.
Over this repentant sinner, at least, there was to be no joy in
heaven. He cursed himself like a less scrupulous Job, as a vehe-
ment man will do when he loses self-respect, the last prop under
mental poverty' (xl).

When we attend closely to what Hardy has been doing with
Henchard's character in chapters xxxiii–xl, it is apparent, then,
that although he exploits situations which depend for their
effects upon our awareness of Henchard's potential for reckless
cruelty, he in fact uses those situations to gradually strip Henchard of the features which earlier in the novel gave rise to 'conjectures of a temperament which would have no pity on weakness'.
But more is involved here than a change of the aspect in which
Henchard's character appears; there is really a marked change in
tragic mode as well – a shift from that fable-like correspondence
of fate and character which earlier in the novel seemed to dramatize a connection between Henchard's moral offense and a just

retribution which followed upon it. Now something less than an ideal justice seems to govern the grim irony of events, unknown to Henchard, through which his decent attempt to return Lucetta's letters is turned to her destruction by the viciousness of Jopp and his degenerate companions from Mixen Lane; and what Hardy repeatedly dramatizes is Henchard's frustrated incapacity to find either the will to destroy or the means to win pardon. It is, finally, the failure of his well-intentioned acts which brings about Henchard's second catastrophe – that loss of self-respect which verges on despair – and in his second fall he appears no longer as a Faust figure but rather, in Hardy's new image, as a 'less scrupulous Job' and a self-tormented 'repentant sinner' who curses himself for the failure of his own redemptive efforts.

The death of Lucetta marks another major turning point in the novel and the opening of a third cycle from hope to catastrophe for Henchard. Shorn of other interests, he now begins to feel his life centering on his stepdaughter and dreams of a 'future lit by her filial presence' (XLI). By one desperate and unthinking lie he turns away Newson and manages for a while to persevere in the hope that he can fulfill his dream. But just as the furmity woman returned to ruin Henchard by her exposure of his past, so Newson now returns to expose Henchard's lie and dash his hope. But the parallel serves mainly to emphasize a difference, for Henchard appears in a greatly altered character, and Hardy's account of his loss of Elizabeth Jane and his withdrawal from Casterbridge as a self-banished outcast is clearly intended to evoke quite another kind of tragic effect. Hardy now presents Henchard in a character so soberly chastened as to seem 'denaturalized' (LXII). He is reduced to suicidal despair at the thought of losing Elizabeth Jane and to anxiously caculating what he says and does in an effort to avoid her displeasure – so much so, Hardy remarks, that 'the sympathy of the girl seemed necessary to his very existence; and on her account pride itself wore the garments of humility' (XLII). Hence, while he looks forward with dread to living like a 'fangless lion' in the back rooms of his stepdaughter's house, Henchard comes to acknowledge that 'for the girl's sake he might put up with anything; even from Farfrae; even snubbings and masterful tongue scourgings. The privilege of being in the house she occupied would almost outweigh the personal humiliation' (xliii).

But it is not only Henchard's pathetic subjection to Elizabeth Jane which Hardy stresses; he now directs attention to Henchard's conscious moral struggles (as opposed to those 'unaccountable' impulses which previously checked his drunken recklessness), and he makes increasingly clear that Henchard now thinks and acts with heightened conscientiousness. Thus, when Henchard is again prompted by his perverse instinct to oppose Farfrae, Hardy pointedly reminds his readers that in the past 'such instinctive opposition would have taken shape in action' but that 'he was not now the Henchard of former days'. Instead, Hardy portrays Henchard's struggle against his instinct : Henchard vows not to interfere with Farfrae's courtship of Elizabeth Jane even though he is convinced that by their marriage he will be 'doomed to be bereft of her', and when the impulse returns, he rejects it as a temptation, wondering, 'Why should I still be subject to these visitations of the devil, when I try so hard to keep him away?' (xlii). At the same time, Henchard now suffers through moments of self-doubt and agonized casuistry in which, after the lie to Newson, his 'jealous soul speciously argued to excuse the separation of father and child' (xli). The problem, Hardy suggests, continues to trouble him :

.To satisfy his conscience somewhat, Henchard repeated to himself that the lie which had retained for him the coveted treasure had not been deliberately told to that end, but had come from him as the last defiant word of an irony which took no thought of consequences. Furthermore, he pleaded within himself that no Newson could love her as he loved her, nor would tend her to his life's extremity as he was prepared to do cheerfully (xlii).

And, finally, when Henchard leaves Casterbridge, Hardy makes clear that he goes as a self-condemned man, hoping that Elizabeth Jane will not forget him after she knows all his 'sins' yet assenting both to the fact of his guilt and the appropriateness of his fate : 'I – Cain – go alone as I deserve – an outcast and a vagabond. But my punishment is *not* greater than I can bear !' (lxii).

In view of the crushed submissiveness, remorse, earnest casuistry and conscious moral effort which have come to figure so prominently in Henchard's character, this self-accusation and self-imposed exile is certainly designed to impress us as excessively harsh. But by having Henchard accept an excessive burden of guilt and determine to bear it, Hardy does enable him to achieve a kind of expiation; and although excessiveness is certainly a constant in Henchard, in his third catastrophe we are brought to see in him a kind of excess which makes claims upon our sympathy in a way that his earlier excesses of moral callousness, antagonism, drunkenness, and frustrated violence have not. In short, Henchard now appears to suffer disproportionately, and he has taken on qualities of character which serve to justify on the moral level the pity and sympathy for him which Hardy evokes in other ways by emphasizing his declining health, his morbid sensitivity, his fears of 'friendless solitude', his character as an 'old hand at bearing anguish in silence', and his lack of friends who will speak in his defense.

The final two chapters of *The Mayor of Casterbridge* form a short coda which, on a still lower level, again involves a movement from hope to catastrophe – from that slightest of hopes which prompts Henchard to consider that he need not be separated from Elizabeth Jane to the rebuke which leads to his second departure from Casterbridge and his lonely death. Despite its brevity, this fourth movement has the important function both of further shifting our perception of Henchard's character and situation and of establishing more explicitly the final meaning of his tragedy. Hardy describes Henchard's journey from Casterbridge to Weydon Priors as a kind of pilgrimage carried out 'as an act of penance'. There Henchard mentally relives his past and retraces the foiled course of his career; and from both Henchard's reflections and Hardy's authorial comment upon his situation there emerges a central point – that Henchard's present situation is a consequence of 'Nature's jaunty readiness to support unorthodox social principles'. For as Henchard grimly reflects on the 'contrarious inconsistencies' of Nature which have nullified his recantation of ambition and foiled his attempts to replace ambition with love, Hardy comments on another of those contrarious inconsistencies – that Henchard, as a result of his suffering, has acquired 'new lights', has become capable of 'achieving higher things', and has found a 'wisdom' to do them precisely when an almost malicious machination in things has caused him to lose his zest for doing (XLIV). Henchard does make a final effort to return to Casterbridge and ask forgiveness of Elizabeth Jane, but now, in being condemned and rebuffed by her, it is he who is made to appear more sinned against than sinning. Even Farfrae, toward whom Hardy has been otherwise sympathetic or at least relatively neutral, is momentarily brought forward to contrast with Henchard's sincere repentance by being put in a hypocritical posture, 'giving strong expression to a song of his dear native country, that he loved so well as never to have revisited it' (XLIV), and, most significantly, Elizabeth Jane comes to regret her own harshness and attempts too late to make amends.

It is in the last chapters of the novel, then, that Hardy emphasizes most strongly the disjunction between Henchard's moral stature and the circumstance which has blindly nullified his repentance, his recantation of ambition, and his new capacity for a higher kind of achievement; and in doing so Hardy seems intent on reversing the fable-like correspondence between character and fate which figures so conspicuously in the first half of the novel. If throughout the opening portion of *The Mayor of Casterbridge* both nature and the course of events seem joined in support of the reassuring belief that the good shall prosper and the wicked fail, the remainder of the novel seems designed to reveal with progressively greater clarity that the fable is false. At its conclusion we are told that Elizabeth Jane has learned the 'secret . . . of making limited opportunities endurable' by 'the cunning enlargement . . . of those minute forms of satisfaction that offer themselves to everybody not in positive pain'. Henchard obviously has not learned that secret, and, by contrast, he remains characteristically excessive and tragically mistaken even in his last acts – in 'living on as one of his own worst accusers' and in executing a will which bears testimony to his final acceptance of a terribly disproportionate burden of guilt. But at the same time, by having Henchard persist in these acts, Hardy continues to dramatize his acceptance of a moral responsibility which now tends to set him quite apart from – and above – the indifferent circumstance which has frustrated his effort and contributed to his defeat. It is appropriate, then, that *The Mayor of Casterbridge* should end with the reflections of Elizabeth Jane, who has found the cunning to make the most of limited opportunities, as she gravely ponders the mysterious 'persistence of the unforeseen' in men's destinies and concludes that 'neither she nor any human being deserved less than was given' while 'there were others receiving less who had deserved much more'. Certainly that pointed distinction with which the novel closes – the distinction between what men deserve (which is a question of worth) and what men receive (which may be enlarged and made endurable by self-control, good sense, and cunning stratagems) is central to the final meaning which Hardy puts upon Henchard's tragedy; for although Hardy makes clear that Henchard fails ultimately because he lacks those qualities of character by which he might make the most of his opportunities, he clearly expects, at the same time, to have brought his readers to see that Henchard must finally be classed among those 'others receiving less who had deserved much more'.

There is, then, a marked contrast between that image of a morally ordered world projected by the long opening movement of *The Mayor of Casterbridge* and the more sombre, disenchanted vision of man's predicament with which the novel closes; and what is suggested about the relationship of Henchard's character to his fate by the first part of the novel is clearly inconsistent with the implications of its conclusion. Yet, considered rhetorically, such an arrangement probably worked to Hardy's advantage, for it enabled him to avoid abruptly confronting many of his readers with a view of life which would have sharply conflicted with their own assumptions and attitudes. Instead, Hardy first met his audience on the more readily acceptable ground of the moral fable; only after he had worked out Henchard's rise and fall on this level did he undertake to bring his readers to face the much more grim image of the human condition with which the novel closes, and even then the change was effected gradually, almost imperceptibly, by those various adjustments in detail and emphasis from movement to movement which I have attempted to trace in the preceding pages.

But, however rhetorically advantageous such an arrangement

might have been, it need not be assumed to have been the outcome of a deliberate and preconceived plan. I think it more likely, rather, that the progressive changes which I have noted in *The Mayor of Casterbridge* came about in the process of its composition and were the result of Hardy's effort to develop his subject and to work out its implications. There is nothing really surprising in the fact that Hardy began *The Mayor of Casterbridge* with an action which strongly implied a connection between Henchard's moral stature and his fate; for, although Hardy had intellectually rejected the traditional belief in an ethically ordered universe, that belief retained a strong and pervasive hold upon his mind at the level of imagination and feeling, and certainly it shaped some of his most deeply rooted and habitual attitudes towards life.[6] But these attitudes remained at variance with his intellectual commitments, and the gradual shift in aspect and emphasis which takes place throughout the second half of *The Mayor of Casterbridge* suggests that, as composition of the novel progressed, Hardy began to exhaust the line of development which stemmed from his more immediate imaginative grasp of his subject and that thereafter he tended to reflect more deliberately upon the implications of Henchard's fall and did so within the framework of his consciously considered views on man's place in a Darwinian world. Yet it is important to note that even then Hardy's treatment of Henchard's character implies his continued respect for an older, pre-scientific conception of man's dignity and worth as a moral agent, and the conclusion of the novel seems to be as much an affirmation of faith in the transcendent worth of the human person as it is an acknowledgment of man's precarious situation in a blind and uncertain universe.

SOURCE: *Nineteenth-Century Fiction*, vol. 21 (1966–7) pp. 249–62.

NOTES

1. See, for example, James R. Baker, 'Thematic Ambiguity in *The Mayor of Casterbridge*', *Twentieth Century Literature*, 1 (April 1955) 13–16; Robert B. Heilman, 'Hardy's "Mayor" and the Problem of Intention', *Criticism*, v (Summer 1963) 199–213.

2. John Paterson, 'The Mayor of Casterbridge as Tragedy', *Victorian Studies*, III (December 1959) 151–72; and Frederick R. Karl, 'The Mayor of Casterbridge: A New Fiction Defined', *Modern Fiction Studies*, VI (Autumn 1960) 195–213.

3. *The Works of Thomas Hardy*, Wessex Edition (London, 1912) I, xii and xviii.

4. *Works*, Wessex Edition, v, ch. ii. All further citations are to this edition and are indicated by chapter numbers inserted parenthetically in the text.

5. Both Hardy's authorial comments and his handling of the action suggest that Henchard's first downfall is the product of a variety of interconnected causes, some related to Henchard's character (as he is variously prompted by instinctive antagonism, superstitiousness, Southern doggedness, disappointment, unconscious cravings, rashness, rivalry in love) and some more clearly matters of chance (coincidental discoveries, inopportune revelations, the vagaries of the weather) : there seems, moreover, no way of establishing any clear causal priority among these.

6. I think that what Delmore Schwartz has had to say about the way belief is involved in Hardy's poetry applies, *mutatis mutandis*, to Hardy's prose fiction as well. See 'Poetry and Belief in Thomas Hardy', *The Southern Review*, VI (Summer 1940) 64–77.

J. C. Maxwell

THE 'SOCIOLOGICAL' APPROACH TO
THE MAYOR OF CASTERBRIDGE (1968)

Ian Gregor recently asked the question 'What kind of Fiction did Hardy write?'[1] Before offering his own answer, he outlines three ways of looking at Hardy which have, successively though with overlaps, been current: the philosophical (Immanent Will and the like), that which takes its cue from Hardy's own formula, 'novels of character and environment', and, most recently, that which treats Wessex 'as actual social history' and credits the power of the novels to 'their imaginative testimony to the gradual destruction of a stable agricultural community by the inroads of nineteenth-century industrialisation'.[2]

This sketch does not, of course, claim to be exhaustive. It ignores, for example, one of Hardy's most stimulating critics, A. J. Guerard, whose Hardy bears an odd resemblance to the Dickens of Edmund Wilson. But the third of his three Hardys is certainly a figure to be reckoned with by any present-day critic. I have chosen to examine fairly closely what the leading champion of this Hardy, Douglas Brown, has made of the novel which he has discussed in the greatest detail, *The Mayor of Casterbridge*.

The Mayor has always been a highly respected novel and has sometimes been described as Hardy's greatest, especially by those who are not over-enthusiastic Hardyans.[3] It is not, moreover, in any obvious way a 'difficult' novel: its qualities are plain and unmistakable in broad outline. There ought, then, to be no distracting subordinate problems in examining what Brown has to say of it, both in his separate monograph,[4] and in his earlier general book on Hardy.[5]

The two poles of Hardy's art, in Brown's view, are the 'sociological' and the 'fabular',[6] and of the latter he writes with great perceptiveness. The sociological emphasis, too, is readily under-standable, and it is a useful corrective for those, if any still exist, who think of Hardy as spending most of his time brooding over Schopenhauer and Hartmann.[7] But to insist that Wessex as it was when he wrote, and as it had been in his boyhood, was a real flesh-and-blood concern to Hardy is one thing. To place this concern in the framework Brown devises is another. And *The Mayor*, as we shall see, presents special difficulties of its own.

Brown formulates the main thesis in *Thomas Hardy*, pp. 30ff. 'The five great novels have a common pattern.' The protagonists, 'strong-natured countrymen, disciplined by the necessities of agricultural life', are brought into relation with 'men and women from outside the rural world, better educated, superior in status, yet inferior in human worth'. Eventually, 'what the situation means becomes more evident: it is a clash between agricultural and urban modes of life'. So far, this might be merely a fictive pattern, no doubt with some basis in reality, but appealing to Hardy principally for artistic reasons. But the next step in the argument is that 'this pattern records Hardy's dismay at the pre-dicament of the agricultural community in the south of England during the last part of the nineteenth century and at the precarious hold of the agricultural way of life', and that it has to be seen in the light, especially, of 'the agricultural tragedy of 1870–1902'.

This is clearly a far-reaching thesis as to what the novels are basically 'about'. And Brown is relatively cautious in his formu-lation. He offers nothing so crude as the statement by Arnold Kettle – 'The subject of *Tess of the d'Urbervilles* is stated clearly by Hardy to be the fate of a 'pure woman'; in fact it is the dest-ruction of the English peasantry'[8] – on which Ian Gregor aptly comments: 'it is interesting, and rather characteristic, that a novel like this must first of all be shown to be socially and historically significant before it can be considered "important".'[9] But Brown is prepared to go a good deal of the way with Kettle. Referring to the latter's essay, he speaks of *Tess* as Hardy's 'most tragic fable of agricultural defeat',[10] and refers to the 'agricultural tragedy' as 'the substance of his narrative art',[11] implying a contrast with something else that is, by comparison, superficial or secondary;

and in discussing *The Mayor* in particular, he shows a tendency to play down the individuality of the protagonist – 'he is agricultural man, defeated'[12] – and Guerard is rebuked for over-psychologizing him as the 'damned and self-destructive individualist'.[13]

I think there are very serious objections to be made to all this, and hope that an examination restricted to *The Mayor of Casterbridge* will at least show that it does not apply at all well to that novel.

Tess, however much we may dissent from what Kettle says about it, is at least not merely written during but set in the period of agricultural depression. In fact, criticism of it on the sociological side might take the line that it paints an insufficiently harsh picture of the life that Tess would in fact have lived at Flintcomb Ash.[14] But with *The Mayor*, Brown is faced with the special difficulty that the main action is played out during the eighteen-forties. This makes Brown understandably uneasy. Henchard, 'agricultural man', falls at a time when, no doubt, many individuals came to disaster in a similar way, but it is hard to see his fate as epitomizing that of English agriculture. Brown is not too happy about the years from the repeal of the Corn Laws to 1870, and is reduced to writing of them as 'two decades of apparent prosperity . . . (Farfrae's decades)'.[15] It is hard to see how prosperity is made merely 'apparent' by the fact that new conditions, especially the opening up of the wheat-growing areas of the New World, prevented it from being more than temporary. Yet without some such notion, Henchard cannot convincingly be given the representative role which Brown wants him to play. Difficulties multiply if we look not just at Henchard but at his relationship to his rival and supplanter, Farfrae.

It is easy to agree in general terms that something impressive and important about the relationship between different generations is being presented through these two characters. Julian Moynahan has, with some plausibility, seen Henchard and Farfrae in the roles of Saul and David,[16] and the main objection to this sort of interpretation is not that it is wrong but that it covers too much : that the 'conflict between generations' is 'so archetypal that it is omnitypal'.[17] But for Brown, Farfrae must stand for something more sociologically distinctive than just the younger generation. In *Thomas Hardy*, the formula is fairly simple : '[Henchard's] story . . . enacts forcefully the tension between the old rural world and the new urban one. Farfrae is the invader, the stranger within the gates.'[18] But there is some rethinking in *Thomas Hardy: The Mayor of Casterbridge* : 'I used to identify Farfrae as the Invader, but I can no longer read *The Mayor* in that way. Farfrae comes from outside, but he joins; he is *for* the agricultural community, not a disrupter; he holds a hope of renovation in his skills and intelligence; created perhaps out of Hardy's truthful acknowledgement of local inadequacies.'[19] Some such modification is obviously called for. Farfrae is certainly not in any literal sense an 'urban' figure, and it would be a rather crude and patronizing stereotype to regard him as alien to the countryside just because he can adapt himself to changing conditions. But Brown modifies his picture of Farfrae without making corresponding adjustments to that of Henchard and what he stands for. If no longer so much an alien, still less an urban invader, Farfrae remains an intruder, and this is all right so long as we do not insist on seeing Henchard in a sharply antithetic role as a fully assimilated and representative member of the community. It is surely important that, as Howard O. Brogan says, 'all of the main characters, male and female, are intruders into a community in which they do not really belong'.[20] Brown is conscious of this when he is emphasizing the 'fabular' side of the book, and writes of the 'fairy-tale transformation' of Henchard 'from skilled labourer migrant in the country to corn factor and mayor in the country town', but hastens to add, less convincingly, that 'he is still the essentially *representative* protagonist'.[21]

What is it to be 'representative' in this sense? Literally, Henchard is a highly individual and very exceptional member of his community, whose fate is all the more impressive because it too is exceptional : the sort of thing that can happen, but very seldom does happen in such a spectacular form. For this purpose, it is important that in one way he should not be 'representative'. Hence, Hardy is right to set the action in a period of relative long-term agricultural stability and prosperity, though the plot requires what Hardy calls in his Preface 'the uncertain harvests

which immediately preceded the repeal of the Corn Laws'. Yet
Brown would have him also 'representative' of a fate that is
later – a good deal later – going to overtake the agricultural
community as a whole. This is surely a very unsatisfactory kind
of juggling both with time and with the relation between
naturalism and something that can hardly be seen as falling
short of allegory. Hardy's art just does not have the feel of being
like this. It is odd that a critic who wants, rightly, to have him
very firmly rooted in the real world of the nineteenth century
should in effect remove him from it. This comes out particularly
in a parenthesis in which Brown writes of *The Mayor* as 'a novel
much concerned with the drama of the Corn Law conflicts'[22]
In any straightforward sense of being 'concerned with', this is
plainly untrue. Brown has to take a panoramic view of the whole
period from the forties to the eighties in order to make out that
Hardy is somehow giving a poetic rendering of the process of
agricultural change. On the very next page, indeed, we read that
'each of the great Wessex novels treats *in imaginative form* of the
defeat of our peasantry and the collapse of our agriculture'[23]
(my italics). Brown seems unable to make up his mind whether to
interpret this in an extreme form, with Kettle – as an assertion
that the novels are not 'really' about the characters they claim to
be about; or as a more modest assertion that Hardy's imagination
works on the social setting as well as on the individual characters,
and that the latter must be seen in the light of what Hardy implies, but does not spell out, about the former. Certainly a reader
who can enter sympathetically and knowledgeably into Hardy's
attitude towards the rural society of his own day, and that of the
earlier period in which some of the novels are set, is likely to be
a better reader than one who approaches them with no historical
knowledge. In fact Brown seems to come to rest half way between
these positions. He is unwilling to sacrifice the individuality of
Hardy's characters, but he moves some way towards the more
radical interpretation because of his belief that 'human relations
and human persons are represented less for their own sakes than
for the clearer focusing of the invasion and the havoc'.[24]

It might still be true that, even if Henchard is scarcely 'agricultural man' in Brown's sense, there is a broad distinction bet-

ween his way of life and that of Farfrae that reflects the distinction
between the old rural world and the world of Hardy's own day.
Brown, we have seen, is prepared to withdraw somewhat from
his earlier contention that this is 'the tension between the old
rural world and the new urban one'.[25] But he still lays stress on
one element of modernity: Farfrae can cope with a market
economy and Henchard cannot.[26] But Hardy's own Preface,
which Brown ignores, suggests a very different attitude towards
market fluctuations as an element in the story. The main reason
for setting the action in the mid-forties is that the harvest was then
much more of a gamble, and a temptation to speculation, than
it later became: 'the home Corn Trade, on which so much of
the action turns, had an importance that can hardly be realized
by those unaccustomed to the sixpenny loaf of the present date
[1895], and to the present indifference of the public to harvest
weather'. The curiously perverse way in which Brown regards
Henchard and Farfrae, and what they respectively stand for, can
be studied in some detail in terms of his treatment of a particular episode.

He quotes[27] Farfrae's account to Lucetta of his dealings (chapter xxiii), which is later said to describe 'the new market ethics
Farfrae boyishly vaunted to Lucetta'.[28] The quotation itself is
preceded by the description of the innocuous sentence 'A man
must live where his money is made' (which in its context is simply
an explanation of why Farfrae left his home) as his 'candid dec-
laration' which 'is a submission to "the market's" terms: accumulation of stock and finance-strategy not to fulfil a necessary
role in trade; not to connect Casterbridge with the agriculture
of its countryside; but for its own sake, or for further reserves of
financial power' – a formidable set of implications to be unrolled
from a casual sentence. But it is on the following more extended
quotation that Brown relies:

'Yet I've done very well this year. O yes. . . . You see that man with
the drab kerseymere coat? I bought largely of him in the autumn
when wheat was down, and then afterwards when it rose a little I sold
off all I had! It brought only a small profit to me; while the farmers
kept theirs, expecting higher figures – yes, though the rats were
gnawing the ricks hollow. Just when I sold the markets went lower,

and I bought up the corn of those who had been holding back at less price than my first purchases. And then,' cried Farfrae impetuously, his face alight, 'I sold it a few weeks after, when it happened to go up again ! And so, by contenting mysel' with small profits frequently repeated, I soon made five hundred pounds – yes !' – (bringing down his hand upon the table, and quite forgetting where he was) – 'while the others by keeping theirs in hand made nothing at all !'

Brown's immediately following comment is : 'The technique extends the traditional wariness of farming communities and reaches out towards the idea of finance corporations'.

Now if Farfrae's methods were to be taken as representative of a new system, with concomitant dangers to an established way of life, one would expect them to be set over against a contrasting practice that fairly represented the healthy functioning of a traditional system and values. What is extraordinary is that Brown does not seem to have noticed how the old-style farmers are in fact described as having behaved. There is no need to idealize Farfrae – Brown's later 'canny moderation, striking just the right equipoise between competing possibilities',[29] is fair enough. But if Farfrae is telling the truth – and we have no reason to doubt it – he has been behaving much better (even if for prudential rather than loftily moral reasons) by the traditional agrarian standards than the farmers : contenting himself with moderate gains, where they have, with short-sighted cunning and avarice, been trying to play the market; they are the lineal descendants of Shakespeare's farmer who hanged himself on the expectation of plenty.

The farmers of chapter xxiii are, of course, less important for their own sakes than as a foreshadowing of Henchard's more disastrous gamble a few chapter later, and it is in connection with this that Hardy elaborates on the point later to be made in the Preface, the dependence of this crucial part of his plot on the old order of things :

The time was in the years immediately before foreign competition had revolutionized the trade in grain, when still, as from the earliest ages, the wheat quotations from month to month depended entirely upon the home harvest. A bad harvest, or the prospect of one, would double the price of corn in a few weeks; and the promise of a good yield would lower it as rapidly. Prices were like the roads of the period, steep in gradient, reflecting in their phases the local conditions, without engineering, levellings, or averages (chapter XXVI).

Nothing could be clearer. Far from choosing a period for his novel in which new market standards are invading a hitherto innocent agrarian economy, Hardy has chosen the *latest* period at which the uncushioned dominance of price fluctuations depending on the home harvest, which had existed 'from the earliest ages', still persisted. Brown's treatment of this passage is extraordinary: 'Hardy chooses to indicate the forces operating on the wheat markets at the time of his tale, as though to throw the whole weight of agricultural change behind Henchard's decline',[30] and Henchard is credited with 'efforts to mimic the new capitalist techniques'.[31]

It would be impossible for an intelligent critic to misrepresent his subject so badly if there were not some correspondence to reality in what he says. A broad contrast between old and new is certainly present in Henchard and Farfrae. One feels that something true and illuminating is being said about Farfrae when Brown remarks that 'negotiation through trade union is not far off, one feels, and Farfrae will do well at it'.[32] But this is more because Farfrae strikes us as adaptable to any changing situation than because he belongs specifically to the new world of Hardy's own day. It is, in fact, one of the skilful things about Hardy's portraiture of him that he is allowed to remain a very limited character, responding to the immediate challenge of the situation rather than creating a new situation – a good mayor of Casterbridge in a better than average year. In terms of Shakespearian parallels, if there is something of Lear in Henchard – 'the oldest hath borne most' – there is also something of the pattern of *Richard II*, and as in that play, a too mechanical pattern of rise and fall is avoided by not giving Farfrae, the Bolingbroke of the novel, the same degree of prominence that belongs to the protagonist. Henchard – it is a commonplace of criticism – remains the unchallengeably dominating figure even in defeat and disaster.

Philip Larkin has expressed dissatisfaction about what has been written on Hardy with the appeal, 'Wanted: Good Hardy Critic'.[33] I am not myself so pessimistic. I think we have had a number of good ones: Brown himself, whom Larkin does not mention, is, at his best, one of them: Guerard is another. I do not find it necessary to supplement this essay, limited and negative though it has been, with a reassessment of *The Mayor of Casterbridge*, because I think it has, on the whole, been justly appreciated, even if some of the commonplaces have worn rather threadbare. Larkin is right, however – it is Arnold Kettle on *Tess* that is immediately in question – in saying that 'the reader feels uncomfortable rather than illuminated' by the sort of criticism that exhorts us to 'trust the tale and not the teller'.[34] True, one must with Hardy as with any other novelist be prepared to follow the tale if it is clearly determined to escape the monitory eye of the teller. But with a plain, intelligent, and articulate writer like Hardy, it is at our peril that we ignore lucid and explicit comments such as he makes in this book – I am thinking particularly of the passages discussed from the Preface and chapter XXVI. At least they are likely to be a safer guide than the critic's judgement of what the historical situation might or ought to have prompted the novelist to offer his readers.

SOURCE : Ian Gregor and Maynard Mack (eds), *Imagined Worlds* (1968), pp. 225–33.

NOTES

1. *Essays in Criticism*, XVI (1966) 290–308.
2. Ibid. p. 291.
3. For example, Frank Chapman, *Scrutiny*, III (1934–5) 30.
4. *Thomas Hardy: The Mayor of Casterbridge* (London, 1962) : hereafter *T.H.M.*
5. *Thomas Hardy* (1954, 1961) : hereafter *T.H.* I have used the 1961 edition. I am sorry that Brown's untimely death prevents this essay from being a contribution to a continuing dialogue.
6. *T.H.M.*, p. 14.
7. This name is misprinted Hauptmann in *T.H.*, p. 22.
8. *An Introduction to the English Novel*, II (1953; Greyfriars ed., 1962) 50.
9. Ian Gregor and Brian Nicholas, *The Moral and the Story* (London, 1962) p. 136.
10. *T.H.M.*, p. 43.

11. *T.H.*, p. 42.

12. *T.H.M.*, p. 62.

13. Ibid. p. 38, citing A. J. Guerard, *Thomas Hardy: The Novels & Stories* (London, 1949) p. 148.

14. See William J. Hyde, *Victorian Studies*, II (1958–9) 51.

15. *T.H.M.*, p. 42; similarly *T.H.*, p. 32.

16. *P.M.L.A.*, LXXI (1956) 118–30.

17. George Wing, *Hardy* (Edinburgh and London, 1963) p. 64.

18. Douglas Brown, *Thomas Hardy* (London, 1954) p. 65.

19. Douglas Brown, *Thomas Hardy: The Mayor of Casterbridge* (London, 1962) p. 31.

20. *E.L.H.*, XVII (1950) 316.

21. *T.H.M.*, p. 15.

22. *T.H.*, p. 35.

23. Ibid. p. 36.

24. Ibid. p. 30.

25. Ibid. p. 65.

26. *T.H.M.*, p. 43.

27. Ibid. pp. 33–4.

28. Ibid. p. 49.

29. *T.H.M.*, p. 50.

30. *T.H.M.*, pp. 49–50.

31. Ibid. p. 50.

32. Ibid. p. 53.

33. *Critical Quarterly*, VIII (1966) 174–9.

34. *Critical Quarterly*, VIII (1966) 174. I might also mention, as relevant to some of the points made in this essay, the article by Raymond Williams in *Critical Quarterly*, VI (1964). [The substance of this article is reprinted in *The English Novel, from Dickens to Lawrence*, an extract from which is included in Part Two.] Though it is only indirectly relevant to the subject of this essay, any reader of *The Mayor* is likely to be interested in an article in the *Economic History Review*, 2 Ser., XX (1967) 280–92, by E. H. Hunt, 'Labour Productivity in English Agriculture, 1850–1914'. This contrasts the high-wage and high-productivity areas (which would include Farfrae's home) and the low-wage and low-productivity areas, in which the low wages, and consequent malnutrition, helped to perpetuate low productivity. Hardy knew what he was doing when he made Christopher Coney say to Farfrae : 'we be bruckle folk here . . . so many mouths to fill, and God-a'mighty sending his little taties so terrible small to fill 'em with' (ch. VIII).

III *Tess of the d'Urbervilles*

Douglas Brown

A NOVEL OF CHARACTER AND ENVIRONMENT (1954)

. . . It is true to say that *Tess* is a flawed performance, but it is little to the purpose. The novel survives its faults magnificently. The simplicity and force of its conception give to it a legendary quality. Here is not merely the tragedy of a heroic girl, but the tragedy of a proud community baffled and defeated by processes beyond its understanding or control. The resonance of the tale makes itself felt over and over again. The superb opening, the death of Prince the horse, the lovely elegiac scene of the harvesting, the sequence in the dairy farm, the scene of the sleepwalking, the episodes of agricultural life at Flintcomb Ash, even the climax at Stonehenge, are powerful and original imaginative inventions. The rather tawdry theatricality of that climax, the deceptive offer of tragic symbolism, reveal themselves only on reflection. We scarcely try to understand – we feel that Hardy himself did not altogether measure this defeat, this calamity. But the insistent tenderness exacts concurrence, by a force like make-believe. The falsities, the intrusive commentaries, the sophisticated mannerisms in the prose, do only local damage.

Hardy composed nothing finer than the opening of *Tess*, and the style of it is entirely his own. The whole invention is at once substantial with social and historical perceptions, and quick with metaphorical life. The May Dance communicates a country mirth sustained by customary traditions and recognition of the seasonal rhythm. The three ominous visitors, one of them later to become an agent of destruction, suggest how the dance of vitality is jeopardized by the thrust of sophisticated urban life. Then the appearance of the spurious country squire adds to the sense of jeopardy. The masquerader, the economic intruder, the representative of processes at work destroying the bases of agricultural security, stands with the spiritual intruder. Alongside this image, there unfolds that of the old father's discovery of his ancient but unavailing ancestry: a disclosure of the community's past which helps to define what Tess represents in the ensuing tale, at the same time as it sharpens the intrusive and invading quality in Alec d'Urberville. We feel the lost independence and the helplessness of agricultural man in his decrepit figure, as also in old South, Durbeyfield's equivalent in the previous novel. The art ordering the whole is marvellously secure of its purpose. The metaphorical terms reside so naturally within the ballad narrative. The preparation for such later scenes as Tess harvesting at Marlott, Tess in the early dawn at Talbothays, is perfect. For Tess is not only the pure woman, the ballad heroine, the country girl: she is the agricultural community in its moment of ruin. For two years preceding the writing of *Tess*, Mrs. F. E. Hardy has recorded, 'Hardy explored in greater detail than ever before the scenes of the story, and was powerfully impressed by the massing evidence of the decay in agricultural life.' Here is the impulse behind the legend. It dramatizes the defeat of Tess, the country girl and representative of an ancient country line, and her ruin by the economic and spiritual invaders of country life. (d'Urberville's farm is as bogus as his villa is ostentatiously civic and unrelated to the countryside.) It takes its origin in a past lively with traditional activity; it ends in Stonehenge, in passivity, the primitive place confirming a sense of doom which has gathered intensity all along. What has happened in the agricultural society is by now irrevocable. It is 1890, in south-west England.

The powerful, if faulty, sleepwalking scene records the passivity and the doom most poignantly. It balances precariously between sentimentality and tragedy, yet its impact transcends its place in the story. Hardy has constructed a perfect imaginative equivalent for the deepest perceptions which inform the novel as a whole. Old John South's paralysis and death had something of this fascinating quality, but here the enacted image proves more distress-

ing. For the most part the narrative issues as if from the consciousness of Tess herself, impotent in the hold and motion of an
alien force. She is awake and strong-willed, yet passive, stunned.
Her passivity (she makes no effort to alter the course of events)
appears to be one facet of her resilience. She is the agricultural
predicament in metaphor, engaging Hardy's deepest impulses of
sympathy and allegiance. Clare is helpless too: a blind, un-
knowing force, carrying the country girl to burial. Hardy's sense
of curt, impersonal powers (such as preside in the world of balladry) who order human destiny, here becomes a strength to his
fiction. Clare, so the narrative implies, is the impassive instrument
of some will, some purpose, stemming from the disastrous life
of the cities, from the intellectual and spiritual awareness – and
confusion – of the world outside the agricultural community, and
rather doomed to destroy, than intending to destroy, the dignity
and vitality of country life. The invention, here, goes beyond
nostalgia. But the image is painful; all the suffering with which
Hardy felt the defeat of agricultural life by nullifying urban forces,
has gone into it, and the private despair that was the novelist's
own inheritance from his sojourn 'outside'.

The movement of this novel, in which the tale develops against
a shifting background instead of growing from one tract of
countryside, also came of those desolate journeyings over the
Wessex countryside. The pattern is deliberate. The unspoiled childhood and the May festivities belong to the village of Marlott.
Tess's first restoration has for setting the dairy farms of the 'lush
Froom Valley'. Her second restoration, when she builds a stoicism
out of despair, occurs among 'the sterile expanses of Flintcomb
Ash farmlands'. The catastrophe is in Sandbourne with its 'fashionable promenades'.

When Tess first returns to agricultural activity after her seduction, in the harvesting at Marlott, the scenes are sufficiently impressive; the passage of her withdrawal from the field to feed her
child is inspired. Yet it is spoiled by a commentary almost vulgar,
as are the scenes describing the baptism and death of the
child. Book Three, *The Rally*, however, sustains its power more
steadily, a revelation of Hardy's sensuous understanding, that
quality of feeling and instinct with which Lawrence thought

Hardy to have been more generously endowed than any other English novelist. Talbothays is no paradisaical dairy farm. Language eager with details of activity, and native to its stated objects, language frank and vivid in sensuous perception, balances Tess's despair. Against the background of farm and dairyhouse, labour in the compact community, and the presence and voices of the workfolk, emerges the story of the fine young lord and the milkmaid and the three forlorn girls whose love is unrequited. To sketch it out like that is to suggest the proper way to take the 'story' element in Hardy's art.

The second movement whose power and beauty are sustained at length, balances the account of life at Crick's dairy farm. It records the life of Flintcomb Ash. The starting point is a matter of agricultural economics.

Of the three classes of village, the village cared for by its lord, the village cared for by itself, and the village uncared for either by its lord or itself (in other words, the village of a resident squire's tenantry, the village of free or copy-holders, and the absentee-owner's village, farmed with the land) this place, Flintcomb Ash, was the third.

Flintcomb Ash directly reflects the new farming, contrasting in every essential with Talbothays. It is as essential to the meaning of the novel as the historical analysis of the opening, or the violent uprooting of the family driven out of the agricultural community at the end. And it affords an apt environment for this bitter part of the narrative. Tess's second recovery is painfully gradual, described in grave and laboured prose. The end of the movement is very moving; it brings us close to Hardy's distinction as a tragic writer. His incipient nostalgia is controlled by a scrutiny of the natural environment and the daily toil of the agricultural 'home', a scrutiny almost fierce in its anxiety. There is deep distress in this contemplation of Tess and the girls and the little labouring society of which they are a part. There is the nagging rigour of this life, and there is the will to endure and to persist and to labour on regardlessly, and the prose vividly reflects both.

An epilogue to this movement of the second recovery balances the harvest scene at Marlott which was prologue to the first.

Harvest tide has returned. But now the human threshers stand side by side with the invading threshing machine. The narrative quality suggests the sleepwalking scene again. The sleepwalker, impersonal agent of destruction, is now the machine. The sleep-walking scene gave a first impression of some mechanical force not to be baulked, once released. Now the impression grows clearer. The helpless Tess of the earlier scene is here the trapped, exhausted Tess whose task is to feed the machine. Her predica-ment gets a richer imagery from the group of labourers of 'an older day' who cannot resist, or accept, the new power, and who are bewildered and defeated. But in this second passage a bitter resentment makes the episode more disquieting. Consider the engineer, for instance.

What he looked, he felt. He was in the agricultural world, but not of it. He served fire and smoke; these denizens of the fields served vegetation, weather, frost, and sun. He travelled with his engine from farm to farm, from county to county, for as yet the steam threshing-machine was itinerant in this part of Wessex. He spoke in a strange northern accent; his thought being turned inwards upon himself, his eye on his iron charge, hardly perceiving the scenes around him, and caring for them not at all. . . . The long strap which ran from the driving-wheel of his engine to the red thresher under the rick was the sole tie-line between agriculture and him.

The description which follows is quieter in its manner, but the use of detail of colour and gesture is more pointed. Hardy sounds a wistful note that suggests a personal disquiet. 'The old men on the rising straw-rick talked of the past days when they had been accustomed to thresh with flails on the oaken barn-floor; when everything, even to winnowing, was effected by hand labour. . . .' Then he emphasizes the less human quality of the life that has replaced that older life, an older life embodied earlier at Talbothays. Tess is again powerless and passive, caught by the machine's noise and motion, unable to speak, un-able to rest.

Into this situation, reinforcing an aspect of its meaning, comes the invader, the son of the merchant from the North, 'dressed in a tweed suit of fashionable pattern, and twirling a gay walking

cane'. Tess in Clare's arms as he sleepwalks, Tess in the clutch of
the threshing machine, Tess before Alec d'Urberville – her predicament is the same. Detail by detail Hardy restores the environment to mind. 'Then the threshing-machine started afresh; and
amid the renewed rustle of the straw Tess resumed her position
by the buzzing drum as one in a dream, untying sheaf after sheaf
in endless succession.'

The marvellous passages that follow have a sensuous force and
a depth of feeling Hardy rarely equalled.

From the west a wrathful shine . . . had burst forth after the cloudy
day, flooding the tired and sticky faces of the threshers, and dyeing
them with a coppery light. . . . A panting ache ran through the rick.
The man who fed was weary, and Tess could see that the red nape
of his neck was encrusted with dirt and husks.

Wrathful takes its force from the mood of the contemplation.
The *tired and sticky faces* seen as the shine breaks out suggest the
weakening before the machine, and the *dyeing* of those faces rein-
forces that: they slip out of human expressions. *Coppery* both
defines the observed tint, and reflects from the machine, holding
the machine there beside their faces.

She still stood at her post, her flushed and perspiring face coated
with the corn-dust, and her white bonnet embrowned by it. She was
the only woman whose place was upon the machine so as to be shaken
bodily by its spinning, and the decrease of the stack now separated
her from Marian and Izz. . . . The incessant quivering, in which
every fibre of her frame participated, had thrown her into a stupefied
reverie, in which her arms worked on independently of her consciousness. She hardly knew where she was, and did not hear Izz Huett tell
her from below that her hair was tumbling down.

By degrees the freshest among them began to grow cadaverous and
saucer-eyed. Whenever Tess lifted her head she beheld always the
great upgrown straw-stack, with the men in shirt-sleeves upon it,
against the gray north sky. . . .

. . . And as the evening light in the direction of the Giant's Hill
by Abbot's-Cernel dissolved away, the white-faced moon of the
season arose from the horizon that lay towards Middleton Abbey and
Shottsford. . . . But Tess still kept going. . . .

. . . She shook her head and toiled on.

The dramatic force with which Hardy's painful insights here find
sensuous expression, is of no ordinary kind. The manner is one of
simple and truthful tenderness; there is a fine adjustment between what the creating mind intends, and what the senses perceive. The truth carries over into the conversation afterwards,
and to this: 'The cold moon looked aslant upon Tess's fagged
face between the twigs of the garden-hedge as she paused. . . .'

Hardy sets the culminating family tragedy against the ominous
background of the Lady Day migration of so many village folk.
The erasure of long local life by these contemporary migrations,
Hardy perceived, was a grave social and spiritual loss. It is no
accident of art that the story of Tess should end amid scenes of uprooting. The narrative of the Durbeyfields' own moving from
home is full of disquiet. The migration of so many others, the
dissolving social order, is not particularly dwelt upon; but the
ironical reception of the forlorn family at Kingsbere, its ancient
home, dramatizes a personal bitterness of spirit. Only a place in
the family vault, a home there, remains to the derelict inheritors.
It is this homeless despair of a family which has lost its rights and
independence in the village community, that gives Tess finally
into the invader's power.

The sensation of moving unresistingly through a dream recurs
in the passages that describe Tess impelled towards her doom and
trapped for the last time. The hints of madness are indecisive
enough to leave a nightmare quality around her experiences.
The situation is blurred for her; the forces that have defeated
her are beyond her comprehension. . . .

S o u r c e : Douglas Brown, *Thomas Hardy* (1954) pp. 90–8.

David Lodge

TESS, NATURE, AND THE VOICES OF HARDY (1966)

Thomas Hardy might be described as an 'in-spite-of' novelist. That is, he figures in literary criticism and literary history as a great novelist 'in spite of' gross defects, the most commonly alleged of which are his manipulation of events in defiance of probability to produce a tragic–ironic pattern, his intrusiveness as authorial commentator, his reliance on stock characters, and his capacity for writing badly. In my view, the last of these alleged faults involves all the others, which, considered in the abstract as narrative strategies, are not necessarily faults. If we have reservations about them in Hardy's work, it must be because of the way they are articulated – or inadequately articulated.

Does Hardy write badly? One method of trying to answer such a question is that of Practical Criticism: the critical analysis of a passage extracted from its context. I therefore begin by citing an example of Practical Criticism *avant la lettre* performed by Vernon Lee upon five hundred words taken at random from *Tess of the d'Urbervilles*.[1] The unsatisfactoriness of her conclusions, I suggest, can only be made good by returning the passage to its context – the whole novel, and by trying to define the linguistic character of the novel in terms of its literary purpose. Using the perspective thus established, I turn to the consideration of another passage from the novel, one which has attracted a good deal of conflicting commentary. My intention is primarily to try and define as clearly as possible the sense in which the author of *Tess* may be said to 'write badly'; and to show that the consideration of this question, even when based on the close examination of short extracts, must inevitably involve us in the consideration of the meaning and artistic success of the novel as a whole.

The passage discussed by Vernon Lee is from Chapter XVI, the first chapter of the third 'Phase' of the novel, entitled 'The Rally'. It follows immediately after Tess, on her journey from her home at Marlott in the Vale of Blackmoor to the dairy of Talbothays, where she hopes to make a new start after her seduction by Alec d'Urberville, breaks into the 148th Psalm; and it describes her descent into the valley of the Var :

However, Tess found at least approximate expression for her feelings in the old *Benedicite* that she had lisped from infancy; and it was enough. Such high contentment with such a slight initial performance as that of having started towards a means of independent living was a part of the Durbeyfield temperament. Tess really wished to walk uprightly, while her father did nothing of the kind; but she resembled him in being content with immediate and small achievements, and in having no mind for laborious effort towards such petty social advancement as could alone be effected by a family so heavily handicapped as the once powerful d'Urbervilles were now.

There was, it might be said, the energy of her mother's unexpended family, as well as the natural energy of Tess's years, rekindled after the experience which had so overwhelmed her for the time. Let the truth be told – women do as a rule live through such humiliations, and regain their spirits, and again look about them with an interested eye. While there's life there's hope is a conviction not so entirely unknown to the 'betrayed' as some amiable theorists would have us believe.

Tess Durbeyfield, then, in good heart, and full of zest for life, descended the Egdon slopes lower and lower towards the dairy of her pilgrimage.

The marked difference, in the final particular, between the rival vales now showed itself. The secret of Blackmoor was best discovered from the heights around; to read aright the valley before her it was necessary to descend into its midst. When Tess had accomplished this feat she found herself to be standing on a carpeted level, which stretched to the east and west as far as the eye could reach.

The river had stolen from the higher tracts and brought in particles to the vale all this horizontal land; and now, exhausted, aged, and attenuated, lay serpentining along through the midst of its former spoils.

Not quite sure of her direction Tess stood still upon the hemmed expanse of verdant flatness, like a fly on a billiard table of indefinite length, and of no more consequence to the surroundings than that fly. The sole effect of her presence upon the placid valley so far had been to excite the mind of a solitary heron, which, after descending to the ground not far from her path, stood with neck erect, looking at her.

Suddenly there arose from all parts of the lowland a prolonged and repeated call –

'Waow! waow! waow!'

From the furthest east to the furthest west the cries spread by contagion, accompanied in some cases by the barking of a dog. It was not the expression of the valley's consciousness that beautiful Tess had arrived, but the ordinary announcement of milking-time – half-past four o'clock, when the dairy men set about getting in the cows.

The interested reader will find it rewarding to read Vernon Lee's commentary in its entirety, but I must confine myself to extracts from it. Her basic objection to this passage is 'that we are *being told about* the locality, not what is necessary for the intelligence of the situation'[2] – the 'then', she argues, poses falsely as a connective between the description of the valley and the meditative commentary that precedes it[3] – and that even as a straightforward description it is awkwardly and untidily written:

Notice how he tells us the very simple fact of how Tess stops to look round: 'Tess . . . stood still upon the hemmed expanse of verdant flatness, like a fly on a billiard-table of indefinite length.' '*Hemmed* expanse,' that implies that the expanse had limits; it is, however, compared to a billiard-table 'of indefinite length'. Hardy's attention has slackened, and really he is talking a little at random. If he visualized that valley, particularly from above, he would not think of it, which is bounded by something on his own higher level (*hemmed*, by which he means *hemmed in*), in connection with a billiard table which is bounded by the tiny wall of its cushion. I venture to add that if, at the instant of writing, he were feeling the variety, the freshness of a valley, he would not be comparing it to a piece of cloth, with which it has only two things in common, being flat and being green; the utterly dissimilar flatness and greenness of a landscape and that of a billiard-table.

We are surely in the presence of slackened interest, when the Writer casts about for and accepts any illustration, without realizing it sufficiently to reject it. Such slackening of attention is confirmed by the poor structure of the sentence, 'a fly on a billiard-table of indefinite length *and* of no more consequence to the surroundings than that fly'. The *and* refers the 'of no more consequence' in the first instance to the billiard-table. Moreover, I venture to think the whole remark was not worth making : why divert our attention from Tess and her big, flat valley, surely easy enough to realize, by a vision of a billiard-table with a fly on it? Can the two images ever grow into one another? is the first made clearer, richer, by the second? How useless all this business has been is shown by the next sentence : 'The sole effect of her presence upon the placid valley so far had been to excite the mind of a solitary heron, which, after descending to the ground not far from her path, stood, with neck erect, looking at her.' Leave out all about the billiard-table, and the sentences coalesce perfectly and give us all we care to know.[4]

Vernon Lee's discussion of the rest of the passage is equally severe, finding everywhere a 'general slackening of attention, the vagueness showing itself in the casual distribution of the subject matter; showing itself, as we . . . see in lack of masterful treatment of the Reader's attention, in utter deficiency of logical arrangement. These are the co-related deficiencies due to the same inactivity and confusion of thought'.[5] In her closing remarks, however, Vernon Lee glaringly declines to accept the critical conclusions which follow from her analysis :

The woolly outlines, even the uncertain drawing, merely add to the impression of primeval passiveness and blind, unreasoning emotion; of inscrutable doom and blind, unfeeling Fate which belong to his whole outlook on life. And the very faults of Hardy are probably an expression of his solitary and matchless grandeur of attitude. He belongs to a universe transcending such trifles as Writers and Readers and their little logical ways.[6]

This disingenuous conclusion conceals either a failure of nerve before the Great Reputation, or an admission that the total effect of *Tess* is rather more impressive than the analysis of the extract suggests. I suspect that the latter is the case, and that if we consider the peculiarities of the passage in the context of the whole novel we shall arrive at a view of Hardy somewhere between the semi-illiterate blunderer exposed by Vernon Lee's commentary and the majestic figure transcending ordinary critical standards postulated in her conclusion. Such a consideration must start with an attempt to describe the function of the 'author's voice' in *Tess*, and proceed to discuss the attitudes of that author to Nature.

Underlying all Vernon Lee's criticism we can detect a prejudice against omniscient narration and in favour of Jamesian 'presentation'; against 'telling' and in favour of 'showing'. Just how dangerously narrowing and exclusive such prescriptive interpretation of Jamesian precept and practice can be, has been fully and persuasively argued by Wayne Booth in *The Rhetoric of Fiction*. But to note the existence of this element in Vernon Lee's approach to Hardy by no means disposes of her objections for a candid appraisal of *Tess* will reveal a fundamental uncertainty about the author's relation to his readers and to his characters, an uncertainty which is betrayed again and again in the language of the novel.

Tess, we are told, 'spoke two languages: the dialect at home, more or less; ordinary English abroad and to persons of quality' (III). To some extent the same is true of Hardy as narrator. There is the Hardy who can recreate dialect speech with flawless authenticity, who shows how closely he is in touch with the life of an agrarian community through being in touch with its idiom; and there is the Hardy speaking to 'the quality' in orotund sentences of laboured syntax and learned vocabulary, the Hardy who studied *The Times*, Addison, and Scott to improve his style.[7] It is probably the second Hardy who is responsible for the most spectacular stylistic lapses. But to regard the second Hardy as a regrettable excrescence superimposed upon the first, 'true', Hardy would be mistaken. For while one aspect of the novelist's undertaking in *Tess* demands a quality of immediacy, of 'felt life', achieved through his empathetic identification with his characters, particularly his heroine – in other words, the voice of the first Hardy – other aspects demand a quality of distance, both of time and space, through which the characters can be seen in their cosmic, historical and social settings – in other words, the voice of the second Hardy. And some of the most effective passages in the book – the description of the mechanical thresher, for instance (XLVII) – are articulated by this second Hardy.

Several accents are mingled in this voice. The author here is a combination of sceptical philosopher, and local historian, topographer, antiquarian, mediating between his 'folk' – the agricultural community of Wessex – and his readers – the metropolitan 'quality'. About the sceptical philosopher critics have had much to say, and most of them have regretted his presence. But if we reject such intrusions *qua* intrusions, we must reject other kinds of intrusion in the novel, in which case we shall not be left with very much in our hand. On the whole I think it will be found that these intrusions offend when they are crudely expressed. The sentence in Vernon Lee's passage, 'While there's life there's hope is a conviction not so entirely unknown to the "betrayed" as some amiable theorists would have us believe', for example, alienates rather than persuades the reader because it attempts to overthrow a social–moral cliché (that sexual betrayal is irredeemable) by nothing more potent than a proverbial cliché ('while there's life there's hope') and an ironic cliché ('amiable'). Compare the bitingly effective comment on the burial of Tess's child :

So the baby was carried in a small deal box, under an ancient woman's shawl, to the churchyard that night, and buried by lantern-light, at the cost of a shilling, and a pint of beer to the sexton, in that shabby corner of God's allotment where He lets the nettles grow, and where all unbaptized infants, notorious drunkards, suicides and others of the conjecturally damned are laid. (XIV)

There is much to admire in this sentence. It begins with a subdued literal description of the pathetic particulars of the child's burial. A hint of irony appears in the shilling and the pint of beer. This becomes overt in the axis of the sentence which marks the transition from impersonal narration to comment – 'That shabby corner of God's allotment where He lets the nettles grow' – where, through the conventional idea that the churchyard is ground dedicated to God, He is held responsible for the behaviour of His earthly representatives – is presented, in fact, as a cynically careless smallholder, a stroke which has particular appropriateness in the agrarian environment of the story. The irony is sustained and intensified in the conclusion of the sentence, in the grouping of unbaptized infants with drunkards and suicides, and in the juxtaposition of the cool 'conjecturally' with the uncompromising 'damned', which effectively shocks us into awareness of the arrogance and inhumanity of presuming to forecast the eternal destiny of souls.

The author of *Tess* as local historian has received less attention than the author as sceptical philosopher, but his presence is unmistakable. The title-page tells us that the story of Tess is 'Faithfully Presented by Thomas Hardy'; and the explanatory note to the first edition of 1891 describes the novel, rather equivocally, 'as an attempt to give artistic form to a true sequence of things'. Although no dates are specified in the novel, we are often made to feel that Tess's story is not taking place in a continuum in which author and reader keep pace with the action and, so to speak, discover its outcome with the protagonists; but that it is already finished, that it took place in living memory, and is being reported to us by someone who lived in the locality, who knew her, though only slightly, who has received much of his information at second-hand, and whose account is one of imaginative reconstruction :

The name of the eclipsing girl, whatever it was, has not been handed down. (II)

. . . the stopt-diapason note which her voice acquired when her heart was in her speech, and which will never be forgotten by those who knew her. (XIV)

It was said afterwards that a cottager of Wellbridge, who went out late that night for a doctor, met two lovers in the pastures, walking very slowly, without converse, one behind the other, as in a funeral procession, and the glimpse he obtained of their faces seemed to denote that they were anxious and sad. (XXXV)

This voice of the author as local historian, dependent upon secondary sources, is in a state of uneasy co-existence with the voice of the author as creator and maker, as one acquainted with the deepest interior processes of his characters' minds. The uneasiness manifests itself notably in Hardy's hesitation about how far to attempt an imitation of the verbal quality of Tess's consciousness. Often he does not attempt it at all : the morning after Angel's sleep-walking, for instance, we are told that, 'It just crossed her mind, too, that he might have a faint recollection of his tender vagary, and was disinclined to allude to it from a conviction that she would take amatory advantage of the opportunity it gave her of appealing to him anew not to go' (xxxvii). That Hardy was not entirely happy about using vocabulary and syntax so far removed from Tess's natural idiom is suggested by this quotation: 'She thought, *without actually wording the thought*, how strange and godlike was a composer's power, who from the grave could lead through sequences of emotion, which he alone had felt at first, a girl like her who had never heard of his name. . . .' (xiii – *my italics*). Of course, in the strict sense, there is no 'real' Tess, and everything we know about her proceeds from the same source. But in terms of literary illusion, the distinction between Tess's consciousness and the author's articulation of it is a real one. Consider for example the account of her disappointment at the appearance of Alec d'Urberville:

She had dreamed of an aged and dignified face, the sublimation of all the d'Urberville lineaments, furrowed with incarnate memories representing in hieroglyphic the centuries of her family's and England's history. But she screwed herself up to the work in hand, since she could not get out of it, and answered –
'I came to see your mother, sir.' (v).

The first sentence is a consciously literary paraphrase of Tess's vague, romantic expectations; whereas the second sentence is tough, simple and idiomatic, precisely rendering the verbal quality of Tess's consciousness. Each sentence is written in a mode which is legitimate and effective. But the transition between the two is too abrupt: a slight disturbance and confusion is created in the movement of the language, of a kind which we experience persistently in Hardy. It is particularly noticeable when he employs free indirect speech, for it would appear that the novelist who uses this device is obliged to be particularly faithful to the linguistic quality of his character's consciousness – the omission of the introductory verb 'he thought', 'he said', etc., seems to break down the literary convention by which we accept that the writer and his characters operate on quite different levels of discourse. Here is an example: 'Was once lost always lost really true of chastity? she would ask herself. She might prove it false if she could veil bygones. The recuperative power which pervaded organic nature was surely not denied to maidenhood alone' (xv). The structure of the last sentence indicates that it is a rendering, in free indirect speech, of Tess's thought; but its vocabulary belongs to the voice of the authorial commentator.

This duality in the presentation of Tess's consciousness is paralleled in the treatment of Nature (understanding Nature in its general cosmic sense and more specific sense of landscape, the earth, flora and fauna). Ian Gregor has commented acutely on the contradiction that exists in *Tess* between a 'Rousseauistic view of Nature' as essentially life-giving, healthy, opposed to the inhibiting, destructive forces of society and convention which alone generate human misery, and the 'deterministic [view] which Hardy runs alongside it', in which the world appears as a 'blighted star' and the three dairymaids in love with Angel 'writhed feverishly under the oppressiveness of an emotion which they neither expected nor desired'.[8] This contradiction applies not only to generalizations about Nature, but also to the treatment of landscape, and Gregor's own assertion that 'at every stage of the tale interior states are visualized in terms of landscape'[9] must be qualified. It would be difficult to refute Vernon Lee's point that in the passage she quotes the description of the landscape does *not* reflect Tess's interior state of mind. On the other hand, we must not assume that such a relationship between character and setting is a necessary feature of imaginative prose, or that Hardy failed to establish it through incompetence. The truth of the matter is rather more complex.

No attentive reader can fail to note how persistently Tess is associated and identified with Nature, on several different levels. On the social level, in terms of the rural/urban or agrarian/industrial antithesis on which the values of the novel are largely based, she is a 'daughter of the soil' (xix), almost timeless and anonymous – 'Thus Tess walks on; a figure which is part of the landscape, a fieldswoman pure and simple, in winter guise' (xlii) (the present tense here having an effect of timelessness rather than of immediacy) – a quasi-symbolic 'object . . . foreign to the gleaming cranks and wheels' of the railway engine (xxx). In

religious or spiritual terms, Tess is a Nature-worshipping pagan.
Her beliefs are 'Tractarian as to phraseology' 'but Pantheistic as
to essence' (xxvII). 'You used to say at Talbothays that I was
a heathen', says Tess to Angel, as she lies on a stone 'altar' at
Stonehenge, 'So now I am at home' (LVIII). 'Did they sacrifice to
God here?' she asks later. 'No . . . I believe to the sun', he replies
(LVIII). And we may recall here, that at their second embrace at
Talbothays the sun had shone through the window 'upon her
inclining face, upon the blue veins of her temple, upon her naked
arm, and her neck, and into the depths of her hair' (xxvII).

This schematic association of Tess with Nature is enforced by
insistent allusion, literal and figurative, to flora and fauna. Early
in the novel she appears with 'roses at her breast; roses in her
hat; roses and strawberries in her basket to the brim' (vI). Her
hair is 'earth-coloured' (v), her mouth 'flower-like' (xIV), and
her breath tastes 'of the butter and eggs and honey on which she
mainly lived' (xxxvI). She is compared to a 'plant' (xxvII) and
a 'sapling' (xx); the dew falls on her as naturally as on the grass
(xx). To Angel, 'her arm, from her dabbling in the curds, was
cold and damp to his mouth as new-gathered mushrooms' (xxvIII).
While her physical appearance finds its metaphorical equivalents
in the vegetable world, her behaviour is often compared to that
of animals, particularly cats and birds. She 'wears the look of a
wary animal' (xxxI). 'There was something of the habitude of the
wild animal in the unreflecting instinct with which she rambled
on' (xLI). She is as unresponsive to sarcasm as a 'dog or cat' (xxxv).
She listens to Angel's harp like a 'fascinated bird', and moves
through an overgrown garden 'as stealthily as a cat' (xIx). After
sleep, 'she was as warm as a sunned cat' (xxvII). When she is
happy her tread is like 'the skim of a bird which has not quite
alighted' (xxxI). She faces d'Urberville with 'the hopeless defiance
of the sparrow's gaze before its captor twists its neck' (xLvII).

This network of imagery and reference encourages us to think
of Tess as essentially 'in touch' with Nature. Her character is
defined and justified by metaphors of flora and fauna, and the
changing face of the earth both directs and reflects her emotional
life. At such moments we are least conscious of the literary *persona* of the author, and of his distance from the story. But it is

equally true that Nature is quite indifferent to Tess and her fate. It is simply 'there', the physical setting against which the story takes place, described by the local historian with a wealth of geological and topographical detail, its moral neutrality emphasized by the sceptical philosopher.

This is surely the case in the passage quoted by Vernon Lee, particularly the two paragraphs beginning, 'The marked difference, in the final particular, between the rival vales now showed itself'. These paragraphs have the very tone of the guide-book, the tone of the parallel description of the Vale of Blackmoor : 'It is a vale whose acquaintance is best made by viewing it from the summits of the hills that surround it – except perhaps during the droughts of summer. An unguided ramble into its recesses in bad weather is apt to engender dissatisfaction with its narrow, tortuous, and miry ways' (II). But this earlier description is deliberately and clearly detached from the narrative, most obviously by its use of the present tense. Whereas in the passage quoted by Vernon Lee there is a fumbling attempt to relate the guide-book view to Tess. It is true that the two valleys might present themselves to Tess as in some sense 'rivals', but not in such impersonal, topographical terms.

A similar problem is raised by the simile of the fly, of which Vernon Lee asks, 'Why divert our attention from Tess and her big, flat valley, surely easy enough to realise, by a vision of a billiard table with a fly on it?' The answer surely is that Hardy, having got Tess into the valley, wants to give us, not a horizontal picture of the situation from her point of view, but a vertical, bird's eye picture; and he wants to do so in order to bring out her defencelessness, her isolation, her insignificance, in the eye of impersonal nature. (One is reminded of the later description of Flintcomb, in which the earth and the sky are compared to two vacant faces, 'the white face looking down on the brown face, and the brown face looking up at the white face, without anything standing between them but the two girls crawling over the surface of the former like flies' (XLIII), and even of the lines from *Lear* quoted in the Preface to the Fifth and later editions : 'As flies to wanton boys are we to the gods;/They kill us for their sport.') The trouble, once again, is that the structure of the sentence is confused and misleading. 'Not quite sure of her direction Tess stood still . . .' arouses expectations that any subsequent image will define her sense of uncertainty, whereas it does nothing of the sort. This confusion in the handling of the point of view, with its consequent disturbance of tone and meaning, is the essential basis of Vernon Lee's criticism; and I do not see how it can be dismissed, here or elsewhere in the novel.

On the other hand her critique can be challenged on two grounds. Firstly, she does not seem to have given her text the careful attention which close criticism demands. Her transcription of the passage (from an unspecified 'cheap edition') runs together the three paragraphs beginning 'Tess Durbeyfield, then', 'The marked difference', and 'The river had stolen', and adds on the following sentence to make one paragraph ending with 'fly'. This considerably increases the confusion in the point of view. For in my text the first of these three paragraphs stands as a self-contained statement of Tess's mood and action, which seems to have a sufficient logical connection with the preceding commentary to justify the use of the connective 'then'; and the third stands as a self-contained statement of the geological history of the valley. The attempt to provide some transition between the two in the second paragraph remains, however, a muddle.*

A more significant limitation of Vernon Lee's critique is her assumption that landscape in fiction must be vividly realized in sensuous terms, and reflect characters' states of consciousness. The fly and billiard table image does neither of these things, and is dismissed as the mechanical gesture of a nodding writer. She does not consider the possibility that it is a deliberately homely and bathetic image, designed to dissociate us from Tess at this point, to check any tendency to find reassurance in the identification of Tess's renewed hope with the fertile promise of the valley.

Ruskin called such identification the 'pathetic fallacy', and Hardy's ambiguous treatment of Nature throughout *Tess* might

* Vernon Lee also omits from her transcription the line 'Waow! waow! waow!'; and when quoting the sentence with the fly simile a second time, she omits the comma after *length*, which removes the grammatical ambiguity of which she complains.

be formulated as his inability to decide whether the pathetic fallacy was fallacious or not. For of course it is Hardy himself who has encouraged us to make this kind of identification between Tess and her environment. A page or two before the passage quoted by Vernon Lee, we have the following description of Tess on a summit overlooking the valley into which she later descends :

The bird's eye perspective before her was not so luxuriantly beautiful, perhaps, as that other one which she knew so well; yet it was more cheering. It lacked the intensely blue atmosphere of the rival vale, and its heavy soils and scents; the new air was clear, bracing, ethereal. The river itself, which nourished the grass and cows of these renowned dairies, flowed not like the streams in Blackmoor. Those were slow, silent, often turbid; flowing over beds of mud into which the incautious wader might sink and vanish unawares. The Froom waters were clear as the pure River of Life shown to the Evangelist, rapid as the shadow of a cloud, with pebbly shallows that prattled to the sky all day long. There the water-flower was the lily; the crowfoot here.

Either the change in the quality of the air from heavy to light, or the sense of being amid new scenes where there were no invidious eyes upon her, sent up her spirits wonderfully. Her hopes mingled with the sunshine in an ideal photosphere which surrounded her as she bounded along against the soft south wind. She heard a pleasant voice in every breeze, and in every bird's note seemed to lurk a joy. (xvi)

Here we have the 'rivalry' of the two valleys defined in a quite different way, a way that is verbally related to Tess's sensuous and emotional experience (the pedantic 'photosphere' striking the only incongruous note). The suggestions of hope and recovery are unmistakable, and appropriate to the first chapter of a 'Phase' of the novel entitled 'The Rally'. And yet, as Tess descends this same valley, the 'Froom waters . . . clear as the pure river of life shown to the Evangelist', become a river exhausted by aeons of geological activity, and we are sharply reminded that Tess was of not the slightest consequence to her natural surroundings, that the sudden burst of sound 'was not the expression of the valley's consciousness that lovely Tess had arrived'. 'Who in his senses would have thought that it was?' asks Vernon Lee. The answer is surely, a Romantic poet – Wordsworth, perhaps, to whom Hardy twice alludes in sarcastic asides elsewhere in the novel (III and LI). Hardy's undertaking to defend Tess as a pure woman by emphasizing her kinship with Nature* perpetually drew him towards the Romantic view of Nature as a reservoir of benevolent impulses, a view which one side of his mind rejected as falsely sentimental. Many Victorian writers, struggling to reconcile the view of Nature inherited from the Romantics with the discoveries of Darwinian biology, exhibit the same conflict, but it is particularly noticeable in Hardy.

A passage which seems especially revealing in this respect is that which describes Tess's gloomy nocturnal rambling in the weeks, following her seduction, where she is explicitly shown entertaining the pathetic fallacy, and her mistake explicitly pointed out by the author :

On these lonely hills and dales her quiescent glide was of a piece with the element she moved in. Her flexuous and stealthy figure became an integral part of the scene. At times her whimsical fancy would intensify natural processes around her till they seemed a part of her own story. Rather they became a part of it; for the world is only a psychological phenomenon, and what they seemed they were. The midnight airs and gusts, moaning amongst the tightly-wrapped buds and bark of the winter twigs, were formulae of bitter reproach. A wet day was the expression of irremediable grief at her weakness in the mind of some vague ethical being whom she could not class definitely as the God of her childhood, and could not comprehend as any other.

But this encompassment of her own characterization, based on shreds of convention, peopled by phantoms and voices antipathetic to her, was a sorry and mistaken creation of Tess's fancy – a cloud of moral hobgoblins by which she was terrified without reason. It was they that were out of harmony with the actual world, not she. Walking among the sleeping birds in the hedges, watching the skipping rabbits on a moonlit warren, or standing under a pheasant-laden bough, she looked upon herself as a figure of Guilt intruding

---

* In the Preface to the 5th edition (1895), Hardy says of readers who had objected to the description of Tess as a 'pure' woman : 'They ignore the meaning of the word in Nature.'

into the haunts of Innocence. But all the while she was making a distinction where there was no difference. Feeling herself in antagonism she was quite in accord. She had been made to break an accepted social law, but no law known to the environment in which she fancied herself such an anomaly. (xiii)

Here we have two paragraphs, one describing Tess's subjective state of mind, and the second describing the objective 'reality'. We are meant to feel that the second cancels out the first, that 'guilt' is a fabrication of social convention, something unknown to the natural order which Tess distorts by projecting her own feelings into it. It seems to me, however, that there is an unresolved conflict in Hardy's rhetoric here. Not only are the 'midnight airs and gusts, moaning amongst the tightly wrapped buds and bark of the winter twigs' images of sorrow and remorse too moving and impressive to be easily overthrown by the rational arguments of the second paragraph; we are explicitly told that 'the world is only a psychological [i.e. subjective] phenomenon', in which case the view expressed in the second paragraph is as 'subjective' as that expressed in the first, and has no greater validity. If Tess felt herself in antagonism she *was* in antagonism. But in fact 'antagonism' is a clumsy formulation of the experience so delicately expressed in the first paragraph. That Nature should present its most sombre aspect to Tess when she is most desolate is, in a way, evidence of how deeply she is 'in accord' with Nature. There are many other places in the book where Hardy 'intensifies natural processes around Tess till they seem part of her story', without suggesting that she is deceiving herself, e.g. – 'She was wretched – O so wretched. . . . The evening sun was now ugly to her, like a great inflamed wound in the sky. Only a solitary cracked-voiced reed-sparrow greeted her from the bushes by the river, in a sad, machine-made tone, resembling that of a past friend whose friendship she had outworn.' (xxi)

There is further ambiguity about the 'actual world' of nature with which, according to the author, Tess is in accord without realizing it. Is she mistaken in thinking herself guilty, or Nature innocent, or both? Elsewhere in the novel it is true to say that when Nature is not presented through Tess's consciousness, it is neither innocent nor guilty, but neutral; neither sympathetic nor hostile, but indifferent. When Tess and her young brother are driving their father's cart through the night, 'the cold pulses' of the stars 'were beating in serene dissociation from these two wisps of human life' (IV). The birds and rabbits skip happily and heedlessly round the defenceless Tess at her seduction (XI); and the Valley of the Var has no interest in her arrival. Is not Tess more human in preferring a sad but sympathetic Nature to a gay but indifferent one?

Hardy, then, here undermines our trust in the reliability of Tess's response to Nature, which is his own chief rhetorical device for defending her character and interesting our sympathies on her behalf. Without this winterpiece, which the author dismisses as a delusion of Tess's mind, we would lose the significance of Tess's renewal of energy in the spring which urges her towards the Valley of the Var and her 'rally':

A particularly fine spring came round, and the stir of germination was almost audible in the buds; it moved her, as it moved the wild animals, and made her passionate to go . . . some spirit within her rose automatically as the sap in the twigs. It was unexpended youth, surging up anew after its temporary check, and bringing with it hope, and the invincible instinct towards self-delight. (XV)

But of course the instinct is, in the event, vincible . . . and so we return to the basic contradiction pointed out by Ian Gregor, of which he says: 'the small measure in which this confusion, which is central to the theme of the novel, really decreases its artistic compulsion, suggests how effectively the latter is protected against the raids of philosophic speculation'.[10] I find myself in some disagreement with this verdict for, as I have tried to show, the confusion is not merely in the abstractable philosophical content of the novel, but inextricably woven into its verbal texture. . . .

SOURCE: David Lodge, *Language of Fiction* (1966), extract from chapter IV.

NOTES

1. Vernon Lee, *The Handling of Words and Other Studies in Literary Psychology* (London, 1923) pp. 222–41. Vernon Lee's

method does not of course anticipate I. A. Richards' procedure in *Practical Criticism* (London, 1929) exactly. His is primarily pedagogic in purpose; hers, critical. He deals with complete short poems, the context from which they are extracted being historical knowledge of the poem's origins; she deals with extracts from novels which are identified, though they are not discussed as wholes. The similarity resides mainly in their mutual reliance on the close analysis of limited pieces by reference to certain constant assumptions about good literary language.

2. Lee, *The Handling of Words*, p. 224.

3. Ibid. p. 233.

4. Ibid. pp. 227–8.

5. Ibid. p. 234.

6. Ibid. pp. 240–1.

7. Douglas Brown, *Thomas Hardy* (London, 1954; reprinted 1961) p. 103.

8. Ian Gregor and Brian Nicholas, *The Moral and the Story* (London, 1962) pp. 143–4.

9. Ibid. p. 137.

10. Ibid. p. 144.

Tony Tanner

COLOUR AND MOVEMENT IN
TESS OF THE D'URBERVILLES (1968)

'the discontinuance of immobility in any quarter suggested confusion' (*The Return of the Native*)

'the least irregularity of motion startled her' (*Tess of the d'Urbervilles*)

I

Every great writer has his own kind of legibility, his own way of turning life into a language of particular saliences, and in Hardy this legibility is of a singularly stark order. If we can think of a novelist as creating, among other things, a particular linguistic world by a series of selective intensifications of our shared vocabulary, then we can say that Hardy's world is unusually easy to read. The key words in his dialect, to continue the image, stand out like braille. It is as though some impersonal process of erosion had worn away much of the dense circumstantial texture of his tales, revealing the basic resistant contours of a sequence of events which Hardy only has to point to to make us see – like ancient marks on a barren landscape. And Hardy above all does make us see. Just as he himself could not bear to be touched, so he does not 'touch' the people and things in his tales, does not interfere with them or absorb them into his own sensibility. When he says in his introduction to *Tess of the d'Urbervilles* that 'a novel is an impression, not an argument', or in his introduction to *Jude the Obscure* that 'like former productions of this pen, *Jude the Obscure* is simply an endeavour to give shape and coherence to a series of seemings, or personal impressions', we should give full stress to the idea of something seen but not tampered with, something scrupulously watched in its otherness, something perceived but not made over. Hardy's famous, or notorious, philosophic broodings and asides are part of his reactions as a watcher, but they never give the impression of violating the people and objects of which his tale is composed. Reflection and perception are kept separate (in Lawrence they often tend to merge), and those who complain about the turgidity of his thoughts may be overlooking the incomparable clarity of his eyes.

II

This illusion that the tale exists independently of Hardy's rendering of it *is* of course only an illusion, but it testifies to art of a rather special kind. For all Henry James's scrupulous indirectness, Hardy's art is more truly impersonal. He goes in for graphic crudities of effect which James would have scorned, yet, as other critics have testified, the result is an anonymity which we more commonly associate with folk-tale, or the ballads. By graphic crudity of effect I am referring, for instance, to such moments as when Tess, shortly after being seduced, encounters a man who is writing in large letters 'THY, DAMNATION, SLUMBERETH, NOT.' There are commas between every word 'as if to give pause while that word was driven well home to the reader's heart'. This is not unlike Hardy's own art which is full of prominent notations, and emphatic pauses which temporarily isolate, and thus vivify, key incidents and objects. On the level of everyday plausibility and probability it is too freakish a chance which brings Tess and the painted words together at this point. In the vast empty landscapes of Hardy's world, peoples' paths cross according to some more mysterious logic – that same imponderable structuring of things in time which brought the *Titanic* and the iceberg together at one point in the trackless night sea. (See the poem 'The Convergence of the Twain'.) A comparable 'crudity' is discernible in the characterisation which is extremely schematic, lacking in all the minute mysteries of individual uniqueness which a writer like James pursued. *Angel* Clare is indeed utterly ethereal; his love is 'more spiritual than animal'. He even plays the harp! On the other hand Alec d'Urberville is almost a stage villain with his 'swarthy complexion . . . full lips . . . well-groomed black moustache with curled points', his cigars and his rakish way with his fast spring-cart. If we turn from character to plot sequence we see at once that the overall architecture of the novel is blocked out with massive simplicity in a series of balancing phases – The Maiden, Maiden No More; The Rally, The Consequence; and so on. Let it be conceded at once that Hardy's art is not subtle in the way that James and many subsequent writers are subtle. Nevertheless I think it is clear that Hardy derives his great power from that very 'crudity' which, in its impersonal indifference to plausibility and rational cause and effect, enhances the visibility of the most basic lineaments of the tale.

III

I want first to concentrate on one series of examples which show how this manifest visibility works. For an artist as visually sensitive as Hardy, colour is of the first importance and significance, and there is one colour which literally catches the eye, and is meant to catch it, throughout the book. This colour is red, the colour of blood, which is associated with Tess from first to last. It dogs her, disturbs her, destroys her. She is full of it, she spills it, she loses it. Watching Tess's life we begin to see that her destiny is nothing more or less than the colour red. The first time we (and Angel) see Tess, in the May dance with the other girls, she stands out. How? They are all in white except that Tess 'wore a red ribbon in her hair, and was the only one of the white company who would boast of such a pronounced adornment'. Tess is marked, even from the happy valley of her birth and childhood. The others are a semi-anonymous mass; Tess already has that heightened legibility, that eye-taking prominence which suggests that she has in some mysterious way been singled out. And the red stands out because it is on a pure white background. In that simple scene and colour contrast is the embryo of the whole book and all that happens in it.

This patterning of red and white is often visible in the background of the book. For instance 'The ripe hue of the red and dun kine absorbed the evening sunlight, which the white-coated animals returned to the eye in rays almost dazzling, even at the distant elevation on which she stood.' This dark red and dazzling white is something seen, it is something there; it is an effect on the retina, it is a configuration of matter. In looking at this landscape Tess in fact is seeing the elemental mixture which conditions her own existence. In the second chapter Tess is described as 'a mere vessel of emotion untinctured by experience'. The use of the word 'untinctured' may at first seem surprising; we perhaps tend to think of people being shaped by experience rather than coloured by it – yet the use of a word connected with dye and paint is clearly intentional. In her youth Tess is often referred to as a 'white shape' – almost more as a colour value in a landscape than a human being. And on the night of her rape she is seen as a 'white muslin figure' sleeping on a pile of dead leaves; her 'beautiful feminine tissue' is described as 'practically blank as snow'. The historic precedent for what is to happen to this vulnerable white shape is given at the start when we read that 'the Vale was known in former times as the Forest of White Hart, from a curious legend of King Henry III's reign, in which the killing by a certain Thomas de la Lynd of a beautiful white hart which the king had run down and spared, was made the occasion of a heavy fine'. Against all social injunctions, white harts are brought down. And in Tess's case the 'tincturing' – already prefigured in the red ribbon – starts very early.

The next omen – for even that harmless ribbon is an omen in this world – occurs when Tess drives the hives to market when her father is too drunk to do the job. When she sets out the road is still in darkness. Tess drifts, sleeps, dreams. Then there is the sudden collision and she wakes to find that Prince, their horse, has been killed by another cart. 'The pointed shaft of the cart had entered the breast of the unhappy Prince like a sword, and from the wound his life's blood was spouting in a stream and falling with a hiss on the road. In her despair Tess sprang forward and put her hand upon the hole, with the only result that she became splashed from face to skirt with the crimson drops. Then she stood helplessly looking on. Prince also stood firm and motionless as long as he could, till he suddenly sank down in a heap.' It is possible to say different things about this passage. On one level the death of the horse means that the family is destitute, which means in turn that Tess will have to go begging to the d'Urbervilles. Thus, it is part of a rough cause and effect economic sequence. But far more graphic, more disturbing and memorable, is the image of the sleeping girl on the darkened road, brutally awakened and desperately trying to staunch a fatal puncture, trying to stop the blood which cannot be stopped and only getting drenched in its powerful spurts. It adumbrates the loss of her virginity, for she, too, will be brutally pierced on a darkened road far from home; and once the blood of her innocence has been released, she too, like the stoical Prince, will stay upright as long as she can until, all blood being out, she will sink down suddenly in a heap. Compressed in that one imponderable scene we can see her whole life.

After this Tess is constantly encountering the colour red – if not literal blood, manifold reminders of it. When she approaches the d'Urberville house we read : 'It was of recent erection – indeed almost new – and of the same rich red colour that formed such a contrast with the evergreens of the lodge.' And the corner of the house 'rose like a geranium bloom against the subdued colours around'. Tess, with her red ribbon, also stood out against 'the subdued colours around'. Mysteriously, inevitably, this house will play a part in her destiny. And if this red house contains her future rapist, so it is another red house which contains her final executioner, for the prison where she is hanged is 'a large red-brick building'. Red marks the house of sex and death. When first she has to approach the leering, smoking Alec d'Urberville, he forces roses and strawberries on her, pushing a strawberry into her mouth, pressing the roses into her bosom. Hardy, deliberately adding to the legibility I am describing, comments that d'Urberville is one 'who stood fair to be the blood-red ray in the spectrum of her young life'. On the evening of the rape, Tess is first aware of d'Urberville's presence at the dance when she sees 'the red coal of a cigar'. This is too clearly phallic to need comment, but it is worth pointing out that, from the first, d'Urberville seems to have the power of reducing Tess to a sort of trance-like state, he envelops her in a 'blue narcotic haze' of which his cigar smoke is the most visible emblem. On the night of the rape, at the dance, everything is in a 'mist', like 'illuminated smoke'; there is a 'float-ing, fusty *débris* of peat and hay' stirred up as 'the panting shapes spun onwards'. Everything together seems to form 'a sort of vegeto-human pollen'. In other words it becomes part of a basic natural process in which Tess is caught up simply by being alive, fecund, and female. D'Urberville is that figure, that force, at the heart of the haze, the mist, the smoke, waiting to claim her when the dance catches her up (we first saw her at a dance and she can scarcely avoid being drawn in). It is in a brilliant continuation of this blurred narcotic atmosphere that Hardy has the rape take place in a dense fog, while Tess is in a deep sleep. Consciousness and perception are alike engulfed and obliterated. When Tess first leaves d'Urberville's house she suddenly wakes up to find that she is covered in roses; while removing them a thorn from a re-maining rose pricks her chin. 'Like all the cottagers in Blackmoor Vale, Tess was steeped in fancies and prefigurative superstitions; she thought this an ill omen.' The world of the book is indeed a world of omens (*not* symbols) in which things and events echo and connect in patterns deeper than lines of rational cause and effect. Tess takes it as an omen when she starts to bleed from the last rose pressed on her by Alec. She is right; for later on she will again wake up to find that he has drawn blood – in a way which determines her subsequent existence.

After the rape we are still constantly seeing the colour red. The man who writes up the words promising damnation is carry-ing 'a tin pot of red paint in his hand'. As a result 'these vermilion words shone forth'. Shortly after, when Tess is back at home, Hardy describes a sunrise in which the sun 'broke through chinks of cottage shutters, throwing stripes like red-hot pokers upon cup-boards, chests of drawers, and other furniture within'. (The con-junction of sun-light and redness is a phenomenon I will return to.) And Hardy goes on : 'But of all ruddy things that morning the brightest were two broad arms of painted wood . . . forming the revolving Maltese cross of the reaping-machine.' We will later see Tess virtually trapped and tortured on a piece of red machinery, and her way will take her past several crosses until she finds her own particular sacrificial place. When Tess is working in the fields her flesh again reveals its vulnerability. 'A bit of her naked arm is visible between the buff leather of the gauntlet and the sleeve of her gown; and as the day wears on its feminine smoothness becomes scarified by the stubble, and bleeds.' Notice the shift to the present tense: Hardy makes us look at the actual surfaces – the leather, the sleeve, the flesh, the blood. One of the great strengths of Hardy is that he knew, and makes us realise, just how very much the surfaces of things mean.

Of course it is part of the whole meaning of the book that there is as much red inside Tess as outside her. Both the men who seek to possess her see it. When Tess defies d'Urberville early on, she speaks up at him, 'revealing the red and ivory of her mouth'; while when Angel watches her unawares, 'she was yawning, and he saw the red interior of her mouth as if it had been a snake's'. When Angel does just kiss her arm, and he kisses the inside vein, we read that she was such a 'sheaf of susceptibilities' that 'her blood (was) driven to her finger ends'. Tess does not so much act as re-act. She would be content to be passive, but something is always disturbing her blood, and all but helplessly she submits to the momentums of nature in which, by her very constitution, she is necessarily involved. As for example when she is drawn by Angel's music 'like a fascinated bird' and she makes her way through, once again, a misty atmosphere ('mists of pollen') of uncontrollable swarming fertility and widespread insemination. It is a place of growth, though not wholly a place of beauty. There are 'tall blooming weeds' giving off 'offensive smells' and some of the weeds are a bright 'red'. 'She went stealthily as a cat through this profusion of growth, gathering cuckoo-spittle on her skirts, cracking snails that were underfoot, staining her hands with thistle-milk and slugslime, and rubbing off upon her naked arms sticky blights which though snow-white on the apple-tree trunks, made *madder* stains on her skin . . .' (my italics). In some of the earlier editions (certainly up to the 1895 edition) that final phrase was 'blood-red stains on her skin'; only later did Hardy change 'blood-red' to 'madder', a crimson dye made from a climbing plant. This change clearly reveals that he intended us once again to see Tess's arm marked with red, though he opted for a word which better suggested something in nature staining, 'tincturing', Tess as she pushes on through 'this profusion of growth'. And once again Hardy presents us with redness and snow-whiteness in the same scene – indeed, in the same plant.

After Tess has been abandoned by Angel and she has to renew her endless journeying the red omens grow more vivid, more violent. She seeks shelter one night under some bushes and when she wakes up : 'Under the trees several pheasants lay about, their rich plumage dabbled with blood; some were dead, some feebly twitching a wing, some staring up at the sky, some pulsating quickly, some contorted, some stretched out – all of them writhing in agony, except for the fortunate ones whose torture had ended during the night by the inability of nature to bear more'. There is much that is horribly apposite for Tess in these bloody writhings. (It is worth noting that Hardy uses the same word to describe the torments of the onset of sexual impulse; thus he describes the sleeping girls at Talbothays who are all suffering from 'hopeless passion'. 'They writhed feverishly under the oppressiveness of an emotion thrust on them by cruel Nature's law – an emotion which they had neither expected nor desired.' The writhings of life are strangely similar to the writhings of death.) Looking at the dying birds Tess reprimands herself for feeling self-pity, saying 'I be not mangled, and I be not bleeding'. But she will be both, and she, too, will have to endure until she reaches 'the inability of nature to bear more'. Like the white hart and the pheasants she is a hunted animal; hunted not really by a distinct human individual, but by ominous loitering presences like the cruel gun-men she used to glimpse stalking through the woods and bushes – a male blood-letting force which is abroad. Later when she makes her fruitless trek to Angel's parents she sees 'a piece of blood-stained paper, caught up from some meat-buyer's dust heap, beat up and down the road without the gate; too flimsy to rest, too heavy to fly away, and a few straws to keep it company'. It is another deliberate omen. Tess, too, is blood-stained, she, too, is beat up and down the road without the gate; too flimsy to rest, too heavy no door opens to her); and she, too, very exactly, is too flimsy to rest, too heavy to fly away. (cf. Eustacia Vye's envy of the heron. 'Up in the zenith where he was seemed a free and happy place, away from all contact with the earthly ball to which she was pinioned; and she wished that she could arise uncrushed from its sur-

face and fly as he flew then.') The blood-stained piece of paper
is not a clumsy symbol; it is one of a number of cumulative omens.
When Alec d'Urberville renews his pressure on Tess, at one point
she turns and slashes him across the face with her heavy leather
gauntlet. 'A scarlet oozing appeared where her blow had alighted
and in a moment the blood began dropping from his mouth upon
the straw.' (Notice again the conjunction of blood and straw.)
The man who first made her bleed now stands bleeding from the
lips. Blood has blood, and it will have more blood. We need only
to see the scene – there, unanalysed, unexplained; a matter of
violent movement, sudden compulsions. Hardy spends more time
describing the glove than attempting to unravel the hidden
thoughts of these starkly confronted human beings. Few other
writers can so make us feel that the world is its own meaning –
and mystery, requiring no interpretative gloss. Seeing the heavy
glove, the sudden blow, the dripping blood, we see all we need
to see.

At one point shortly before her marriage, Tess comes into proximity with a railway engine. 'No object could have looked more
foreign to the gleaming cranks and wheels than this unsophisticated girl, with the round bare arms. . . .' This feeling that her
vulnerable flesh is somehow menaced by machinery is realised
when she is later set to work on that 'insatiable swallower', the
relentless threshing machine. It is a bright red machine, and the
'immense stack of straw' which it is turning out is seen as 'the
faeces of the same buzzing red glutton'. Tess is 'the only woman
whose place was upon the machine so as to be shaken bodily by
its spinning'. She is beaten into a 'stupefied reverie in which her
arm worked on independently of her consciousness' (this separation, indeed severance, of consciousness and body is a crucial part
of Tess's experience). Whenever she looks up 'she beheld always
the great upgrown straw-stack, with the men in shirt-sleeves upon it, against the grey north sky; in front of it the long red elevator
like a Jacob's ladder, on which a perpetual stream of threshed
straw ascended . . .'. There it is. We see Tess, trapped and stupefied
in the cruel red man-made machine. Whenever she looks up in
her trance of pain and weariness she sees – the long red elevator,
the growing heap of straw, the men at work against the grey

sky. It is a scene which is, somehow, her life : the men, the movement, the redness, the straw (blood and straw seem almost to be
the basic materials of existence in the book – the vital pulsating
fluid, and the dry, dead stalks). At the end of the day she is as a
'bled calf'. We do not need any enveloping and aiding words;
only the legibility of vibrant, perceived detail.

The end of the book is sufficiently well known, but it is worth
pointing out how Hardy continues to bring the colour red in front
of our eyes. The landlady who peeps through the keyhole during
Tess's anguish when Angel has returned reports that, 'her lips
were bleeding from the clench of her teeth upon them'. It is the
landlady who sees 'the oblong white ceiling, with this scarlet blot
in the midst', which is at once the evidence of the murder and the
completion of a life which also started with a red patch on a
white background, only then it was simply a ribbon on a dress.
The blood stain on the ceiling has 'the appearance of a gigantic
ace of hearts'. In that shape of the heart, sex and death are merged in utmost legibility. After this we hardly need to see the
hanging. It is enough that we see Tess climb into a vast bed with
'crimson damask hangings', not indeed in a home, for she has no
home, but in an empty house to be 'Let Furnished'. And in that
great crimson closed-in bed she finds what she has wanted for so
long – rest and peace. Apart from the last scene at Stonehenge,
we can say that at this point the crimson curtains do indeed fall
on Tess; for if she was all white at birth, she is to be all red at
death. The massed and linking red omens have finally closed in
on Tess and her wanderings are over.

Tess is a 'pure woman' as the subtitle, which caused such outrage, specifically says. The purest woman contains tides of blood
(Tess is always blushing), and if the rising of blood is sexual passion
and the spilling of blood is death, then we can see that the purest
woman is sexual and mortal. Remember Tess watching Prince
bleed to death – 'the hole in his chest looking scarcely large
enough to have let out all that animated him'. It is not a large hole
that Alec makes in Tess when he rapes her, but from then on the
blood is bound to go on flowing until that initial violation will
finally 'let out all that animated her'. Hardy is dealing here with
the simplest and deepest of matters. Life starts in sex and ends in

death, and Hardy constantly shows how closely allied the two
forms of blood-letting are in one basic, unalterable rhythm of
existence.

I V

I have suggested that the destiny of Tess comes to us as a cumu-
lation of visible omens. It is also a convergence of omens and to
explain what I mean I want to add a few comments on the part
played in her life by the sun, altars and tombs, and finally walking
and travelling. When we first see Tess with the other dancing girls
we read that they are all bathed in sunshine. Hardy, ever conscious of effects of light, describes how their hair reflects various
colours in the sunlight. More, 'as each and all of them were warmed without by the sun, so each of them had a private little sun
for her soul to bask in'. They are creatures of the sun, warmed
and nourished by the sources of all heat and life. Tess starts sun-
blessed. At the dairy, the sun is at its most active as a cause of the
fertile surgings which animate all nature. 'Rays from the sunrise
drew forth the buds and stretched them into stalks, lifted up sap
in noiseless streams, opened petals, and sucked out scents in in-
visible jets and breathings.' This is the profoundly sensuous atmosphere in which Tess, despite mental hesitations, blooms into
full female ripeness. Hardy does something very suggestive here
in his treatment of the times of day. Tess and Angel rise very
early, before the sun. They seem to themselves 'the first persons
up of all the world'. The light is still 'half-compounded, aqueous',
as though the business of creating animated forms has not yet
begun. They are compared to Adam and Eve. As so often when
Tess is getting involved with the superior power of a man, the atmosphere is misty, but this time it is cold mist, the sunless fogs
which precede the dawn. In this particular light of a cool watery
whiteness, Tess appears to Angel as 'a visionary essence of woman',
something ghostly, 'merely a soul at large'. He calls her, among
other things, Artemis (who lived, of course, in perpetual celibacy).
In this sunless light Tess appears to Angel as unsexed, sexless, the
sort of non-physical spiritualised essence he, in his impotent spirit-
uality, wants. (At the end he marries 'a spiritualized image of

Tess'). But Tess is inescapably flesh and blood. And when the sun does come up, she reverts from divine essence to physical milk-maid : 'her teeth, lips and eyes scintillated in the sunbeams, and she was again the dazzlingly fair dairymaid only. . . .' (That placing of 'only' is typical of the strength of Hardy's prose.) Soon after this, the dairyman tells his story of the seduction of a young girl; 'none of them but herself seemed to see the sorrow of it'. And immediately we read, 'the evening sun was now ugly to her, like a great inflamed wound in the sky'. Sex is a natural instinct which however can lead to lives of utter misery. The same sun that blesses, can curse.

Tess drifts into marriage with Angel (her most characteristic way of moving in a landscape is a 'quiescent glide'), because 'every wave of her blood . . . was a voice that joined with nature in revolt against her scrupulousness', but meanwhile 'at half-past six the sun settled down upon the levels, with the aspect of a great forge in the heavens'. This suggests not a drawing-up into growth, but a slow inexorable downward crushing force, through an image linked to that machinery which will later pummel her body. It is as though the universe turns metallic against Tess, just as we read when Angel rejects her that there is in him a hard negating force 'like a vein of metal in a soft loam'. This is the metal which her soft flesh runs up against. Other omens follow on her journey towards her wedding. Her feeling that she has seen the d'Urber-ville coach before; the postillion who takes them to church and who has 'a permanent running wound on the outside of his right leg'; the ominous 'afternoon crow' and so on. I want to point to another omen, when the sun seems to single out Tess in a sinister way. It is worth reminding ourselves that when Angel finally does propose to Tess she is quite sun-drenched. They are standing on the 'red-brick' floor and the sun slants in 'upon her inclining face, upon the blue veins of her temple, upon her naked arm, and her neck, and into the depths of her hair'. Now, on what should be the first night of her honeymoon we read : 'The sun was so low on that short, last afternoon of the year that it shone in through a small opening and formed a golden staff which stretched across to her skirt, where it made a spot like a paint-mark set upon her'. She has been marked before – first, with the blood of a dying

beast, now with a mark from the setting sun. We find other descriptions of how the sun shines on Tess subsequently, but let us
return to that crimson bed which, I suggested, effectively marked
the end of Tess's journey. 'A shaft of dazzling sunlight glanced
into the room, revealing heavy, old-fashioned furniture, crimson
damask hangings, and an enormous four-poster bedstead. . . .'
The sun and the redness which have marked Tess's life, now con-
verge at the moment of her approaching death. Finally Tess takes
her last rest on the altar of Stonehenge. She speaks to Angel –
again, it is before dawn, that sunless part of the day when he can
communicate with her.

> 'Did they sacrifice to God here?' asked she.
> 'No', said he.
> 'Who to?'
> 'I believe to the sun. That lofty stone set away by itself is in
> the direction of the sun, which will presently rise behind it.'

When the sun does rise it also reveals the policemen closing in, for
it is society which demands a specific revenge upon Tess. But in
the configuration of omens which, I think, is the major part of
the book, Tess is indeed a victim, sacrificed to the sun. The
heathen temple is fitting, since of course Tess is descended from
Pagan d'Urberville, and Hardy makes no scruple about asserting
that women 'retain in their souls far more of the Pagan fantasy of
their remote forefathers than of the systematized religion taught
their race at a later date'. This raises an important point. Is Tess
a victim of society, or of nature? Who wants her blood, who is
after her, the policemen, or the sun? Or are they in some sadistic
conspiracy so that we see nature and society converging on Tess
to destroy her? I will return to this question.

To the convergence of redness and the sun we must add the
great final fact of the altar, an altar which Tess approaches almost
gratefully, and on which she takes up her sacrificial position with
exhausted relief. She says (I have run some of her words to Angel
together): 'I don't want to go any further, Angel. . . . Can't we
bide here? . . . you used to say at Talbothays that I was a heathen.
So now I am at home . . . I like very much to be here.' Fully to be
human is partly to be heathen, as the figure of Tess on the altar

makes clear. (And after all what did heathen originally mean? – someone who lived on the heath; and what was a pagan? – someone who lived in a remote village. The terms only acquire their opprobrium after the advent of Christianity. Similarly Hardy points out that Sunday was originally the sun's day – a spiritual superstructure has been imposed on a physical source.) Tess's willingness to take her place on the stone of death has been manifested before. After she returns from the rape we read 'her depression was then terrible, and she could have hidden herself in a tomb'. On her marriage night, Angel sleepwalks into her room, saying 'Dead! Dead! Dead! . . . My wife – dead, dead!' He picks her up, kisses her (which he can now only manage when he is unconscious), and carries her over a racing river. Tess almost wants to jog him so that they can fall to their deaths : but Angel can negotiate the dangers of turbulent water just as he can suppress all passion. His steps are not directed towards the movement of the waters but to the stillness of stone. He takes Tess and lays her in an 'empty stone coffin' in the 'ruined choir'. In Angel's life of suppressed spontaneity and the negation of passional feeling, this is the most significant thing that he does. He encoffins the sexual instinct, then lies down beside Tess. The deepest inclinations of his psyche, his very being, have been revealed.

Later on, when things are utterly desperate for Tess's family and they literally have no roof over their heads, they take refuge by the church in which the family vaults are kept (where 'the bones of her ancestors – her useless ancestors – lay entombed'). In their exhaustion they erect an old 'four-post bedstead' over the vaults. We see again the intimate proximity of the bed and the grave. This sombre contiguity also adumbrates the ambiguous relief which Tess later finds in her crimson four-post-bed which is also very close to death. On this occasion Tess enters the church and pauses by the 'tombs of the family' and 'the door of her ancestral sepulchre'. It is at this point that one of the tomb effigies moves, and Alec plays his insane jest on her by appearing to leap from a tomb. Again, we are invited to make the starkest sort of comparison without any exegesis from Hardy. Angel, asleep, took Tess in his arms and laid her in a coffin. Alec, however, seems to wake up from the tomb, a crude but animated threat to Tess

in her quest for peace. Angel's instinct towards stillness is countered by Alec's instinct for sexual motion. Together they add up
to a continuous process in which Tess is simply caught up. For it
is both men who drive Tess to her death : Angel by his spiritualised rejection, Alec by his sexual attacks. It is notable that both
these men are also cut off from any fixed community; they have
both broken away from traditional attitudes and dwellings. Angel
roams in his thought; Alec roams in his lust. They are both drifters
of the sort who have an unsettling, often destructive impact in
the Hardy world. Tess is a pure product of nature; but she is
nature subject to complex and contradictory pressures. Angel
wants her spiritual image without her body (when he finds out
about her sexual past he simply denies her identity, 'the woman I
have been loving is not you'); Alec wants only her body and is
indifferent to anything we might call her soul, her distinctly
human inwardness. The effect of this opposed wrenching on her
wholeness is to induce a sort of inner rift which develops into
something we would now call a schizophrenia. While still at Talbothays she says one day : 'I do know that our souls can be made
to go outside our bodies when we are alive.' Her method is to
fix the mind on a remote star and 'you will soon find that you are
hundreds and hundreds o' miles away from your body, which you
don't seem to want at all'. The deep mystery by which consciousness can seek to be delivered from the body which sustains it, is
one which Hardy had clearly before him. That an organism can
be generated which then wishes to repudiate the very grounds of
its existence obviously struck Hardy as providing a very awesome
comment on the nature of nature. Tess is robbed of her integrated singleness, divided by two men, two forces. (This gives
extra point to the various crosses she passes on her travels; the
cross not only indicating torture, but that opposition between
the vertical and the horizontal which, as I shall try to show, is
ultimately the source of Tess's – and man's – sufferings in Hardy.)
It is no wonder that when Alec worries and pursues her at the
very door of her ancestors' vault, she should bend down and whis-
per that line of terrible simplicity – 'Why am I on the wrong side
of this door?' (A relevant poem of great power is 'A Wasted Illness'
of which I quote three stanzas which are very apt for Tess :

'Where lies the end
To this foul way?' I asked with weakening breath.
Thereon ahead I saw a door extend –
The door to Death.

It loomed more clear:
'At last!' I cried. 'The all-delivering door!'
And then, I know not how, it grew less near
Than theretofore.

And back slid I
Along the galleries by which I came,
And tediously the day returned, and sky,
And life – the same.)

Tess at this moment is utterly unplaced, with no refuge and no comfort. She can only stumble along more and rougher roads; increasingly vulnerable, weary and helpless, increasingly remote from her body. Her only solution is to break through that 'all-delivering door', the door from life to death which opens on the only home left to her. This she does, by stabbing Alec and then taking her place on the ritual altar. She has finally spilled all the blood that tormented her; she can then abandon the torments of animateness and seek out the lasting repose she has earned.

v

This brings me to what is perhaps the most searching of all Hardy's preoccupations – walking, travelling, movement of all kinds. Somewhere at the heart of his vision is a profound sense of what we may call the mystery of motion. *Tess of the d'Urbervilles* opens with a man staggering on rickety legs down a road, and it is his daughter we shall see walking throughout the book. Phase the Second opens, once again, simply with an unexplained scene of laboured walking. 'The basket was heavy and the bundle was large, but she lugged them along like a person who did not find her especial burden in material things. Occasionally she stopped to rest in a mechanical way by some gate or post; and then, giving the baggage another hitch upon her full round arm, went steadily

on again.' Such visualised passages carry the meaning of the novel,
even down to the material burdens which weigh down that
plump, vulnerable flesh : the meaning is both mute and unmistakable. At the start of Phase the Third, again Tess moves : 'she
left her home for the second time'. At first the journey seems easy
and comfortable in 'a hired trap'; but soon she gets out and walks,
and her journey again leads her into portents of the life ahead
of her. 'The journey over the intervening uplands and lowlands
of Egdon, when she reached them, was a more troublesome walk
than she had anticipated, the distance being actually but a few
miles. It was two hours, owing to sundry turnings, 'ere she found
herself on a summit commanding the long-sought-for vale. . . .'
The road to the peaceful vale of death is longer and harder than
she thinks. Always Tess has to move, usually to harsher and more
punishing territories, and always Hardy makes sure we *see* her.
After Angel has banished her : 'instead of a bride with boxes and
trunks which others bore, we see her a lonely woman with a basket
and a bundle in her own porterage. . . .' Later she walks to Em-
minster Vicarage on her abortive journey to see Angel's parents.
She starts off briskly but by the end she is weary, and there are
omens by the way. For instance, from one eminence she looks
down at endless little fields, 'so numerous that they look from this
height like the meshes of a net'. And again she passes a stone
cross, Cross-in-Hand, which stands 'desolate and silent, to mark
the site of a miracle, or murder, or both'. (Note the hint of the
profound ambivalence and ambiguity of deeds and events.) At
the end of this journey there is nobody at home and there follows the incident of Tess losing her walking boots, another physical reminder that the walking gets harder and harder for her.
'Her journey back was rather a meander than a march. It had
no sprightliness, no purpose; only a tendency.' Her movements
do get more leaden throughout, and by the end Hardy confronts
us with one of the strangest phenomena of existence – motion
without volition. (Interestingly enough, Conrad approaches the
same phenomenon in *The Secret Agent* where walking is also the
most insistent motif.) The only relief in her walking is that as
it gets harder it also approaches nearer to darkness. Thus when
she is summoned back to her family : 'She plunged into the

chilly equinoctial darkness . . . for her fifteen miles' walk under the steely stars'; and later during this walk from another eminence she 'looked from that height into the abyss of chaotic shade which was all that revealed itself of the vale on whose further side she was born'. She is indeed returning home, just as Oedipus was returning home on all his journeyings. Perhaps the ultimate reduction of Tess, the distillation of her fate, is to be seen when she runs after Angel having murdered Alec. Angel turns round. 'The tape-like surface of the road diminished in his rear as far as he could see, and as he gazed a moving spot intruded on the white vacuity of its perspective.' This scene has been anticipated when Tess was working at Flintcomb-Ash: 'the whole field was in colour a desolate drab; it was a complexion without features, as if a face, from chin to brow, should be only an expanse of skin. The sky wore, in another colour, the same likeness; a white vacuity of countenance with the lineaments gone. So these two upper and nether visages confronted each other all day long . . . without anything standing between them but the two girls crawling over the surface of the former like flies.' In both cases we see Tess as a moving spot on a white vacuity. And this extreme pictorial reduction seems to me to be right at the heart of Hardy's vision.

VI

To explain what I mean I want to interpose a few comments on some remarkable passages from the earlier novel, *The Return of the Native*. Chapter I describes the vast inert heath. Chapter II opens 'Along the road walked an old man'. He in turn sees a tiny speck of movement – 'the single atom of life that the scene contained'. And this spot is a 'lurid red'. It is, of course, the reddleman, but I want to emphasise the composition of the scene – the great stillness and the tiny spot of red movement which is the human presence on the heath. Shortly after, the reddleman is scanning the heath (Hardy's world is full of watching eyes) and it is then that he first sees Eustacia Vye. But how he first sees her is described in a passage which seems to me so central to Hardy that I want to quote at length.

There the form stood, motionless as the hill beneath. Above the plain rose the hill, above the hill rose the barrow, and above the barrow rose the figure. Above the figure there was nothing that could be mapped elsewhere than on a celestial globe.

Such a perfect, delicate, and necessary finish did the figure give to the dark pile of hills that it seemed to be the only obvious justification of their outline. Without it, there was the dome without the lantern; with it the architectural demands of the mass were satisfied. The scene was strangely homogeneous. The vale, the upland, the barrow, and the figure above it amounted to unity. Looking at this or that member of the group was not observing a complete thing, but a fraction of a thing.

The form was so much like an organic part of the entire motionless structure that to see it move would have impressed the mind as a strange phenomenon. Immobility being the chief characteristic of that whole which the person formed portion of, the discontinuance of immobility in any quarter suggested confusion.

Yet that is what happened. The figure perceptibly gave up its fixity, shifted a step or two, and turned round.

Here in powerful visual terms is a complete statement about existence. Without the human presence, sheer land and sky seem to have no formal, architectural significance. The human form brings significant outline to the brown mass of earth, the white vacuity of sky. But this moment of satisfying formal harmony depends on stillness, and to be human is to be animated, is to move. Hardy's novels are about 'the discontinuance of immobility'; all the confusions that make up his plots are the result of people who perceptibly give up their fixity. To say that this is the very condition of life itself is only to point to the elemental nature of Hardy's art. All plants and all animals move, but much more within rhythms ordained by their native terrain than humans – who build things like the *Titanic* and go plunging off into the night sea, or who set out in a horse and cart in the middle of the night to reach a distant market, in both cases meeting with disastrous accidents. Only what moves can crash. Eustacia moves on the still heath, breaking up the unity: there is confusion ahead for her. Not indeed that the heath is in a state of absolute fixity; that would imply a dead planet: 'the quality of repose appertaining to the scene . . . was not the repose of actual stagnation, but the apparent repose of incredible slowness'. Hardy often reminds us of the mindless insect life going on near the feet of his bewildered human protagonists; but to the human eye, which after all determines the felt meaning of the perceptible world, there is a movement which is like stillness just as there is a motion which seems to be unmitigated violence. The 'incredible slowness' of the heath, only serves to make more graphic the 'catastrophic dash' which ends the lives of Eustacia and Wildeve. And after the 'catastrophic dash' – 'eternal rigidity'.

The tragic tension between human and heath, between motion and repose, between the organic drive away from the inorganic and, what turns out to be the same thing, the drive to return to the inorganic, provides Hardy with the radical structure of his finest work. The human struggle against – and temporary departure from – the level stillness of the heath, is part of that struggle between the vertical and the horizontal which is a crucial part of Hardy's vision. We read of the 'oppressive horizontality' of the heath, and when Eustacia comes to the time of her death Hardy describes her position in such a way that it echoes the first time we saw her, and completes the pattern of her life. She returns to one of those ancient earthen grave mounds, called barrows. 'Eustacia at length reached Rainbarrow, and stood still there to think . . . she sighed bitterly and ceased to stand erect, gradually crouching down under the umbrella as if she were drawn into the Barrow by a hand from underneath.' Her period of motion is over; her erect status above the flatness of the heath terminates at the same moment; she is, as it were, drawn back into the undifferentiated levelness of the earth from which she emerged. At the same time, you will remember, Susan is tormenting and burning a wax effigy of Eustacia, so that while she seems to be sinking back into the earth Hardy can also write 'the effigy of Eustacia was melting to nothing'. She is losing her distinguishing outline and features. Hardy describes elsewhere how a woman starts to 'lose her own margin' when working the fields. Human life is featured and contoured life : yet the erosion of feature and contour seems to be a primal activity of that 'featureless convexity' of the heath, of the earth itself.

VII

This feeling of the constant attrition, and final obliteration, of the human shape and all human structures, permeates Hardy's work. Interviewed about Stonehenge he commented that 'it is a matter of wonder that the erection has stood so long', adding however that 'time nibbles year after year' at the structure. Just so he will write of a wind 'which seemed to gnaw at the corners of the house'; of 'wooden posts rubbed to a glossy smoothness by the flanks of infinite cows and calves of bygone years'. His work is full of decaying architecture, and in *The Woodlanders* there is a memorable picture of the calves roaming in the ruins of Sherton Castle, 'cooling their thirsty tongues by licking the quaint Norman carving, which glistened with the moisture'. It is as though time, and all the rest of the natural order, conspired to eat away and erase all the structures and features associated with the human presence on, or intrusion into, the planet. Of one part of the heath Hardy says, in a sentence of extraordinarily succinct power, 'There had been no obliteration, because there had been no tending'. Tess working at Flintcomb-Ash in a landscape which is 'a complexion without features', and Tess running after Angel, 'a moving spot intruding on the white vacuity', is a visible paradigm of the terms of human life – a spot of featured animation moving painfully across a vast featureless repose. Like Eustacia, and like her wounded horse Prince, having remained upright as long as possible, she, too, simply 'ceases to stand erect' and lies down on the flat sacrificial stone, as though offering herself not only up to the sun which tended her, but to the obliterating earth, the horizontal inertia of which she had disturbed.

Life is movement, and movement leads to confusion. Tess's instinct is for placidity, she recoils from rapid movements. Yet at crucial times she finds herself in men's carriages or men's machines. She has to drive her father's cart to market and Prince is killed. Alec forces her into his dog-cart which he drives recklessly at great speed. Of Tess we read 'the least irregularity of motion startled her' and Alec at this point is disturbing and shaking up blood which will only be stilled in death. Angel, by contrast, takes

Tess to the wedding in a carriage which manages to suggest something brutal, punitive, and funereal all at once – 'It had stout wheel-spokes, and heavy felloes, a great curved bed, immense straps and springs, and a pole like a battering-ram.' All these man-made conveyances, together with the ominous train, and that 'tyrant' the threshing machine, seem to threaten Tess. And yet she is bound to be involved in travelling, and dangerous motion, because she has no home. At the beginning the parson telling Tess's father about his noble lineage says an ominous thing. To Jack's question, 'Where do we d'Urbervilles live?' he answers : 'You don't live anywhere. You are extinct – as a county family.' Tess does not live anywhere. The one home she finds, Angel turns her out of. That is why she is bound to succumb to Alec. He provides a place but not a home. Alec takes her to Sandbourne, a place of 'detached mansions', the very reverse of a community. It is a 'pleasure city', 'a glittering novelty', a place of meretricious fashion and amusement. "Tis all lodging-houses here. . . .' This is the perfect place for the modern, deracinated Alec. It is no place at all for Tess, 'a cottage girl'. But we have seen her uprooted, forced to the roads, ejected from houses, knocking on doors which remain closed to her; we have seen the process by which she has become an exhausted helpless prey who is finally bundled off to a boarding house. Her spell in this place is a drugged interlude; she seems finally to have come to that state of catatonic trance which has been anticipated in previous episodes.

Angel realises that 'Tess had spiritually ceased to recognize the body before him as hers – allowing it to drift, like a corpse upon the current, in a direction dissociated from its living will'. Tess has been so 'disturbed' by irregularities of motion, so pulled in different directions, that she really is sick, split, half dead. Hardy was very interested in this sort of split person – for instance, people with primitive instincts and modern nerves, as he says in another book – and we can see that Tess is subjected to too many different pressures, not to say torments, ever to achieve a felicitous wholeness of being.

VIII

This brings me to a problem I mentioned earlier. We see Tess
suffering, apparently doomed to suffer; destroyed by two men, by
society, by the sun outside her and the blood inside her. And we
are tempted to ask, what is Hardy's vision of the *cause* of this tale
of suffering. Throughout the book Hardy stresses that Tess is
damned, and damns herself, according to man-made laws which
are as arbitrary as they are cruel. He goes out of his way to show
how Nature seems to disdain, ignore or make mockery of the
laws which social beings impose on themselves. The fetish of chastity is a ludicrous aberration in a world which teems and spills
with such promiscuous and far-flung fertility every year (not to say
a brutal caricature of human justice in that what was damned in
the woman was condoned in the man). So, if the book was an
attempt to show an innocent girl who is destroyed by society
though justified by Nature, Hardy could certainly have left the
opposition as direct and as simple as that. Social laws hang Tess;
and Nature admits no such laws. But it is an important part of
the book that we feel Nature itself turning against Tess, so that we
register something approaching a sadism of *both* the man-made
and the natural directed against her. If she is tortured by the man-
made threshing machine, she is also crushed by the forge of the sun;
the cold negating metal in Angel is also to be found in the 'steely
stars'; the pangs of guilt which lacerate her are matched by the
'glass splinters' of rain which penetrate her at Flintcomb-Ash.
Perhaps to understand this feeling of almost universal opposition
which grows throughout the book, we should turn to some of
Hardy's own words, when he talks of 'the universal harshness
. . . the harshness of the position towards the temperament, of the
means towards the aims, of today towards yesterday, of hereafter
towards today'. When he meditates on the imminent disappearance of the d'Urberville family he says, 'so does Time ruthlessly
destroy his own romances'. This suggests a universe of radical
opposition, working to destroy what it works to create, crushing
to death what it coaxes into life. From this point of view society
only appears as a functioning part of a larger process whereby the

vertical returns to the horizontal, motion lapses into stillness and structure cedes to the unstructured. The policemen appear as the sun rises : Tess is a sacrifice to both, to all of them. Hardy's vision is tragic and penetrates far deeper than specific social anomalies. One is more inclined to think of Sophocles than, say, Zola, when reading Hardy. The vision is tragic because he shows an ordering of existence in which nature turns against itself, in which the sun blasts what·it blesses, in which all the hopeful explorations of life turn out to have been a circuitous peregrination towards death. 'All things are born to be diminished' said Pericles at the time of Sophocles; and Hardy's comparable feeling that all things are tended to be obliterated, reveals a Sophoclean grasp of the bed-rock ironies of existence.

Tess is the living demonstration of these tragic ironies. That is why she who is raped lives to be hanged; why she who is so physically beautiful feels guilt at 'inhabiting the fleshly taber-nacle with which Nature had endowed her'; why she who is a fertile source of life comes to feel that 'birth itself was an ordeal of degrading personal compulsion, whose gratuitousness nothing in the result seemed to justify'. It is why she attracts the incom-patible forces represented by Alec and Angel. It is why she who is a lover is also a killer. Tess is gradually crucified on the oppug-nant ironies of circumstance and existence itself, ironies which centre, I have suggested, on the fact of blood, that basic stuff which starts the human spot moving across the white vacuity. Blood, and the spilling of blood; which in one set of circum-stances can mean sexual passion and the creation of life, and in another can mean murderous passion and death – two forms of 'red' energy intimately related – this is the substance of Tess's story. And why should it all happen to her? You can say, as some people in the book say fatalistically, 'It was to be'. Or you could go through the book and try to work out how Hardy apportions the blame – a bit on Tess, a bit on society, a bit on religion, a bit on heredity, a bit on the Industrial Revolution, a bit on the men who abuse her, a bit on the sun and the stars, and so on. But Hardy does not work in this way. More than make us judge, Hardy makes us see; and in looking for some explanation of why all this should happen to Tess, our eyes finally settle on that red ribbon marking out the little girl in the white dress, which already foreshadows the red blood stain on the white ceiling. In her beginning is her end. It is the oldest of truths, but it takes a great writer to make us experience it again in all its awesome mystery.

I X

Hardy specifically rejected the idea of offering any theory of the universe. In his General Preface to his works, he said 'Nor is it likely, indeed, that imaginative writings extending over more than forty years would exhibit a coherent scientific theory of the universe even if it had been attempted – of that universe concerning which Spencer owns to the "paralyzing thought" that possibly there exists no comprehension of it anywhere. But such objectless consistency never has been attempted. . . .' Hardy 'theorizes' far less than Lawrence, but certain images recur which serve to convey his sense of life – its poignancy and its incomprehensibility – more memorably than any overt statement. Death, the sudden end of brilliance and movement, occupied a constant place in his thoughts. 'The most prosaic man becomes a poem when you stand by his grave and think of him' he once wrote; and the strange brightness of ephemeral creatures is something one often meets in his fiction – pictorially, not philosophically. 'Gnats, knowing nothing of their brief glorification, wandered across the shimmer of this pathway, irradiated as if they bore fire within them, then passed out of its line, and were quite extinct.' Compare with that the description of the girls returning from the dance : 'and as they went there moved onward with them . . . a circle of opalized light, formed by the moon's rays upon the glistening sheet of dew. Each pedestrian could see no halo but his or her own. . . .' Hardy is often to be found stressing the ephemeral nature of life – 'independent worlds of ephemerons were passing their time in mad carousal', 'ephemeral creatures, took up their positions where only a year ago other had stood in their place when these were nothing more than germs and inorganic particles' – and it often seems that the ephemeral fragments of moving life are also like bubbles of light, temporary illuminations of an encroaching darkness. One of the great scenes in all of Hardy is in *The Return of the Native* when Wildeve and Venn, the reddleman, gamble at night on the heath. Their lantern makes a little circle of light which draws things out of the darkness towards it. 'The light of the candle had by this time attracted heath-flies, moths and other winged creatures of night, which floated round the lantern, flew into the flame, or beat about the faces of the two players.' Much more suggestivly as they continue to throw dice : 'they were surrounded by dusky forms about four feet high, standing a few paces beyond the rays of the lantern. A moment's inspection revealed that the encircling figures were heath-croppers, their heads being all towards the players, at whom they gazed intently.' When a moth extinguishes the candle, Wildeve gathers glow worms and puts them on the stone on which they are playing. 'The incongruity between the men's deeds and their environment was great. Amid the soft juicy vegetation of the hollow in which they sat, the motionless and the uninhabited solitude, intruded the chink of guineas, the rattle of dice, the exclamations of the reckless players.' Again, it is one of those scenes which seems to condense a whole vision of human existence – a strange activity in a small circle of light, and all round them the horses of the night noiselessly gathering at the very perimeter. And in *Tess of the d'Urbervilles* Hardy develops this scene into a metaphor of great power. He is describing how Tess's love for Angel sustains her : 'it enveloped her as a photosphere, irradiated her into forgetfulness of her past sorrows, keeping back the gloomy spectres that would persist in their attempts to touch her – doubt, fear, moodiness, care, shame. She knew that they were waiting like wolves just outside the circumscribing light, but she had long spells of power to keep them in hungry subjection there. . . . She walked in brightness, but she knew that in the background those shapes of darkness were always spread.'

I have singled out this image not only because I think there is something quintessentially Hardyan in it, but also because I think it is an image which profoundly influenced D. H. Lawrence. Here is a final quotation, taken from the culmination of perhaps his greatest novel, *The Rainbow*. Ursula is trying to clarify her sense of her own presence in the world.

This world in which she lived was like a circle lighted by a lamp. This lighted area, lit up by man's completest consciousness, she thought was all the world : that here all was disclosed for ever. Yet all the time, within the darkness she had been aware of points of light, like the eyes of wild beasts, gleaming, penetrating, vanishing. And her soul had acknowledged in a great heave of terror only the outer darkness. This inner circle of light in which she lived and moved, wherein the trains rushed and the factories ground out their machine-produce and the plants and the animals worked by the light of science and knowledge, suddenly it seemed like the area under an arc lamp, wherein the moths and children played in the security of blinding light, not even knowing there was any darkness, because they stayed in the light.

But she could see the glimmer of dark movement just out of range, she saw the eyes of the wild beast gleaming from the darkness, watching the vanity of the camp fire and the sleepers; she felt the strange, foolish vanity of the camp, which said 'Beyond our light and our order there is nothing', turning their faces always inwards toward the sinking fire of illuminating consciousness, which comprised sun and stars, and the Creator, and the System of Righteousness, ignoring always the vast shapes that wheeled round about, with half-revealed shapes lurking on the edge. . . .
Nevertheless the darkness wheeled round about, with grey shadow-shapes of wild beasts, and also with dark shadow-shapes of the angels, whom the light fenced out, as it fenced out the more familiar beasts of darkness.

Lawrence, more insistent as to the torments and sterilities of consciousness, confidently ascribes positive values to the shapes prowling around the perimeter of the circle of light. But Lawrence's *interpretation* – itself an act of consciousness – of the population of the dark, is only something overlayed on the *situation*, that irreducible configuration which is to be found, I suggest, at the heart of Hardy's work. 'She walked in brightness, but she knew that in the background those shapes of darkness were always spread.'

S o u r c e : *Critical Quarterly*, 10 (Autumn 1968).

IV *Jude the Obscure*

Robert B. Heilman

HARDY'S SUE BRIDEHEAD (1965)

In *Jude the Obscure*, a novel in which skillful characterization eventually wins the day over laborious editorializing, Thomas Hardy comes close to genius in the portrayal of Sue Bridehead. Sue takes the book away from the title character, because she is stronger, more complex, and more significant, and because her contradictory impulses, creating a spontaneous air of the inexplicable and even the mysterious, are dramatized with extraordinary fullness and concreteness, and with hardly a word of interpretation or admonishment by the author. To say this is to say that as a character she has taken off on her own, sped far away from a conceptual role, and developed as a being whose brilliant and puzzling surface provides only partial clues to the depths in which we can sense the presence of profound and representative problems.

Sue's original role, of course, is that of counterpoint to Arabella : spirit against flesh, or Houyhnhnm against Yahoo. Sue and Arabella are meant to represent different sides of Jude, who consistently thinks about them together, contrasts them, regards them as mutually exclusive opposites (e.g. III, 9, 10; IV, 5). Early in their acquaintance he sees in Sue 'almost an ideality' (II, 4), 'almost a divinity' (III, 3); the better he gets to know her, the more he uses, in speech or thought, such terms as 'ethereal' (III, 9; IV, 3; VI,.3), 'uncarnate' (III, 9), 'aerial' (IV, 3), 'spirit, . . . disembodied creature . . . hardly flesh' (IV, 5), 'phantasmal, bodiless creature' (V, 1), 'least sensual', 'a sort of fay, or sprite' (VI, 3). She herself asks Jude to kiss her 'incorporeally' (V, 4), and she puts Mrs. Edlin 'in mind of a sperrit' (VI, 9).

[handwritten annotation:] ✓ Sue takes away the book on the 2nd + 3rd readings but by the 4th it is firmly and unreadably Jude's. (Cloud 9 ? ?)

The allegorical content in Hardy's delineation of Sue has also
a historical base : she is made a figure of Shelleyan idealism. When
Phillotson describes the rather spiritualized affinity that he perceives between Jude and Sue, Gillingham exclaims 'Platonic !'
and Phillotson qualifies, 'Well, no. Shelleyan would be nearer
to it. They remind me of Laon and Cythna' (IV, 4), the idealized
liberators and martyrs in *The Revolt of Islam* (which is quoted
later in another context – v, 4). Sue asks Jude to apply to her
certain lines from Shelley's 'Epipsychidion' – '. . . a Being whom
my spirit oft/Met on its visioned wanderings far aloft. . . . A seraph
of Heaven, too gentle to be human' (IV, 5) – and Jude later calls
Sue a 'sensitive plant' (VI, 3).

Deliberately or instinctively Hardy is using certain Romantic
values as a critical instrument against those of his own day, a free
spirit against an oppressive society, the ethereal against commonplace and material. But a very odd thing happens : in conceiving
of Sue as 'spirit', and then letting her develop logically in such
terms, he finds her coming up with a powerful aversion to sex –
in other words, with a strong infusion of the very Victorianism
that many of her feelings and intellectual attitudes run counter
to. On the one hand, her objection to allegorizing the Song of
Solomon (III, 4) is anti-Victorian; but when, in refusing to have
intercourse with Jude, she says, 'I resolved to trust you to set my
wishes above your gratification', her view of herself as a supra-
sexual holder of prerogative and of him as a mere seeker of 'gratification' is quite Victorian. She calls him 'gross', apparently both
for his night with Arabella and for desiring her physically, and
under her pressure he begs, 'Forgive me for being gross, as you
call it !' (IV, 5). Again, he uses the apologetic phrase, 'we poor unfortunate wretches of grosser substance' (v, 1). All of Sue's terms
for Arabella come out of middle-class propriety : 'fleshy, coarse
woman', 'low-passioned woman', 'too low, too coarse for you',
as does her argument that Jude should not go to help her because
'she's not your wife. . . .' Jude is not entirely pliant here; in fact,
there is some defiance in his saying that perhaps he is 'coarse, too,
worse luck !' But even while arguing against her refusal of sex he
can say that 'your freedom from everything that's gross has elevated me', accepting the current view of the male as a lower being

who needs to be lifted up to a higher life (v, 2). Even when, near the end, he is vehemently urging Sue not to break their union, he can entertain the possibility that in overturning her proscription of sex he may have 'spoiled one of the highest and purest loves that ever existed between man and woman' (vi, 3); the 'average sensual man' all but gives up his case to a conventional opinion of his own time. Other aspects of Sue's vocabulary betray the Victorian tinge : when she first calls marriage a 'sordid contract' (iv, 2) it seems fresh and independent, but the continuing chorus of 'horrible and sordid' (v, 1), 'vulgar' and 'low' (v, 3), 'vulgar' and 'sordid' (v, 4) suggests finally an over-nice and complacent personality. The style is a spontaneous accompaniment of the moral elevation which she assumes in herself and which in part she uses – Hardy is very shrewd in getting at the power-sense in self-conscious 'virtue' – to keep Jude in subjection.

There is a very striking irony here : perhaps unwittingly Hardy has forged or come upon a link between a romantic idea of spirit (loftiness, freedom) and a Victorian self-congratulatory 'spiritual-ity' – a possibly remarkable feat of the historical imagination. He has also come fairly close to putting the novel on the side of the Houyhnhnms, a difficulty that he never gets around quite satis-factorily. But above all he has given a sharp image of inconsistency in Sue, for whatever the paradoxical link between her manifesta-tions of spirit, she nevertheless appears as the special outsider on the one hand and as quite conventional on the other. In this he continues a line of characterization that he has followed very skillfully from the beginning. Repeatedly he uses such words as 'perverseness', 'riddle' (iii, 1), 'conundrum' (iii, 2), 'unreason-able . . . capricious' (iii, 5), 'perverse', 'colossal inconsistency' (iii, 7), 'elusiveness of her curious double nature', 'ridiculously inconsistent' (iv, 2), 'logic . . . extraordinarily compounded', 'puzzling and unpredictable' (iv, 3), 'riddle' (iv, 4), 'that mys-tery, her heart' (iv, 5), 'ever evasive' (v, 5). With an inferior novelist, such an array of terms might be an effort to do by words what the action failed to do; here, they only show that Hardy knew what he was doing in the action, for all the difficulties, puzzles, and unpredictability have been dramatized with utmost variety and thoroughness. From the beginning, in major actions and lesser ones, Sue is consistently one thing and then another: reckless, then diffident; independent, then needing support; severe, and then kindly; inviting, and then offish. The portrayal of her is the major achievement of the novel. It is an imaginative feat, devoid of analytical props; for all of the descriptive words that he uses, Hardy never explains her or places her, as he is likely to do with lesser characters. She simply is, and it is up to the reader to sense the inner truth that creates multiple, lively, totally conflicting impressions. With her still more than with the other characters Hardy has escaped from the allegorical formula in which his addiction to such words as 'spirit' might have trapped him.

From the beginning her inconsistency has a pattern which teases us with obscure hints of an elusive meaningfulness. Her first action characterizes her economically; she buys nude statues of classical divinities, but 'trembled', almost repented, concealed them, misrepresented them to her landlady, and kept waking up anxiously at night (II, 3). She reads Gibbon but is superstitious about the scene of her first meeting with Jude (II, 4). She criticizes unrestrainedly the beliefs of Jude and Phillotson, but is wounded by any kind of retort (II, 5); repeatedly she can challenge, censure, and deride others but be hypersensitive to even mild replies, as if expecting immunity from the normal reciprocities of argument and emotion (III, 4; IV, 5; VI, 3, 4, 8). She reacts excessively to the unexpected visit of the school inspector, snaps at Phillotson 'petulantly', and then 'regretted that she had upbraided him' (II, 5). Aunt Drusilla reports that as a girl Sue was 'pert . . . too often, with her tight-strained nerves', and an inclination to scoff at the by-laws of modesty; she was a tomboy who would suddenly run away from the boys (II, 6).

These initial glimpses of Sue prepare for the remarkable central drama of the novel: her unceasing reversals, apparent changes of mind and heart, acceptances and rejections, alternations of warmth and offishness, of evasiveness and candor, of impulsive acts and later regrets, of commitment and withdrawal, of freedom and constraint, unconventionality and propriety. She is cool about seeing Jude, then very eager, then offish (III, 1). She escapes from confinement at school but appears increasingly

less up to the exploit already concluded (III, 3–5). She tells Jude,
'You mustn't love me', then writes 'you may', quarrels with him,
and writes, 'Forgive . . . my petulance. . . .' (III, 5). Before and
after marriage she resists talking about Phillotson ('But I am not
going to be cross-examined . . .') and then talks about him almost
without reserve (III, 6, 9; IV, 2). Again she forbids Jude to come
to see her (III, 9), then 'with sweet humility' revokes the prohibi-
tion (III, 10), is changeable when he comes, invites him for the
next week (IV, 1), and then cancels the invitation (IV, 2). She 'tear-
fully' refuses to kiss Jude, and then suddenly kisses him (IV, 3).
Hardy identifies, as a natural accompaniment of her shifting
of attitude and mood, a tendency to shift ground under pressure.
Since she dislikes firm reply, argument, or questioning from others,
she may simply declare herself 'hurt'. Another ploy is to make a
hyperbolic statement of desolation or self-condemnation. 'I *wish*
I had a friend here to support me; but nobody is ever on my
side!' (III, 5), 'I am in the wrong. I always am!' (IV, 3), 'I know
I am a poor, miserable creature' (IV, 5). Another self-protective
situation-controlling move is to fall back directly on her emotional
responsiveness to a difficult moment. She will not sleep with Jude
but is jealous of Arabella; so she simply tells Jude, '. . . I don't like
you as well as I did!' (IV, 5). When she will not acknowledge
loving him and he remarks on the danger of the game of elusiveness, her reply, 'in a tragic voice', is 'I don't think I like you today
so well as I did . . .' (V, 1). For all of her intellectual freedom,
she seems to accept the ancient dogma of 'women's whims' (IV, 5)
and calls Jude 'good' because 'you give way to all my whims!' (V,
4).

   Through all the sensitiveness, fragility, and caprice there appears an impulse for power, for retaining control of a situation,
very delicately or even overtly, in one's own terms. The Victorian
acceptance of woman's pedestal implies a superiority to be acknowledged. Early in the story, just after Jude sees 'in her almost
a divinity' (III, 3), Sue states candidly that she 'did want and long
to ennoble some man to high aims' (III, 4) – which might be pure
generosity or an idealism infected with egoism.* She trusts Jude

   * Just a little before *Jude* Ibsen was investigating this operation of
the power-sense beneath the appearance of exerting a noble in-

not to pursue her with a desire for 'gratification' (IV, 5). She would rather go on 'always' without sex because 'It is so much sweeter – for the woman at least, and when she is sure of the man' (V, 1). The reappearance of Arabella so disturbs Sue's confidence in ownership that she tries to get rid of Arabella without Jude's seeing her, and when that fails, accepts the sexual bond only as a necessary means of binding Jude to her (V, 2). This gives her new confidence – 'So I am not a bit frightened about losing you, now . . .' – and hence she resists marriage (V, 3). Behind this near-compulsion to prescribe terms is a need which Sue states three different times: 'Some women's love of being loved is insatiable' (IV, 1); 'But sometimes a woman's *love of being loved* gets the better of her conscience . . .' (IV, 5); 'the craving to attract and captivate, regardless of the injury it may do the man' (VI, 3). Here again Hardy avoids both allegory and that idealizing of a character whom her own associates find it easy to idealize.

At the center of hypersensitivity he perceives a self-concern which can mean a high insensitivity to others and hence a habit of hurting them which may actually embody an unconscious intention (another version of the power-sense). Despite her formal words of regret and self-censure, Sue seems almost to relish the complaint of the student that she 'was breaking his heart by hold-ing out against him so long at such close quarters' (III, 4). Though she resents criticism of or even disagreement with her, all that Jude believes in and holds dear she attacks with an unrestraint that ranges from inconsiderateness to condescension to an out-right desire to wound – the church, the university, and their traditions (III, 1, 2, and 4). Always careless of Phillotson's feelings, she does not even let him know about her expulsion from school (III, 6). Hardy presents her desire to leave Phillotson as under-standable and defensible, but at the same time he portrays her style with Phillotson as fantastically inconsiderate. For instance, as he 'writhed', she upbraided him in a doctrinaire style for not

---

fluence on a man – in *Rosmersholm* (1886) and *Hedda Gabler* (1890). In Rebecca West, the chief woman character in *Rosmersholm*, Ibsen was also noting the presence of irrational impulses in a woman strongly committed to modernist and rationalist views.

having a free mind as J. S. Mill advised (IV, 3); later, he lies 'writhing like a man in hell' (IV, 6) as she lets him think that her relation with Jude is adulterous. She is indifferent to Jude's feelings when she refuses to have sexual intercourse with him. She insists that Jude must 'love me dearly' (V, 3), but when he gives her an opening for speaking affectionately to him, she says only, 'You are always trying to make me confess to all sorts of absurdities' (V, 5). She moves variously toward self-protection, self-assertion, and self-indulgence. One of the most remarkable cases of giving way to her own feelings in complete disregard of their impact on others is her telling Father Time, 'vehemently', that 'Nature's law [is] mutual butchery!' (V, 6) – a view that with any imagination at all she would know him utterly unfitted to cope with. It prepares for her thoughtless reply of 'almost' to his statement that it 'would be better to be out o' the world than in it' and her total ineptitude in dealing with his surmise that all their trouble is due to the children and with his desperation in finding that there is to be another child. Sue actually provides the psychological occasion, if not the cause, of the double murder and suicide (VI, 2) – the disasters that, with massive irony, begin her downward course to death-in-life.

The final touch in Sue as Victorian is her 'I can't explain' when Father Time is driven frantic by the news that there will be another child. This is a lesser echo of 'Sue's embarrassment in all matters of sex – a disability the more marked in one who enters into otherwise intimate relations with a series of men. In her feeling free to deny the very center of the relationship what looks like naiveté or innocence masks a paradoxical double design of self-interest: she wants to be sexually attractive and powerful but to remain sexually unavailable. Sue has something of La Belle Dame Sans Merci, leaving men not 'palely loitering' but worse off than that: of the three men who have desired her, one finally has her but only as a shuddering sacrificial victim, and the other two die of 'consumption', which modern medical practice regards as predominantly of psychosomatic origin. She does give in to Jude, indeed, but immediately begins campaigning against marriage, and in terms so inapplicable – she repeatedly argues from the example of their earlier marriages, which are simply not relevant (e.g. v, 4) – that they exist not for their own sake but as a symbolic continuation of the resistance to sex. They secretly help to prepare us for her eventual flight from Jude, and to keep us from crediting her later statement that she and Jude found a pagan joy in sensual life (Hardy's belated effort to do something for sex, which he has hardly moved an inch from the most conventional position). True, she declares, just before resuming sexual relations with Phillotson, 'I find I still love [Jude] – oh, grossly!' (vi, 9), but at this time the words seem less an intuition of truth than a reaction from the horror of her penitential life; and it is noteworthy that, in whatever sense they may be true, they are spoken by her only when the action they imply is now finally beyond possibility.

La Belle Dame Sans Merci cannot practice mercilessness without being belle – beautiful, or charming, or fascinating. Though Sue may be, as Arabella puts it, 'not a particular warm-hearted creature' and 'a slim, fidgety little thing' who 'don't know what love is' (v, 5), even Gillingham feels what the three men in her life respond to, her 'indefinable charm' (vi, 5). She is always spontaneous, often vivacious, occasionally kindly and tender. More important, Hardy has caught a paradoxical and yet powerful kind of charm: the physical attractiveness of the person who seems hardly to have physical existence and hence evokes such terms as 'aerial' and 'ethereal'. The possibility that she unconsciously holds out to men in the enrichment of the ordinary sensual experience by its very opposite: all modes – or rather, the two extremes – of relationship are present at once in an extraordinary fusion. But this special charm is tenuously interwoven with the much more evident charm, the sheer power to fascinate, of an unpredictable personality. Though Sue may, as she herself theorizes, get into 'these scrapes' through 'curiosity to hunt up a new sensation', she does not have in her very much of the cold experimenter. Jude senses sadistic and masochistic elements in her (elements much noted by more recent critics). He theorizes that she 'wilfully gave herself and him pain' for the pleasure of feeling pity for both, and he suspects that she will 'go on inflicting such pains again and again, and grieving for the sufferer again and again' (iii, 7). Her selfishness is never consistent; she can be virtually ruthless in seeking ends, and then try to make reparation. She can be contemptuous and cutting, and then penitent and tearful. She can be daring and then scared ('scared' and 'frightened' are used of her repeatedly); inconsiderate, and then generous; self-indulgent, and then self-punishing; callous, and then all but heartbroken – always with a kind of rushing spontaneity. Such endless shifts as these, which Hardy presents with unflagging resourcefulness, make Jude call Sue a 'flirt' (IV, I). Jude merely names what the reader feels on page after page : the unconscious coquetry that Sue practices. The novel is, in one light, a remarkable treatment of coquetry, for it implicitly defines the underlying bases of the style. The ordinary coquette may tease and chill by plan, invite and hold off deliberately, heighten desire by displaying readiness and simulating retreat : the piquant puzzle. This is what Arabella offers with great crudity in the beginning ; Hardy's preparation, by contrast, for the brilliant unconscious tactics of Sue.

The true, ultimate coquette, the coquette in nature, has no plans, no deliberations, no contrived puzzles. Her inconsistency of act is the inconsistency of being. She goes this way, and then that way, for no other reason than that she cannot help it. She acts in terms of one impulse that seems clear and commanding, and is then pulled away by another that comes up and, though undefined, is not subject to her control. On the one hand, she freely puts conventional limitations behind her; on the other, she hardly comes up to conventional expectations. She has freedom of thought but not freedom of action and being. She is desirable but does not desire. She wishes to be desirable, which means making the moves that signify accessibility to desire; the cost of love is then a commitment from which she must frantically or stubbornly withdraw. She is thoughtless and even punitive, but she has pangs of conscience; yet to be certain that she has conscience, she must create situations that evoke pity for others and blame of self. Hardy catches very successfully the spontaneity of each of her acts and gestures; they are authentic, unprogrammed expressions of diverse elements in her personality. Coquetry is, in the end, the external drama of inner divisions, of divergent impulses each of which is strong enough to determine action at any time, but not

at all times or even with any regularity. The failure of unity is
greater than that of the ordinary personality, and the possibilities
of trouble correspondingly greater. If the coquette is not fortunate in finding men with great tolerance for her diversity – and
ordinarily she has an instinct for the type she needs – and situations that do not subject her to too great pressure, she will hardly
avoid disaster.

The split that creates the coquette is not unlike the tragic
split; the latter, of course, implies deeper emotional commitments
and more momentous situations. Yet one might entitle an essay
on Sue 'The Coquette as Tragic Heroine'. Because she has a
stronger personality than Jude, has more initiative, and endeavors
more to impose her will, she is closer to tragic stature than he.
Like traditional tragic heroes, she believes that she can dictate
terms and clothe herself in special immunities; like them, she
has finally to reckon with neglected elements in herself and in
the order of life. If the catastrophe which she helps precipitate is
not in the first instance her own, nevertheless it becomes a turning
point for her, a shock that opens up a new illumination, a new
sense of self and of the moral order. After the death of the children
Sue comes into some remarkable self-knowledge. She identifies
precisely her errors in dealing with Father Time (vi, 2). Her
phrase 'proud in my own conceit' describes her style as a free-
swinging critic of others and of the world. She recognizes that her
relations with Jude became sexual only when 'envy stimulated
me to oust Arabella'. She acknowledges to Jude, '. . . I merely
wanted you to love me . . . it began in the selfish and cruel wish
to make your heart ache for me without letting mine ache for
you.' Such passages, with their burden of tragic self-understand-
ing, predominate over others in which Sue looks for objects of
blame, falls into self-pity, or frantically repeats her ancient self-
protective plea, 'Don't criticize me, Jude – I can't bear it!' (vi, 3).

But the passages that indicate growth by understanding are
predominated over, in turn, by others in which Sue violently and
excessively blames herself and pronounces on herself a life sentence of the severest mortification that she can imagine. Under
great stress the precarious structure of her divided personality
has broken down, and it has been replaced by a narrow, rigid

unity under the tyrannical control of a single element in the personality – the self-blaming, self-flagellating impulse which Sue now
formulates in Christian terms but which has been part of her all
along. In place of the tragic understanding there is only black
misery. Hence she ignores all Jude's arguments; Hardy may sympathize with these, but he knows what development is in character for Sue. A basic lack of wholeness has been converted, by heavy
strains, into illness. Not that an imposition of a penalty is in itself pathological; we see no illness in the self-execution of Othello,
or, more comparably, in the self-blinding of Oedipus. Facts become clear to them, and they accept responsibility by prompt and
final action. Sue not only judges her ignoble deeds but undis-
criminatingly condemns a whole life; she converts all her deeds
into vice, and crawls into an everlasting hell on earth. Remorse has
become morbid, and punishment seems less a symbolic acknowledgement of error than the craving of a sick nature.

The problem is, then, whether the story of Sue merely touches
on tragedy, with its characteristic reordering of a chaotic moral
world, or becomes mainly a case history of clinical disorder, a
sardonic prediction of an endless night. As always, the problem of
illness is its representativeness : have we a special case, interesting
for its own sake, pitiable, shocking, but limited in its relevance,
or is the illness symbolic, containing a human truth that transcends its immediate terms? There is a real danger of reading Sue's
story as if its confines were quite narrow. If she is simply taken as
an undersexed woman, the human range will not seem a large
one. If she is simply defined as 'sado-masochistic', we have only
an abnormality. If she appears only as the victim of conventions
which the world should get rid of, the romantic rebel unjustly
punished, the intellectual range will seem too narrow, wholly
without the comprehensiveness of George Eliot, who could see at
once the pain inflicted by, and the inevitability of, conventions. If
she seems simply a person of insufficient maturity – and Hardy
uses the words *child* and *children* repeatedly of Jude and Sue, and
makes Sue say, '. . . I crave to get back to the life of my infancy
and its freedom' (III, 2) – we will seem to have only the obvious
truth that it is risky for a child to be abroad in a man's world. If
she seems simply an innocent or idealist done in by a harsh world,

the story will seem banal, if not actually sentimental. A Christian apologist might argue that her history shows the inescapability of Christian thought; an anti-Christian, that she is the victim of wrong ideas without which she would have been saved. The answer to the former is that such a Christian triumph would be a melancholy and hardly persuasive one, and to the latter that Sue's nature would find in whatever system of values might be available, religious or secular, the doctrinal grounds for acting out her own disorder.

She does not strike us, in the end, as of narrow significance. She is the rather familiar being whose resources are not up to the demands made upon them. This is not so much a matter of weakness and bad luck as it is of an impulsiveness and wilfulness that carry her beyond her depth; even as a child she shows signs of strain and tension. She has many of the makings of the nun, but she wants the world too; she is peculiarly in need of protection, but she wants always to assert and attack. She works partly from an unrecognized egotism, sometimes from an open desire to wound and conquer; her aggressiveness leads her into injurious actions not unlike those of tragic protagonists. Aside from inflicting unfulfilled relationships upon three men, she does a subtler but deeper injury to Jude : with a mixture of the deliberate and the wanton she helps undermine the beliefs that are apparently essential to his well-being; she cannot stand that he should have any gods but her own. She has the style of the blue-stocking who has found a new key to truth and is intolerant of all who have not opened the same door. Though she is sympathetic with Jude in many ways, she lacks the imagination to understand the real needs of his nature; instead of understanding either him or her substantial indifferences to his well-being, she volubly pities him because the university and the world are indifferent to him. Having lost his faith and hope, he leans heavily on her; then she takes that support away when her own needs set her on another course. Symbolically, she comes fairly close to husband-murder.

In them Hardy activates two important, and naturally hostile, strains of nineteenth-century thought and feeling. Jude is under the influence of the Tractarian Movement, which, appealing to some of the best minds in university and church, displayed great vitality in pursuing its traditionalist and anti-liberal aims. Yet his allegiance does not hold up under the blows of Sue's modernist criticism; she looks at Jude as a sort of archaelogical specimen, 'a man puzzling out his way along a labyrinth from which one had one's self escaped' (III, 2) and refers sarcastically to his 'Tractarian stage' as if he had not grown up (III, 4). So he falls into a secular liberalism which simply fails to sustain him. Sue, on the other hand, has felt the influence of utilitarianism (she quotes Mill to Phillotson very dogmatically); but her skepticism wilts under catastrophe, and she falls into an ascetic self-torment which utterly distorts the value of renunciation (the reduction of hubris to measure). Sue often talks about charity, but, despite her moments of sweetness and kindliness, it is hardly among her virtues; as a surrogate for charity to others she adopts a violent unchariteble-ness to herself.

Hardy may be intentionally commenting on the inadequacy of two important movements, perhaps because neither corresponds enough to human complexity. But as novelist he is rather exhibiting two characters who in different ways fail, despite unusual conscious attention to the problem, to find philosophical bases of life that are emotionally satisfactory. They like to think of them-selves as ahead of their times, but this is rather a device of self-reassurance in people who are less ahead of their times than not up to them. One suspects that in the twentieth century, which has done away with the obstacles that loomed large before their eyes, they would be no better off – either because they lack some essential strength for survival or because they elect roles too oner-ous for them. Hardy, indeed, has imagined characters who could hardly survive in any order less than idyllic.

In Sue the inadequacy of resources is a representative one that gives her character great resonance. The clue is provided by a crucial experience of her intellectual hero, John Stuart Mill: under the strain of a severe logical discipline he broke down and discovered the therapeutic value of poetry. Sue, so to speak, never finds a therapy. In all ways she is allied with a tradition of intellect; she is specifically made a child of the eighteenth century. She dislikes everything medieval, admires classical writers and architecture, looks at the work of neo-classical secular painters,

conspicuously reads eighteenth-century fiction and the satirists
of all ages. Jude calls her 'Voltairean', and she is a devotee of
Gibbon. She is influenced, among later figures, by Shelley as intellectual rebel, by Mill's liberalism, and by the new historical
criticism of Christianity. Rational skepticism, critical intelligence
are her aims; in his last interview with her, Jude attacks her for
losing her 'reason', 'faculties', 'brains', 'intellect' (vi, 8). Much as
she is an individual who cannot finally be identified by categories,
she is a child of the Enlightenment, with all its virtues and with
the liabilities inseparable from it. Hardy was very early in in-
tuiting, though he did not expressly define it, what in the twentieth century has become a familiar doctrine : the danger of trying
to live by rationality alone.

In Sue, Hardy detects the specific form of the danger : the
tendency of the skeptical intelligence to rule out the nonrational
foundations of life and security. Sue cuts herself off from the two
principal such foundations – from the community as it is expressed in traditional beliefs and institutions and from the physical reality of sex. The former she tends to regard as fraudulent
and coercive, the latter as 'gross'; in resisting marriage she resists
both, and so she has not much left. Her deficiency in sex, whatever
its precise psychological nature (we need not fall into the diag-
nositis of looking for a childhood trauma), is a logical correlative of
her enthroning of critical intellect; thus a private peculiarity takes
on a symbolic meaning of very wide relevance. The rationalist
drawing away from nonrational sources of relationship creates
the solitary; Sue is that, as she implies when, considering marriage
because of the arrival of Father Time, she remarks, sadly, '. . . I
feel myself getting intertwined with my kind' (v, 3). Precisely.
But she is unwilling to be quite the solitary, and for such a person,
the anchorite in search of an appropriate society, the natural
dream is a private utopia – an endless unconsummated idyll with a
single infinitely devoted lover.

At the heart of the drama of Sue is the always simmering revolt
of the modes of life which she rejects, the devious self-assertion of
the rejected values. Hence much of her inconsistency, of the
maddening reversals that constitute a natural coquetry, the wonderfully dramatized mystery that simply stands on its own until

the clues appear in the final section. Sue cannot really either reject
or accept men, and in attempting to do both at once she leaves
men irritated or troubled or desperate, and herself not much better
off. She revolts against conventions, but never without strain;
and here Hardy introduces an inner drama of conventions far
more significant than the criticisms leveled by Jude and Sue. He
detects in conventions, not merely inflexible and irrational pressures from without, but a power over human nature because of
the way in which human nature is constituted. Sue is one of the
first characters in fiction to make the honest mistake of regarding
a convention as only a needless constraint and forgetting that it
is a needed support, and hence of failing to recognize that the
problem admits of no easy pros or cons. As a social critic Hardy
may deplore the rigidity of conventions or the severity of their
impact, but as an artist he knows of their ubiquity in human experience and of their inextricability from consciousness. They are
always complexly present in the drama. At first Jude thinks that
there is 'nothing unconventional' in Sue (III, 2); then he decides
that 'you are as innocent as you are unconventional' (III, 4); still
later he accuses her of being 'as enslaved to the social code as any
woman I know' (IV, 5). The Sue who is devastatingly witty about
institutions finds herself constantly acting in terms of traditional
patterns. On one occasion she assures Jude that 'she despised herself for having been so conventional' (III, 10); on another she has
to acknowledge, 'I perceive I have said that in mere convention'
(IV, 1); and above all she says to Phillotson, '. . . I, of all people,
ought not to have cared what was said, for it was just what I
fancied I never did care for. But . . . my theoretic unconventionality broke down' (IV, 3). Then Jude, shocked when she joins
him but will not sleep with him, finds relief in the thought that
she has 'become conventional' rather than unloving, 'Much as,
under your teaching, I hate convention . . .' (IV, 5). Here she is
not clear herself, and she falls back mainly upon a concept whose
conventionality she appears not to recognize, 'woman's natural
timidity'. It is then that Jude accuses her of being 'enslaved to
the social code' and that she replies, 'Not mentally. But I haven't
the courage of my views . . .'. Her words betray the split between
reason and feeling, between the rational critique of the forms and

the emotional reliance upon them. This steady trail of comments, clashes, and partial acknowledgments leads up to the key event : in Christminster, she catches sight of Phillotson on the street, and she tells Jude, '. . . I felt a curious dread of him; an awe, or terror, of conventions I don't believe in' (vi, 1). It is the turning point; her suppressed emotions, her needs, so long harried by her 'reason', are seriously rebelling at last. 'Reason' can still phrase her assessment of the event : 'I am getting as superstitious as a savage !' Jude can lament the days 'when her intellect played like lambent lightning over conventions and formalities' (vi, 3) and somewhat complacently attack her for losing her 'scorn of convention' (vi, 8). But the defensiveness behind these criticisms soon emerges : as the defender of reason, Jude has also failed to find emotional anchorage, and his new independence of mind has provided him with no sustaining affirmations; and so he must blame Sue for deserting him.

Hardy has faithfully followed the character of Sue and has not let himself be deflated by his own sermonizing impulses. From the beginning he senses the split in her make-up – between rejections made by the mind, and emotional urgencies that she cannot deny or replace. If she is an 'epicure in emotions', it may partly be, as she says apologetically, because of a 'curiosity to hunt up a new sensation' (iii, 7), but mostly it is that a turmoil of emotions will not let the mind, intent on its total freedom, have its own way. Much more than he realizes Jude speaks for both of them when he says, 'And [our feelings] rule thoughts' (iv, 1). Sue's sensitivity, her liability to be 'hurt', is real, but she uses it strategically to cut off Jude's and Phillotson's thoughts when they run counter to those that she freely flings about; understandably Jude exclaims, 'You make such a personal matter of everything !' (iii, 4). Exactly; what appears to be thought is often personal feeling that must not be denied. Answerability, in ordinary as well as special situations, shakes her. On buying the Venus and Apollo she 'trembled' and at night 'kept waking up' (ii, 3). When the school inspector visits, she almost faints, and Phillotson's arm around her in public makes her uncomfortable (ii, 5). Repeatedly her feelings are very conventional : her embarrassment when Jude comes into the room where her wet clothes are hanging

(III, 3), her discomfort after rebelling at school (III, 5), her jealousy of Arabella (III, 6; v, 2, 3). She is 'evidently touched' by the hymn that moves Jude, she finds it 'odd . . . that I should care about' it, and she continues to play it (IV, 1). She is 'rather frightened' at leaving Phillotson (IV, 5). When she refuses to sleep with Jude, it is less that she is 'epicene' and 'boyish as a Ganymede' (III, 4) or that her 'nature is not so passionate as [his]' (IV, 5) than that joining Jude is an act of mind, of principled freedom, that does not have emotional support. Hence her singular scruple that 'my freedom has been obtained under false pretences!' (v, 1) – a rationalizing of feelings that, for all of her liking of Jude, run counter to their mode of life. Hardy rightly saw that only some very powerful emotional urgency could get her over the barrier between Jude and herself, and he supplies that in her jealousy of Arabella. It is a common emotion that her mind would want to reject; and it is notable that after giving in to Jude she gives voice to another conventional feeling – assuring him, and herself, that she is 'not a cold-natured, sexless creature' (v, 2).

In a series of penetrating episodes whose cumulative effect is massive, Hardy shows that her emotions cannot transcend the community which her mind endeavors to reject. With a deficiency of the feeling needed to sustain the courses laid out by the detached critical intellect, she would predictably return under pressure, to whatever form of support were available, to those indeed to which, while professing other codes, she has regularly been drawn. Though it would not take too much pressure, Hardy serves several ends at once by introducing the violent trauma of the death of the children. From here on he has only to trace, as he does with devastating thoroughness and fidelity, the revenge of the feelings that, albeit with admirable intellectual aspirations, Sue has persistently endeavored to thwart. They now counterattack with such force that they make her a sick woman. Although her self-judgements take the superficial form of tragic recognition, what we see is less the recovery that accompanies the tragic anagnorisis than the disaster of a personality distorted by the efforts to bear excessive burdens and now blindly seeking, in its misery, excessive punishments. Illness is something other than tragic.

Whatever Hardy may have felt about the course ultimately

taken by Sue, he was utterly faithful to the personality as he imagined and slowly constructed it. That is his triumph. His triumph, however, is not only his fidelity to the nature of Sue, but the perception of human reality that permitted him to constitute her as he did. We could say that he envisaged her, a bright but ordinary person, attempting the career that would be possible only to the solitary creative intellect, the artist, the saint, whose emotional safety does lie in a vision somewhere beyond that of the ordinary community. Sue does not have that vision; she is everyman. She is everyman entirely familiar to us: her sense of the imperfections around her leads her into habitual rational analysis that tends to destroy the forms of feeling developed by the historical community and to be unable to find a replacement for them. The insistence on the life of reason has become increasingly emphatic in each century of modern life, and Sue as the relentless critic of institutions incarnates the ideal usually held up to us in abstract terms. On the other hand, as if in defiance of rationalist aspirations, the twentieth century has seen destructive outbreaks of irrational force that would have been supposed incredible in the nineteenth. But a still more impressive modern phenomenon, since it entirely lacks the air of aberration, is a growing concern with the threat of intellect to the life of feelings and emotions. From some of the most respected guides of modern thought come warnings against arid rationality, and visions of a reconstructed emotional life essential to human safety and well-being. The present relevance of such cultural history is that it contributes to our understanding of Hardy: in *Jude the Obscure*, and primarily in the portrayal of Sue, he went to the heart of a modern problem long before it was understood as a problem. Yet the 'modern' is not topical, for the problem is rooted in the permanent reality of human nature. Neurotic Sue gives us, in dramatic terms, an essential revelation about human well-being.

S o u r c e : *Nineteenth-Century Fiction*, 20 (1965–6).

Ian Gregor

A SERIES OF SEEMINGS (1974)

From one point of view we feel that *Jude* is the work of a man for whom the universe makes – or ought to make – rational sense; it is something 'out there' to be interrogated, pondered over. And the interrogator, though he may be sceptical in his enquiry, frustrated and disappointed by his conclusions, is never in doubt about the validity or the importance of his undertaking. An entry in Hardy's journal for January 1890, catches the mood: 'I have been looking for God for 50 years, and I think that if he had existed I should have discovered him. As an external personality, of course – the only true meaning of the word.'¹ It is the note of a detective in search of a Missing Person, confident that nothing has been overlooked and with no doubt as to the 'true meaning' of clues. But it is not the particulars of Hardy's scepticism that makes us think of *Jude* as a nineteenth-century novel, so much as the more generalised feeling that the novelist, with all his assurances and doubts, hopes and fears, is present in his work in a very direct way, and yet in a way which quite forbids us to confuse fiction with autobiography. There is a grandeur of conception, a completeness of commitment, a quality of caring, which has all been transmuted into art, and yet which we feel impelled to describe in personal terms; for the integrity of the art has about it a transparency which makes the integrity of the artist an inseparable part of our reading experience. With this kind of fiction before us we have no difficulty in understanding the positive quality there might be in the description 'the novelist as sage'. Nevertheless, it is this element which marks out *Jude* as not of our own time, and of course it is a quality which extends into every detail of the fiction.

Within this firm and articulated structure, however, there glim-

mers another kind of novel which could only be described in
terms very different from these we have been using. Far from the
characters in *Jude* seeming fixed, they are seen in constantly shifting emphases and depths, taking themselves – and us – by surprise; the plot is less a narrative line made up of interlocking
events, than a series of significant but isolated moments : the ideas
debated seem integral to the characters rather than on loan from
the author. Though the novel is structured in terms of places,
they hardly seem to matter, and as the characters move restlessly
from one place to another, the world of the novel seems to be less
in Wessex than at the nerves' end. Above all, the novel is conceived in terms of rhythm, markedly seen in the elaborate contrasting and counterpointing of character and incident, but even
more significantly felt in the rhythm of the whole, where in the
evolving relationship of section to section, the central themes
gradually reveal themselves. If *Jude* prompts us to think of 'the
novelist as sage', it prompts us no less to think of 'the novel as process', and with that description we think of the fiction of our own
time, with its multiplicity of techniques, its interior landscapes,
its careful irresolutions.

Implicit in this dualistic impression which the novel makes is
a tension, but unlike the tension present in the Wessex novels, it
is now present in the very form the novel takes. From one point
of view, it is quite clear that in *Jude* Hardy wanted to evoke a
sense of cosmic tragedy, with a novel claiming epic status; from
another point of view, however, that is by no means so clear, if
we see it, not in its compositional totality, but as an unfolding
process. Here the sources of the tragedy are more complex, the
ironies more subtle, the tone more wry and more detached.

In the pages that follow I would like to argue that the power of
Hardy's last singular achievement was shaped by a conflict
between a kind of fiction which he had exhausted and a kind
of fiction which instinctively he discerned as meeting his need,
but which, imaginatively, he had no access to.

There occurs an incident in Jude's boyhood which both focuses
this duality of emphasis and provides an image which serves to
introduce a reading of the novel as a whole. Jude, pursuing his

dream of learning, has sent to Christminster for some Greek and Latin grammars :

Ever since his first ecstasy or vision of Christminster and its possibilities, Jude had meditated much and curiously on the probable sort of process that was involved in turning the expressions of one language into those of another. He concluded that a grammar of the required tongue would contain, primarily, a rule, prescription, or clue of the nature of a secret cipher, which, once known, would enable him, by merely applying it, to change at will all words of his own speech into those of the foreign one. . . . He learnt for the first time that there was no law of transmutation, as in his innocence he had supposed. . . .

'He learnt for the first time that there was no law of transmutation' – this is a lesson which is to preoccupy Hardy, no less than Jude, as the novel develops. The language in which men seek to make clear to themselves their metaphysical questions, their educational needs, their emotional longings, is in constant need of interpretation. One idiom must be found to complement another. To feel as Jude does that here is some 'secret cipher, which, once known, would enable him, by merely applying it' to master his problem, is a dangerous illusion – whether that illusion finds expression in the prophesyings of Aunt Drusilla, the cynical pragmatism of Arabella, or the fervent idealism of Sue. The incident of the grammar initiates Jude into a life-long education in which he is to learn that there is no simple law of transmutation by which one kind of experience can be simply translated into another, there is only 'a series of seemings' – a phrase which directs us both to the manner and the matter of his novel.

One of the most remarkable things about *Jude* is the tone of the first part – 'At Marygreen'. It is a tone intimately related to the pace of the narrative, uncomfortably reminiscent at times of early silent films. At the still centre is Jude – lying in a field looking through the interstices of his straw hat at 'something glaring, garish, rattling, and the noises and glares hit upon the little cell called your life, and shook it, and warped it'. 'Events did not rhyme quite as he thought' – that sentence could well stand as an epigraph for the section as a whole. Unlike the Wessex novels, which generally build up gradually, *Jude* plunges us directly into tra-

gedy, or at least the potentialities of tragedy, *con brio*. From the
opening pages, Aunt Drusilla reminds us of Jude's luckless existence, 'It would ha' been a blessing if Goddy-mighty had took thee
too, wi' thy mother and father, poor useless boy'; we have Jude
deserted by Phillotson, his only friend, thrown out of his job by
Farmer Troutham, deceived by Vilbert – so that long before he
has even met Arabella he has felt 'his existence to be an un-
demanded one', and indeed wished 'that he had never been born'.
The second half of this opening section drives home these feelings
without pause – he meets Arabella at the point when his self-
education is beginning to take shape, she tricks him into marriage,
they have a brutally short and cynical life together, and then
she leaves him. We are hardly surprised that Jude – knowing him
as we do – walks out to the centre of a frozen pond and seeks
to drown himself. From the moment of his arrival at his aunt's
house, orphaned and alone, to the moment when Arabella deserts
him some seven or eight years later, he would hardly seem to have
known more than the most fleeting moments of happiness. Looked
at simply in the light of events and the speed with which they
succeed each other, the whole opening section is so relentless that
it operates dangerously near the area of black farce.

And yet, as we read, it does not strike us in this way. The reason
is not far to seek. It is because we find in Jude, playing directly
against the forces of these events, an instinctive resilience : 'Like
the natural boy, he forgot his despondency, and sprang up' –
that too is the note struck by the first section, and if the background contains the Clytemnestra-like tones of Aunt Drusilla,
there is also the persistent glow of Christminster on the distant
horizon with its promise of a life elsewhere. Perhaps what is so
striking about the Marygreen section of the novel is the way in
which everything is pushed to extremes – the ugliness of the immediate scene contrasted with the city of light glimpsed through
the surrounding mists, Jude's absorption with the birds and the
clout from the Farmer, and most of all, the juxtaposition of Jude's
dream of learning 'Livy, Tacitus, Herodotus, Aeschylus, Sophocles, Aristophanes – ' with the sounds on the other side of the
hedge, 'Ha, ha, ha! Hoity-toity!' What is interesting to note
however is that, while the substance of this first section may not

seem uncharacteristic of Hardy, it is all accelerated in such a way that the impression it makes is laconic, faintly off-hand, as if Hardy feels that these extremities of tragedy and unfocused aspiration are much too simple a rendering of experience. 'Events did not rhyme as he had thought', this theme is to be caught again and again in the novel, but in a way which makes us increasingly aware that the apocalyptic tones of the opening will become subdued, as Christminster transforms itself from 'a glow in the sky', an ideal to be lived for, into buildings, streets, people.

'It was a windy, whispering, moonless night. To guide himself he opened under a lamp a map he had brought' – and so Jude begins his exploration of Christminster. His first encounter is not with the present of Christminster, but with its past; and as he wanders through the deserted streets in the moonless night he hears the voice of the university in the accents of Addison, Gibbon, Peel, Newman and, most clearly, in Arnold's famous apostrophe, 'Beautiful city! so venerable, so lovely, so unravaged by the fierce intellectual life of our century, so serene!' The clash intimated by Arnold, between the serenity of Oxford and its remoteness from contemporary intellectual concern, foreshadows the stance to be taken by Sue and indeed it is ironically caught in Jude's first glimpse of her at work in the Anglican bookshop – 'A sweet, saintly, Christian business, hers' – while her thoughts dwell on the pagan deities she has bought to decorate her room and the books of Gibbon and Mill which provide her nightly reading. But for Jude, it is not the intellectual remoteness but the social remoteness which strikes him. 'Only a wall divided him from those happy young contemporaries of his with whom he shared a common mental life : . . . Only a wall – but what a wall!' That is the note which is struck throughout this section, and when Jude eventually comes to write to the Master of one of the colleges, the reply expresses in its address the reason for rejection, 'To Mr. J. Fawley, Stone-mason'. For the Master, Jude is not there as a person but as a trade, a trade which should not seek to go beyond the walls it is committed to restoring. The social criticism of this section is direct and unequivocal, and the authorial sentiment none the less trenchant for its familiarity : 'here in the stone yard was a centre of effort as worthy as that dignified by the name of scholarly

study within the noblest of the colleges'. But the criticism of Christminster goes beyond a defence of the dignity of labour, it extends
to its self-conscious medievalism 'as dead as a fern-leaf in a lump
of coal?' The social astringencies of this section, while they are not
remarkable in themselves and, are, indeed, commonplaces in the
social writings of critics like Arnold, Ruskin and Morris, nevertheless evoke a very different mood from the first section of the
novel with its large metaphysical gestures, its sustained air of
cosmic gloom. While this is a mood in which precise social criticisms are emphatically made, nevertheless other notes are being
struck in a quiet way which subtilise that criticism. There is a
naïveté about Jude which is difficult to gainsay. While he might
have failed to recognise that 'mediaevalism was as dead as a fern-
leaf in a lump of coal', he might have made a more effective communication with the colleges if he had chosen a more profitable
method of selection than walking the city looking for the heads of
colleges and then selecting 'five whose physiognomies seemed to say
to him that they were appreciative and far-seeing men. To these
five he addressed letters . . .'. This does not blunt the edge of
criticism about the attitude of the colleges, but it gives an addi-
tional nuance to the epigraph which prefaces the section, 'Save
his own soul he hath no star'. The exclusiveness of that statement
is something that Hardy is to look at several times in the course
of the novel, but here it is offered in its simplest form. Jude's
naïveté, while being related to a fundamental honesty, is also
disabling in that it prevents him from taking an adequate measure of the situation in which he finds himself. So that as the
section concludes with Jude seeking solace for his rejection in a
Christminster pub and being challenged to recite the Nicene Creed
to a public for whom it might as well have been 'the Ratcatcher's
Daughter in double Dutch', our response is not simply that the
Christian creed is incomprehensible to 'the real life of Christminster', but that Jude himself has a great deal to learn about
himself and the world in which he lives.

   Is it right to equate education with formal learning? Might
an education not be found in a vocation pursued away from the
college world of Christminster? It is with questions like these in
mind that Jude goes to Melchester to the theological college, with

a vague intention to enter the Church, but primarily to be near Sue.

Up to this point, Sue's role, lightly sketched in as it has been, would seem clear and unequivocal. She is, among other things, the sceptical voice of the present age, at ease in Christminster, but scornful of its social exclusiveness and even more of its attachment to a creed outworn. The pieties she respects are those of the free spirit; she is wary of the dead hand of the past, sensitive and open to change. For her, Jude is enslaved to a false dream of learning and an idle religious superstition. The kind of conflict which exists between them is succinctly expressed in this exchange :

'Shall we go and sit in the Cathedral?' he asked, when their meal was finished.

'Cathedral? Yes. Though I think I'd rather sit in the railway station,' she answered, a remnant of vexation still in her voice. 'That's the centre of the town life now. The Cathedral has had its day !'

'How modern you are !'

'So would you be if you had lived so much in the Middle Ages as I have done these last few years ! The Cathedral was a very good place four or five centuries ago; but it is played out now. . . .'

The unhesitating sharpness of Sue's replies might perhaps alert us to an authorial irony here, but it is a measure of the feeling of the novel that, at this stage, it is Jude's reactions which take our attention. With our reading of the Christminster section behind us, he would still seem to be the victim of a romantic *naïveté*, a nostalgic addiction to the past. And so when sometime later Sue says, 'the mediaevalism of Christminster must go, be sloughed off, or Christminster itself will have to go', we feel that diagnostic confidence evokes sympathy in the author. When Sue falls foul of the rules governing her training college, we suppose that the kind of criticism against educational institutions operative in the Christminster sections is simply being extended here – the intellectual rigidities of the one being replaced by the moral rigidities of the other.

But it is just here, at the centre of the Melchester section, when the pattern of authorial feeling would seem to be becoming increasingly defined, that the novel begins to change tack in an extremely interesting and unexpected way.

Sue having escaped from the confining discipline of the college
takes refuge with Jude, and begins to recall her past: 'My life
has been entirely shaped by what people call a peculiarity in me.
I have no fear of men, as such. . . .' For the first time we are given
a perspective on Sue other than that of the free spirit, the devoted
Hellene, the admiring follower of Mill. This new impression is
developed quickly, so that when she says to Jude, 'You mustn't
love me. You are to like me – that's all', we feel a vibration here
which is not that of Sue delicately preserving her commitment to
Phillotson, but rather that of her inability to achieve a commitment of any kind. The 'freedom' she has been at such pains to
assert, and which up to this stage in the novel would seem to have
provided an unequivocal point of vantage for criticising Jude's
dream and the institutions which thwart it, is now seen as something much more ambivalent, a nervous self-enclosure, the swift
conceptualising, safeguarding the self against the invasions of experience. Sue's scrutiny is keen, but it is judiciously angled. The
effect of this interplay between her public and private self emerges
in this exchange :

'At present intellect in Christminster is pushing one way, and
religion the other; and so they stand stock-still, like two rams butting
each other.'
'What would Mr. Phillotson – '
'It is a place full of fetichists and ghost-seers !'
He noticed that whenever he tried to speak of the schoolmaster she
turned the conversation to some generalizations about the offending
University.

This is an interesting passage because we can gauge the effect of
the personal pressures being exerted on Sue. Her opening remark is
of a piece with her general criticism about the intellectual sterility
of Christminster and the simile exhibits the familiar self-confidence
in her analysis. The effect of Jude's mention of Phillotson is
immediately to make that analysis shrill and strained, 'it is a place
full of fetichists and ghost-seers'. Gradually we begin to see that
for Sue the pursuit of the idea becomes a surrogate for the presence of personal feeling. The effect of this is not to invalidate
the idea, but to make us increasingly aware that, by the end of
the Melchester section, the centre of Hardy's interest has moved

from the world Jude sees – and with it the criticism provoked by that world – to Sue and 'that mystery, her heart'.

At the very end of the Melchester section there occurs an incident, insignificant in the general development of the novel, but which expresses in a modest but beautifully precise way the 'series of seemings' which the novel as a whole is building up. Greatly moved by a hymn being sung that Easter, 'At the Foot of the Cross', Jude feels that the composer is a man who will understand the problems that beset him, and characteristically, resolves to pay him a visit. The meeting is a crushing disappointment – the composer is interested only in his royalties and has turned to the wine trade for greater financial comfort. The ironies are strident and would seem a further variant on the deceptions of appearance, and generally to be taking up the kind of social criticism present in the Christminster section; there is, besides, a gentle deflating of Jude's *naïveté*. The episode however is to have further implications.

Settled in Shaston – 'the ancient British Palladour . . . the city of a dream' – Sue prepares to met Jude for the first time as Mrs. Phillotson. The afternoon is growing dark and Jude makes his way to the schoolroom where he expects to find her. Seeing it empty he proceeds to play idly on the piano the opening bars of 'At the Foot of the Cross' :

A figure moved behind him, and thinking it was still the girl with the broom Jude took no notice, till the person came close and laid her fingers lightly upon his bass hand. The imposed hand was a little one he seemed to know, and he turned. 'Don't stop,' said Sue, 'I like it. I learnt it before I left Melchester . . .'

Jude then asks her to play it for him :

Sue sat down, and her rendering of the piece, though not remarkable, seemed divine as compared with his own. She, like him, was evidently touched – to her own surprise – by the recalled air; and when she had finished, and he moved his hand towards hers, it met his own half-way. Jude grasped it . . .

It is the renewal of the relationship which is to culminate in Sue's leaving Phillotson and going to live with Jude. The darkening room and the rich melancholy music conspire to weave the spell which enables their relationship to take on an added intensity, an intensity made possible by the fact that the music succeeds in awakening Sue's emotions, but at the same time provides a suitably 'spiritual' mode of expression. This episode, coming at the beginning of the Shaston section, initiates an ever-increasing concern with Sue which is to dominate the remainder of the novel.

'We were too free, under the influence of that morbid hymn and the twilight.' Sue's self-reproach and resolution to withdraw from Jude's company has a fugitive life, and at Shaston we see the break-up of her marriage with Phillotson and the elopement with Jude. When we look at the series of conversations with Phillotson we can see how far Hardy has now taken us into the area of personal relationships. We can catch it revealingly in this exchange, where Sue is attempting some kind of defence of her marital attitudes to Phillotson :

> 'But it is not I altogether that am to blame !'
> 'Who is then? Am I?'
> 'No – I don't know! The universe, I suppose – things in general, because they are so horrid and cruel !'
> 'Well, it is no use talking like that.'

That Sue's reference to 'the universe' should come over as limply rhetorical – an unfocused irritation – and Phillotson's pragmatism as both just and solicitous, is an index of the change in mood and direction since the opening sections of the novel. Sue's critical intelligence may still be on display, but we feel that she is now very much its victim, in the sense that having announced her wish to leave Phillotson and live with Jude, she quotes Mill by way of justifying her action : 'J. S. Mill's words, those are. I have been reading it up. Why can't you act upon them? I wish to, always.' If this was not so clearly dictated by emotional desperation, it would simply strike us as callow and grossly insensitive to the situation in which she finds herself. This is enforced by the increasing sympathy with which Phillotson is presented throughout the section. The account of his final evening with Sue is one of the most deeply felt passages in the novel, and all the more so for the restraint and delicate precision of its feeling.

If Jude formally commits himself to Sue now, he does so with an increasing awareness of her enigmatic nature. And Phillotson's generous farewell tones 'You are made for each other', echo hollowly in the railway carriage as Sue leaves her husband, only to tell Jude that they are not to be lovers in the way he anticipated. He sees her now in a way that he has not seen her before, and though this does not affect his love, a new sharpness of insight is unquestionably present : 'Sue, sometimes, when I am vexed with you, I think you are incapable of real love'; 'under the affectation of independent views you are as enslaved to the social code as any woman'; 'you spirit, you disembodied creature, you dear, sweet, tantalizing phantom – hardly flesh at all; so that when I put my arms round you I almost expect them to pass through you as through air'. And characteristically, Sue's supreme moment of committing herself to Jude is to enter her hotel room – alone.

The deepening analysis of Sue, this is the main preoccupation and drive of this section of the novel, but if we are to understand the remainder of the novel it is important to see that analysis in its context. And it is a context which is increasingly concerned to ponder the meaning of 'freedom'. All the characters in the Shaston section are, in one way or another, asked to ponder this, Sue, Jude, Phillotson and Gillingham. And this meditation is given sharp emphasis by the incident of the rabbit caught in the gin and mercifully killed by Jude. When Jude comes to reflect on his ruined career at the hands of two women, he uses precisely this imagery. 'Is it that the women are to blame; or is it the artificial system of things, under which the normal sex-impulses are turned into devilish domestic gins and springes to hold back those who want to progress?' 'The artificial system of things' – it would seem precisely that which Sue, Jude and Phillotson are brought to recognise in Shaston and to be able to set aside. Phillotson gives Sue her 'freedom', first to be able to go and live with Jude, and then, if she desires, to marry him. Sue begins a life with Jude and appears to be able to call the terms on which it will be lived. Jude formally turns his back on his ambitions, burning his books, and going to live with the woman he loves. Arabella, by marrying again, removes any obstacles about his remarriage to Sue. Connections with the past too are formally severed as Aunt Drusilla dies, and with her the old Wessex of legend and 'the family curse'. In

Shaston then, Hardy would appear to wipe the slate clean, to give
the characters precisely that freedom of decision they have constantly desired and that definition of self they have longed for.
Even in the case of Phillotson, where unhappiness has prompted
his action, there is a power of resolution, a revelation of self-
knowledge which previously had not been open to him. 'The
artificial system of things' has now been openly challenged and a
fresh significance is given to human decision. It is significant that
Aunt Drusilla dies in this section of the novel, because it marks the
opposite pole from the doom-laden world of Marygreen; it is the
moment when the free and untrammelled self seems triumphant.

This then is the context in which we must see the deepening
analysis of Sue – that fine instance of 'freedom', the supremely
individual case. With her we find displayed the consciousness of
self, the innate uncertainties, the psychic disturbance with which
the fiction of our own day is to make us so familiar. And the end
of the Shaston section of *Jude* is the ending of a characteristically
modern fiction. The wounded rabbit has been set free from the
gin, the artificial system of things has been challenged, the individual will has been triumphantly exercised and, though the
past may be painful and the future unknown, the self has been
validated.

But for Hardy that picture would be radically incomplete. He
does not share the views of a later age. Lawrence voiced the representative twentieth-century criticism when he remarked that
Hardy's characters were all cowed by 'the mere judgement of man
upon them, and when all the while by their own souls they were
right'. That antithesis would have been alien to Hardy, and the
last two sections of *Jude* are there to show that 'the mere judgement of man' is for him an inextricable part of man's soul. They
enable us to look at 'the artificial system of things' from an aspect
different from any we have had so far – to draw a distinction
between the tragedy of a rabbit and the tragedy of a man. The
epigraph to the fifth section establishes the emphasis of the section : 'Thy aerial part, and all the fiery parts which are mingled
in thee, though by nature they have an upward tendency, still in
obedience to the disposition of the universe they are overpowered
here in the compound mass the body.' 'The aerial part', 'the body',

this is the .dichotomy to be explored, and with the Phillotson decree made absolute and Arabella marrying again, Sue and Jude are in her words, 'just as free now as if we had never married at all'. For Jude this has its own significance : 'Now we'll strut arm and arm like any other engaged couple. We've a legal right to.' But for Sue, such legality is inimical to the freedom she has just painfully re-acquired – it implies a gesture of public commitment which she, and in effect Jude too, are reluctant to make. Her aversion to marriage has nothing to do with uncertainty about her feelings for Jude, but she fears that those feelings will be debased by 'the government stamp', by a construct which is no more than 'a licence to be loved on the premises'. Faced with the idea of a marriage ceremony, she can see only a sequence of external gestures from which all inner significance has been drained. It marks the high points of her self-enclosure – a self-enclosure not disturbed by the widow Edlin's sardonic reminders of a world beyond herself : 'Nobody thought o' being afeared o' matrimony in my time, nor of much else but a cannon ball or empty cupboard ! Why when I an my poor man were married we thought no more o't than of a game o' dibs !'

Two events however do conspire to modify it. The first is the arrival of Arabella, when feelings of jealousy precipitate Sue into sharing her bed with Jude. The second is more far-reaching – the arrival of Father Time, the natural son of Arabella and Jude, and it is with this figure that Hardy gives his narrative the last decisive shift.

From his introduction Father Time stands apart from the narrative, and of course at the level of realistic presentation he is very awkwardly accommodated indeed. But Hardy leaves us in no doubt that his role is to be choric : 'He was Age masquerading as Juvenility, and doing it so badly that his real self showed through the crevices.' And as he sits in the railway compartment he 'seemed to be doubly awake, like an enslaved and dwarfed Divinity, sitting passive and regarding his companions as if he saw their whole rounded lives rather than their immediate figures'. It would be foolish to deny that the attempt to integrate Father Time into the novel is not a success; Hardy has set aside the conventions of realism too easily, so that the child appears to have

strayed into the novel from another art form, Lady Macduff's
son unnervingly encountered on 'The Great Western'. But that
Hardy should be prepared to risk so much with him is an indication both of the necessity of what he is trying to say at this
stage of the novel and of his difficulty in finding a satisfactory
way of saying it. In a phrase, he is introducing with Father Time
the processes of history into the lives of Jude and Sue – his sorrowful contemplative eyes become ours as we watch them desperately
attempting to cheat time, repudiating the past, evading the social
commitments of the present, indifferent, with their ever increasing family, to the demands of the future. With Father Time
their 'dreamless paradise' fades into the light of common day.

This is poignantly revealed in the visit which Jude and Sue pay
to the Great Wessex Agricultural Show. It is one of the rare
moments when happiness seems to prevail, and it is also one of
the rare moments when we see Jude and Sue through the eyes
of others, in this case those of Arabella and Cartlett. The effect
is that of a brightly lit picture, darkly framed. Wessex, once a
whole way of life, is now present merely as 'a show' for itinerant
observers. Jude and Sue arrive by excursion and wander through
the exhibition ground. Entirely lost in each other's company,
they are oblivious of the people around them :

'Happy?' he murmured.
She nodded.
'Why? Because you have come to the great Wessex Agricultural
Show – or because *we* have come?'
'You are always trying to make me confess to all sorts of absurdi-
ties. Because I am improving my mind, of course, by seeing all these
steam-ploughs, and threshing-machines, and chaff-cutters, and cows,
and pigs, and sheep.'

What was once a way of life, a history, has now become an in-
ventory for 'the improvement' of the mind, and a mind exercised
not by things in use, but by things exhibited. Jude, trying to find
in the event a crystallisation of his feelings, only moves Sue to a
characteristic withdrawal of hers as she marks out, with firm lines
of demarcation, the observer from the world observed. If the
world observed is to extend her feelings, then it must not be

through a shared experience, but through one in which she participates alone.

And so we find her pausing to admire the roses, 'I should like to push my face quite into them – the dears!' Like Miriam in *Sons and Lovers*, she can encounter the sensual world only when she can impose herself upon it, when it cannot make reciprocal demands, but is simply there to feed the contemplative soul. Such a moment cannot be sustained, and Father Time reflects that in a few days the flowers will all be withered.

The moment of joy is precarious and the shadows of Arabella and Father Time, cast emblematically at the Show, begin to acquire a social reality. Ironically, Jude's and Sue's trouble begins with a return to the law which they have both, in their various ways, tried to set aside – a law at once human and divine. Jude, commissioned to re-letter the Ten Commandments in a nearby church, causes a scandal when he is joined in his work by the pregnant, unmarried Sue, and is duly dismissed. His life of wandering now begins, his home is uprooted for the second time, his goods are sold. Father Time asks why they must go, and Jude replies sardonically, 'Because of a cloud that has gathered over us; though "we have wronged no man, corrupted no man, defrauded no man." ' To which Father Time might have added that they have sought to meet no man either. They have neglected 'the disposition of the universe', and in consequence the 'aerial part' and 'the body' have been kept at war.

In Jude's decision to return to Christminster we find a summoning of will and a recognition of the disposition of the universe which has never been present in Sue. For Sue the place still remains what it has always been, 'a nest of commonplace schoolmasters whose characteristic is timid obsequiousness to tradition'. But for Jude, though he recognises himself as permanently excluded from it, 'it is still the centre of the universe. . . . Perhaps it will soon wake up, and be generous'. This acceptance of possibilities, of change, is a note which characterises Jude throughout the last tragic section of the novel, a section drawing out a radical difference in response, as Jude and Sue become increasingly enmeshed in the society they have sought to reject.

Once again the epigraph catches the main emphasis, 'And she

humbled her body greatly, and all the places of her joy she filled
with her torn hair'. The 'aerial part' now seeks to annihilate 'the
body', and the freedom it seeks is the last freedom of all – the
freedom of self-destruction. But 'the body' can no longer be
thought of as 'the individual body', and in destroying herself, Sue
destroys the lives of those around her. The full meaning of Father
Time is to become clear in this last section where the social body
and the individual body become inextricably united, a recall to
Hardy's abiding theme that the human race is 'one great network
or tissue which quivers in every part when one point is shaken,
like a spider's web if touched'.[2]

Jude's attitude of mind in returning to Christminster is made
clear in his speech to the crowd who have gathered for Remem-
brance Day. Though it is certainly not free from bitterness, it is
clear in its emphasis :

It was my poverty and not my will that consented to be beaten. It
takes two or three generations to do what I tried to do in one. . . .
Eight or nine years ago when I came here first, I had a neat stock
of fixed opinions, but they dropped away one by one; and the further
I get the less sure I am . . . I perceive there is something wrong somewhere in our social formulas. . . .

These sentiments give a suggestively defining edge to the way
in which Jude has evolved throughout the successive stages of his
life – the early metaphysical glooms, the unfocused intellectual
and theological ambitions, the formal disavowals and the retreat
into self, and now the attempt to come to terms with a social
reality which, harsh and forbidding as it might be, is resistant to
prophecy and to judgement. As with the Greek and Latin grammars which he received as a boy, there is no simple law of transmutation, there is only a series of seemings. It is this view which
Sue is to reject, and the extent of her negation will make plain
what is at stake. In the last analysis, by a sad irony, assertions of
the free spirit are to catch the inflexible tones if not the substance
of Aunt Drusilla's curse.

The narrative now leads into the most terrible scene in Hardy's
fiction, indeed it might reasonably be argued in English fiction –
the killing of the children by Father Time. Although the scene is

brutally disturbing in a way which the novel can hardly accommodate, nevertheless its animating purpose is rooted deep within the evolving structure of the novel, and it does not represent a deflection of Hardy's into a momentary despair, resulting in an episode more akin to *grand guignol* than realistic fiction. The scene is obviously an attempt at the same kind of choric effect as that represented by Father Time himself, a reaching out beyond the particulars of the narrative to an impersonal tragic dimension, a dimension where Time ceases to be a child and becomes 'the whole tale of their situation'. So that the author can go on to say : 'On that little shape had converged all the inauspiciousness and shadow which had darkened the first union of Jude, and all the accidents, mistakes, fears, errors of the last. He was their nodal point, their focus, their expression in a single term.' The scene is 'the action' of such a figure, the only action he is capable of performing.

To say this is not to argue for the success of the scene, but merely to suggest its nature. It also directs attention to the way in which it arises out of the previous narrative, though its relationship is more with the inner drama than with overt incident. And because it is a drama related to Sue rather than to Jude, it demands a new directness of treatment, now that the two characters are treading rather different paths.

To establish a context for the scene we might go back to a conversation at Shaston, referred to earlier, where Sue asks Phillotson for her freedom. To support her point she quotes Mill :

'She, or he "who lets the world, or his own portion of it, choose his plan of life for him, has no need of any other faculty than the ape-like one of imitation." J. S. Mill's words, those are. I have been reading it up. Why can't you act upon them? I wish to, always.'
'What do I care about J. S. Mill !' moaned he.

The ironies cut deep. Hardy, like Sue a warm admirer of Mill, chooses this passage – in which the variety and independence of human behaviour are defended – to expose Sue's rigidities and intolerance of opinions other than her own. And encompassing that is her total inability to enter into Phillotson's feelings; her intellect is at odds with her sensibility. The point is emphasised

later when having left Phillotson, she comes to visit him in his
illness, though she 'did not for a moment, either now or later,
suspect what troubles had resulted to him from letting her go; it
never once seemed to cross her mind . . .'.

It is precisely this mixture of insensibility and forthright state-
ment that she displays again in her conversation with Father
Time when they are frustrated in their search for lodgings at
Christminster. He begins by asking :

'Can I do anything?'
'No! All is trouble, adversity and suffering !'
'Father went away to give us children room, didn't he?'
'Partly.'
'It would be better to be out o' the world than in it, wouldn't it?'
'It would almost, dear.'
' 'Tis because of us children, too, isn't it, that you can't get a good
lodging?'
'Well – people do object to children sometimes.'
'Then if children make so much trouble, why do people have 'em?'
'O – because it is a law of nature.'
'But we don't ask to be born?'
'No indeed.'

She then goes on to tell the boy that there is to be another baby,
but, through a mistaken sense of delicacy, does nothing to remove
his impression that she has deliberately sought its arrival. The
effect of this on the child – the combination of the indifference of
nature's law with the apparent indifference of his mother – is
overwhelming. Just as in her previous conversation with Phillotson, Sue is blind to the effect her words will have, and she makes
no attempt to go behind the letter of what she is saying. For her,
words alone seem certain good.

The situation is now set for the tragedy, and however grotesque
the actual incidents that follow, Sue has established a structure of
feeling which the boy will carry to a remorseless conclusion, ex-
changing in his pencilled note of explanation, 'Done because we
are to menny', literalism for literalism. 'The letter killeth' has
been made fact. In the icy language of that 'explanation', Sue
reads her own indictment, and her world is shattered. But im-

prisoned within extremes, she can only exchange the letter of
freedom for the letter of renunciation, and though she recognises
that her literalness has provoked the boy's action, she is unable to
assimilate the recognition into behaviour, so that she remains un-
moved by Jude's agonised response to her proposed remarriage to
Phillotson, 'Sue, Sue! we are acting by the letter; and "the
letter killeth" !'

The deaths of the children are a decisive point for her, driving
her ever deeper into herself, so that although her behaviour is now
in striking contrast to her previous conduct – the return to the
church, the remarriage to Phillotson – her fundamental disposition is unchanged. 'The aerial part' and 'the body' are still
held together only by a fanatical act of will, her 'enslavement to
forms' of self-renunciation replacing her earlier enslavement to
forms of self-assertion. Enclosed within herself, she seals herself
off almost literally from human communications; 'clenching her
teeth she uttered no cry' when Phillotson takes her into his bed-
room, and when Jude leaves her for the last time she 'stopped
her ears with her hands till all possible sound of him had passed
away'. She has transformed herself into pure will.

To turn to Jude is to find that he has continued to move in a
significantly different direction. Since his return to Christminster
he has increasingly perceived his tragedy to be inextricably involved with time, place and person. 'Events did not rhyme as they
should', that sentiment stands, but the cause is no longer abstract,
metaphysical, nor as Aunt Drusilla said 'sommat in our blood'.
It is Sue, the free spirit, who now voices that position :

'All the ancient wrath of the Power above us has been vented upon
us, His poor creatures, and we must submit. There is no choice. We
must. It is no use fighting against God !'

to which Jude replies :

'It is only against man and senseless circumstance.'

And that remains his attitude to the end. He recognises with perfect clarity his differences from Sue, that 'events which had enlarged his own view of life, laws, customs, and dogmas, had not
operated in the same manner on Sue's', and more generally :

'Strange difference of sex, that time and circumstance, which enlarge the views of most men, narrow the views of women almost invariably.' His remarriage with Arabella is a black parody of Sue's with Phillotson, the one made possible only by will, the other through torpor. And it is Jude's remarriage that drives home his own personal tragedy. However much he has come to recognise his tragedy as contingent on circumstance, 'the time was not ripe for us! Our ideas were fifty years too soon to be any good to us'; however much he has sought to keep the letter informed by spirit, his own tragedy is stark and unrelieved. Truly, as Hardy says in his preface, Jude's is a tragedy of 'unfulfilled aims', and that unfulfilment is both public and private, educational and sexual. It is interesting to notice that in these closing pages Arabella for all her harshness and cynicism, gives us a sense of being a married woman in a way that Sue never does, and in Jude's refusal to let Sue visit him in his last illness, we feel that finally, he has come to recognise that she could never fulfil that need of his which, however tortuously and casually, is fulfilled by Arabella. His remarriage, of course, can hardly be said to exist at all in its own right, but it is capable nevertheless of casting a harsh retrospective light on Sue, and significantly, the last words of the novel are of Sue's self-deception, and they are spoken not by Jude but by Arabella.

Despite the harsh ironies that attend Jude's death – the cheers from the river sports counter-pointing his recital of verses from the Book of Job, Arabella already preparing herself a future with Vilbert – we feel that Hardy has now opened up perspectives which go beyond the individual tragedy, which reveal the individual as belonging to a wider history, and that it is Jude's singular achievement, despite his personal suffering, to have perceived this.

He never gives up the effort to translate his dream and, even when he returns to Christminster, having seen Sue for the last time, the place is still alive for him with figures of the past. For Arabella, the street is empty, 'There's neither living nor dead hereabouts except a damn policeman!' To Arabella, and to Sue in her very different kind of way, Jude's sense of history has no meaning. For the former, the only time is the present, for the latter, time is to be transcended, but for Jude the past is alive in the way that it was for his creator. For them both, things,

> That nobody else's mind calls back,
> Have a savour that scenes in being lack,
> And a presence more than the actual brings . . .[3]

In that 'presence more than the actual' Jude finds, however obscurely, his pledge for the future, and if he comes to reject a Power above us whether beneficent or malevolent, he senses in a recognition of the Spirit of the Years a clue to a proper humanity.

SOURCE: from 'An End and a Beginning' in *The Great Web* (1974) pp. 208–28.

NOTES

Professor Gregor adds 'a last perspective' in which he suggests that there is a 'plurality of meaning' in the novel, encompassing Jude's tragedy as something inevitable in itself and yet also 'contingent on human institutions'. The criticism made by D. H. Lawrence (see extract, pp. 71–2, and Introduction, pp. 16–17) is thus countered by suggesting that both kinds of tragedy are included in the novel, the result for the reader being an ending which gives a double sense of finality *and* continuity. Lawrence himself, says Gregor, was to develop the possibilities of this sense of continuity in his own fiction : 'where *Jude* ends *The Rainbow* begins'. [Ed.]

1. Hardy, *Life*, p. 224.
2. *Life*, p. 177.
3. Hardy, 'Places', *Collected Poems*, p. 332.

SELECT BIBLIOGRAPHY

For further reading students are advised to consult, first of all, F. E. Hardy, *The Life of Thomas Hardy* (one volume edition, Macmillan, 1962) and Harold Orel (ed.), *Thomas Hardy's Personal Writings* (Macmillan, 1967); and, secondly, the complete books from which extracts have been reprinted in this collection. In addition the following books and articles are also recommended.

Richard C. Carpenter, *Thomas Hardy*, Twayne's English Authors Series (Twayne, New York, 1964).

R. G. Cox (ed.), *Thomas Hardy, the Critical Heritage* (Routledge & Kegan Paul, 1970).

Louis Crompton, 'The Sunburnt God : Ritual and Tragic Myth in *The Return of the Native*', *Boston University Studies in English*, vol. 4 (1960) pp. 229–40.

D. A. Dike, 'A Modern Oedipus', *Essays in Criticism*, vol. 2 (1952) pp. 169–79.

David J. de Laura, ' "The Ache of Modernism" in Hardy's Later Novels', *English Literary History*, vol. 34 (1967) pp. 380–99.

Terry Eagleton, 'Thomas Hardy : Nature as Language', *Critical Quarterly* (Summer 1971) pp. 155–62.

Albert J. Guerard, *Thomas Hardy: The Novels and Stories* (Oxford University Press, 1949).

—— (ed.), *Hardy, A Collection of Essays*, Twentieth Century Views (Prentice-Hall Inc., Englewood Cliffs, N.J., 1963).

John Holloway, *The Victorian Sage* (Macmillan, 1953).

Irving Howe, *Thomas Hardy* (Weidenfeld & Nicolson, 1966).

Frederick R. Karl, '*The Mayor of Casterbridge*: A New Fiction Defined', *Modern Fiction Studies*, vol. 6 (1960) pp. 195–213.

Michael Millgate, *Thomas Hardy, His Career as a Novelist* (Bodley Head, 1971).

Roy Morrell, *Thomas Hardy, the Will and the Way* (University of Malaya and Oxford University Press, 1965).

Julian Moynahan, '*The Mayor of Casterbridge* and the Old Testament's First Book of Samuel', *PMLA*, vol. 71 (1965) pp. 118–30.

J. I. M. Stewart, *Thomas Hardy, A Critical Biography* (Longman, 1971).

Southern Review, vol. 6, 1940–1 (Hardy centennial issue).

The following are also useful for reference :

Helmut E. Gerber and W. Eugene Davis (eds), *Thomas Hardy, An Annotated Bibliography of Writings About Him* (Northern Illinois University Press, 1973).

F. B. Pinion, *A Hardy Companion: A Guide to the Works of Thomas Hardy and Their Background* (Macmillan, 1968).

R. L. Purdy, *Thomas Hardy: A Bibliographical Study* (Oxford University Press, 1954).

NOTES ON CONTRIBUTORS

JEAN BROOKS. Senior Lecturer and Head of the Department of English, Rose Bruford College of Speech and Drama, Kent. Author, besides *Thomas Hardy: the Poetic Structure*, of a thesis on 'Darwinism in Thomas Hardy's Major Novels'.

DOUGLAS BROWN. Senior Lecturer in English at the University of Reading and, when he died in 1964, Professor elect at the University of York. Author of *Thomas Hardy* (1954) and a study of *The Mayor of Casterbridge* (1964).

LEONARD W. DEEN. Associate Professor of English, Queen's College, City University of New York. Author of articles on Carlyle, Newman, Dickens, Byron and Coleridge. Work in progress includes a study of 'Identity' in Romantic poetry.

IAN GREGOR. Professor of Modern English Literature, University of Kent. Besides *The Great Web*, author, with B. Nicholas, of *The Moral and the Story* (1962), and, with M. Kinkead-Weekes, of *William Golding* (1967).

ROBERT B. HEILMAN. Professor of English, University of Washington. Publications include books on *King Lear* (*This Great Stage*, 1948) and *Othello* (*Magic in the Web*, 1956) and studies of tragedy and melodrama.

DAVID LODGE. Professor of English Literature, University of Birmingham. Novelist and critic, whose works include, besides *Language of Fiction, The Novelist at the Crossroads* (1971), essays on *Graham Greene* (1966) and *Evelyn Waugh* (1971), and a Casebook on *Emma* (1968).

J. C. MAXWELL. Reader in Renaissance English Literature, University of Oxford, at the time of his death in 1976. He edited *Notes and Queries*, several Shakespeare plays and Wordsworth's *The Prelude*.

JOHN PATERSON. Professor of English, University of California, Berkeley. Publications include *The Making of 'The Return of the Native'* (1960) and *The Novel as Faith* (1973). Editor of Harper & Row's Standard Edition of Hardy's novels.

ROBERT C. SCHWEIK. Professor of English, State University College, Fredonia, N.Y. With Joseph Schwartz, author of *Hart Crane, A Descriptive Bibliography* (1972). Various articles on Hardy and other nineteenth-century topics.

TONY TANNER. Fellow of King's College and Lecturer in English, University of Cambridge. Publications include *The Reign of Wonder* (1965), *Three Novels by James* (1968), *City of Words* (1971), and collections on Jane Austen and James.

RAYMOND WILLIAMS. Fellow of Jesus College and Professor of Drama, University of Cambridge. Numerous works on literature and society, including *Drama from Ibsen to Eliot* (1952), *Culture and Society* (1958), *The Long Revolution* (1961), *Modern Tragedy* (1966), *The English Novel from Dickens to Lawrence* (1970), and *The Country and the City* (1973).

INDEX